Women, Religion and
Culture in Iran

Royal Asiatic Society Books

The Royal Asiatic Society was founded in 1823 'for the investigation of subjects connected with, and for the encouragement of science, literature and the arts in relation to, Asia'. Informed by these goals, the policy of the Society's Educational Board is to make available in appropriate formats the results of original research in the humanities and social sciences having to do with Asia, defined in the broadest geographical and cultural sense and up to the present day.

The Man in the Panther's Skin
Shota Rustaveli
Translated from the Georgian by M. S. Wardrop

Women, Religion and Culture in Iran

Edited by

Sarah Ansari and Vanessa Martin

CURZON
in association with
THE ROYAL ASIATIC SOCIETY OF GREAT BRITAIN AND IRELAND

First Published in 2002
by Curzon Press
Richmond, Surrey
http://www.curzonpress.co.uk

© 2002 Sarah Ansari and Vanessa Martin

Typeset in Minion by LaserScript Ltd, Mitcham, Surrey
Printed and bound in Great Britain by
Biddles Ltd, Guildford and King's Lynn

British Library Cataloguing in Publication Data
A catalogue record of this book is available from the British Library

Library of Congress Cataloguing in Publication Data
A catalogue record for this book has been requested

ISBN 0–7007–1509–6

Contents

Acknowledgements

The Editors gratefully acknowledge the support of the British Academy, the Royal Asiatic Society, and the History Department, Royal Holloway, University of London.

one

Introduction

Sarah Ansari

It is undeniable that, over the course of the twentieth century and in many parts of the world, women and issues connected with them have steadily moved centre stage much more publicly than had been the case in earlier times. Gender, of course, has always been crucial in the shaping of social, economic and political relations, but now any pretence that this has ever been otherwise has been stripped away to allow a much clearer view of the ways in which gender and society interact. Misperceptions persist, however, particularly concerning women living in Muslim societies. As often as not, the dominant image of a 'typical' Muslim woman combines powerlessness and passivity on an individual level with what seems like a fierce and active loyalty to her community and its shared values, especially religion and culture. That certain groups of Muslim women have always had access to power by virtue of kinship or marriage connections confounds 'traditional', often western, ideas about divisions separating the so-called 'public' and 'private' spheres in Muslim societies and the distribution of effective influence between them.[1] Revealing the range of realities involved in the lives of Muslim women past and present, in effect deconstructing the notion of 'Muslim woman' as a homogeneous category, has become a priority for historians and others concerned to challenge the kinds of myths and misconceptions that endure. At the same time, there is a need to recognize that commentators, fired by the excitement of these new insights, can sometimes err too far in the opposite direction, putting a kind of retrospective pressure on women of earlier times to prove themselves in ways acceptable to or expected by people of today. The challenge for anyone writing on issues concerning women, therefore, is to reflect and analyse developments accurately but realistically, whilst recognizing that the years since the nineteenth century

1

have arguably represented a distinct period when it comes to the changing status of women in societies such as Iran.

In Iran, as elsewhere, the reality is that 'religion has been a source of power for women, or a source of subordination, or both'.[2] And Iranian history has certainly confirmed the very close interconnections that exist between religion, culture and women's lives, complicated further by the impact of political developments on all three. The fact that more than two decades have passed since the 1979 Islamic revolution offers a timely opportunity for fresh perspectives on the effect that this particular important adjustment in the balance of power within Iranian society has had on matters connected with the position of women there. From a lengthier point of view as well, the conclusion of the twentieth century demands assessments of the ways in which, and the reasons why, the experiences of Iranian women have shifted over the last 100 or so years. Echoing the words of Haideh Moghissi, just how far have Iranian women been forced to 'jump fences' blocking their progress and how far have 'gates' been opened, either for them or by them, to make it possible to renegotiate the roles demanded of women by Iranian society?[3]

This volume of articles, encompassing differences in approach and methodology on the part of their authors, investigates the inter-relationship between women, religion and culture in Iran in both the shorter and the longer term, and underlines the value of interdisciplinary thinking and exchange. The liveliness of the contributions on these themes (which also include writing, education and beliefs), together with their imaginative grasp of the diverse possibilities involved in studying Iranian women, highlights the way in which the discussion on women's roles has been expanding. Thus, the collection reflects a broader shift in contemporary approaches to scholarship that allows a wider range of voices than ever to make themselves heard.

In many ways, the study of Iranian women has begun to enter its mature phase. While, for instance, there is still enormous interest in the impact and aftermath of the 1979 Islamic revolution on the experiences of Iranian women, there is also much 'healthy' concern to develop a better appreciation of how these particular, relatively recent, developments can be fitted into longer cycles of change. Parvin Paidar's *Women and the Political Process in Twentieth Century Iran* reflects this. Building on the earlier work produced by scholars such as Janet Afary, Joanna de Groot and (in relation to more contemporary developments) Valentine Moghadam, Paidar examines in panoramic fashion the role of women in the Iranian political process, a role which she emphasizes has not been passive and marginalized but active and central to political change over the last one hundred years.[4] Identifying, contextualizing and scrutinizing the position of women in contemporary Iran are challenges which also occupy political scientists, sociologists and anthropologists, many of whom have homed in on the kinds of exchange which have been taking place in Iran since 1979 between 'secular' and Islamist feminists, between feminists and the state, and between different interpreters of religious law. Hence, Haleh Afshar, for instance, has explored the politics of the Islamic government towards women and also so-called feminist fundamentalism while Haideh Moghissi has likewise attempted to dissect the complex relationship between feminism and Islamism.[5] Afsaneh Najmabadi, following her perceptive analysis of the transformation of women's language in turn-of-the-century Iran, has more recently evaluated the status of women in post-revolutionary Iran by analysing on-going debates as mediated through *Zanan,* an explicitly feminist journal. In the same way Hisae Nakanishi has investigated the ways in which Islamist women have debated the rights of women in a reformist journal, *Payam-i Hajar,* and Maryam Poya has probed the conceptual relations between state, capital and gender ideology.[6] Indeed, authors included in *Women, Religion and Culture in Iran,* such as Azadeh Kian-Thiébaut and Ziba Mir-Hosseini, have themselves already made valuable contributions in their earlier published work to the general reappraisal which has been taking place in post-1979 Iran as far as the nature and extent of the status and rights of women there is concerned.[7]

Two dominant themes which connect many of the articles in this collection are the role of religion, and Shi'i Islam in particular, in Iranian society, and the influence of the state. These represent essential strands of influence which have interacted with each other to varying degrees to shape a specifically Iranian culture and identity. The relationship between women and society in Iran has been profoundly affected by these interactions and the contest for power that has often accompanied them. For much of the last century, from the late Qajar period, through the years of Pahlavi dominance, and since the Islamic revolution, representatives of religion and the state have competed with each other to secure their own visions of Iranian society. In the process of this struggle to configure Iranian identity, matters involving women have been drawn into the heart of debates and policy changes by advocates and critics of reform alike.

The centrality of Shi'i Islam to the character of Iranian culture and social life is explored by Shireen Mahdavi in her article 'Women, Shi'ism and Cuisine in Iran' which investigates connections between the evolution of Persian cooking from the time of the Safavid period onwards, and the position of women within Persian/Iranian society. Employing an innovative long-term perspective on this issue, Mahdavi is able to place the developments under scrutiny within a framework of trends that have taken place, not just over decades, but over centuries. Mahdavi's main focus is on the way in which the cultural norms established by religious belief and practice affect crucial day-to-day aspects of the lives of certain kinds of elite Iranian women, but she also highlights the importance of the nature of the state under the Safavids, and later the Qajars, in helping to establish conditions which favoured the emergence of an elaborate and highly specialized cuisine.

In the late nineteenth century, Iranian women by all accounts lived largely secluded lives. Iran, however, was not isolated from political developments taking place outside its borders, and had been drawn increasingly into the contest between imperial powers for supremacy within the region. As a result, the Qajar state came under pressure not just to resist foreign political control but also to fortify Iranian society, its culture and traditions, against unwelcome foreign interference. One particularly sensitive area was the whole question of the status of Iranian womanhood. Iranian women, like their counterparts in other societies which encountered the challenges of western political dominance and western notions of what being 'civilized' meant, had the spotlight cast on them, exposing every presumed blemish associated with their lives as well as highlighting their supposed virtues. They became the targets of reformers, Iranian and foreign. Their emancipation was a heated topic of discussion. As with other Muslim societies at the turn of the twentieth century, the merits and dangers of introducing reforms were vigorously disputed.[8]

Christian missionaries in Iran, not surprisingly perhaps, were included among those who participated in this debate. As Gulnar Francis-Dehqani underlines in her 'CMS Women Missionaries in Iran, 1891–1934: Attitudes towards Islam and Muslim Women', seeking to reform what they perceived as the 'pitiable' status of Iranian women provided much of the *raison d'être* for British women who came out to Iran to work as missionaries, even when the impetus for their mission was complicated, and had more to do with social developments back home than what was taking place abroad. Much the same could be said for American missionaries working in Iran during the same period. Michael Zirinsky, in 'A Presbyterian Vocation to Reform Gender Relations in Iran: the Career of Annie Stocking Boyce', explores how far the social agenda brought with these missionaries translated into the actual experiences and initiatives of one individual missionary. Boyce served in Iran from 1906 to 1941, and during that time worked as hard to encourage Iranian women to become more 'American' in life-style as she did to convert them, in contrast to the British missionaries, who, according to Dehqani, sought to 'Christianize' rather than westernize Iranian society. In the regular reports written by Boyce, it is also possible to trace, albeit through the eyes of an 'outsider', the extent to which the state under Reza Shah Pahlavi sought to control the way in which Iranian womanhood developed, attempting to fashion the kind of female individual who could reinforce Iran's claims to be a modern society as well as retain the cultural and moral independence which Iran was seeking for itself during the interwar years.

The main instrument which Boyce employed to get her messages across to as wide an audience as possible was a magazine entitled *Alam-i-Nesvan* which was dedicated to the 'uplift' of Iranian women. In Iran, again in similar fashion to what was happening in other Muslim societies, the first half of the twentieth century witnessed a relative explosion in the number of women who learned to read and write. Opportunities for girls to receive a formal education, while generally limited to those from families with the necessary financial resources, increased, and this trend was reflected in greater numbers of women making their voices heard *via* the printed word. Indeed, there has been a great deal of scholarly interest in the impact of growing female literacy on debates on the position of women in these Muslim societies, how far men spoke for women, and how far women took the initiative and spoke for themselves. In both Egypt and Muslim South Asia, for example, concerned male social reformers and, to a lesser extent, independent-minded women alike, used newspapers, magazines and journals as channels through which to address issues affecting women's lives and, usually by implication, the well-being of society as a whole.[9]

The growth in female literacy and literary activities similarly played a key role in developments in Iran. Hossein Shahidi's 'Women and Journalism in Iran' reviews the role of Iranian women in journalism from their first forays into this world through to the present day, and analyses their growing involvement in relation to increased female literacy, the enhancement of female social, political and economic participation and the impact of rising urbanization. Likewise, Anna Vanzan in 'From the Royal Harem to a Post-Modern Islamic Society: Some Considerations on Women Prose Writers in Iran from Qajar Times to the 1990s' casts a long-term perspective on the patterns of prose writing associated with Iranian women writers over the century. This intensely individual activity eventually offered Iranian women opportunities to explore their own society critically while, as Vanzan argues, remaining firmly rooted within it, and this is also evident in the themes and styles expressed by female writers since 1979 in which 'traditional' and 'modern' cultural models have been closely intertwined. Farian Sabahi continues the theme of female literacy in her study of how the state in Iran tackled the question of female education during the Pahlavi period and the momentum which had developed by the time of Muhammad Reza Shah's White Revolution of the 1960s and 1970s. 'Gender and the Army of Knowledge in Pahlavi Iran (1969–1979)' in addition provides valuable insights into the strategies of the Pahlavi state for dealing with and containing Iranian 'feminism', efforts which mirrored those of other Muslim states, such as Nasser's Egypt and Ayub Khan's Pakistan, where during the 1950s and 1960s officially-blessed government-sponsored organizations and initiatives allowed hardly any space for independent women's movements to operate and develop.[10]

The 1979 watershed which separated the Pahlavi period from that of the Islamic republic has proved to be a decisive moment in Iranian history from the point of view of the sensitive triangular relationship between women, religion and culture. The 'aftershocks' generated by the Islamic revolution made a profound impact on the lives of particular groups of Iranian women, especially those for whom the freedom to move outside the 'traditional' sphere of activities reserved for women of their class had increased under the Shah. In the years immediately following the revolution, much attention was focused by critics of the new government on what were perceived to be the negative consequences of its policies for women, the introduction of compulsory *hijab*, the limiting of female employment and educational opportunities, and the generally con-servative rhetoric which characterized official pronouncements on the position and role of women in post-1979 Iranian society.[11]

A generation later, developments on the gender front in Iran have not stood still. Indeed by the late 1990s, the Iranian political context seemed to have created conditions for an extraordinarily lively debate on issues concerning gender, something not found to anything like the same degree in other societies with a theocratic government in power. In 'From Islamization to the Individualization of Women in Post-Revolutionary Iran', Azadeh Kian-Thiébaut reflects on this in her discussion of the ways in which the implementation of the *shari'a* by the Islamic state after 1979 triggered greater autonomy, and a sense of individualism among Iranian women. This was linked to the efforts of social and legal activists, religious as well as secular, to reform laws which emphasize the identity of Iranian women as wives and mothers rather than as individuals in their own right. Kian-Thiébaut's research shows how women in contemporary Iran have been able to take advantage of the situation in which they find themselves and so challenge the state with greater confidence. While they may still be 'behind the veil', these women, it seems, behave like women in any secular society with the necessary difference or proviso that they must cope with the Islamic state's vision of correct moral behaviour. Indeed, women in Iran have been busy taking advantage of opportunities generated by economic and educational change to demand that their role in society be reassessed and reassigned in line with this changing reality.

Images of women acting 'independently' and making choices for themselves are reinforced by Azam Torab's study, 'The Politicization of Women's Religious Circles in Post-revolutionary Iran', which compares and contrasts women's religious circles with men's formal religious associations, and links politicized female religiosity to the bid by Iranian women for greater political participation in recent years. Across the Muslim world, the religious practices and rituals of women still remain relatively hidden: on the whole, Muslim women do not tend to worship 'in public' in the mosque like men, but rather they act out their religious lives 'in private', at home or within restricted circles. With the increase in politicized Islam, women have been linked to the upsurge in religious fervour, but it is often taken for granted that they participate as 'hangers-on', exploited to a large degree by male leaders or family members who seek the moral sanction endowed by their involvement. Torab challenges both this assumption that Muslim women have had little to contribute, as well as the dominant portrayal of Iranian women as first and foremost victims, and demonstrates very clearly the extent to which they have pursued an active role in the growing politicization of religion both before and after 1979. Their separate organizations and activities have given these Iranian women a discrete space within which they have been able to express a range of opinions distinct from, as well as supportive of, those of their male counterparts.

Yet the practices and rituals undertaken by Muslim women, Iranian or otherwise, have always been important in preserving religious identity and traditions. Muslim reformers in different parts of the world from the late nineteenth century onwards were acutely aware of the decline in Muslim confidence and so placed renewed emphasis on the responsibilities of individual

Muslims as the way for the community to overcome its crisis of faith. Conscious of the importance of the role filled by women in the lives of their families, these reformers deliberately targeted women, perceived to be weak links in the chain, as key players in this process of reform. Usually, however, it was a matter of male reformers deciding that they knew what was best for their community, with little sense of any dialogue between men and women. A particularly interesting aspect, therefore, of contemporary developments in Iran is the growing evidence of the extent to which male religious experts have had to take female concerns on board. Whether these concerns are articulated by post-revolutionary secular or so-called Islamic feminists, representatives of the Islamic ruling order have had to make room within their ideological parameters for women to be endowed with greater religio-political significance than they were prepared to concede in the past. This important shifting of ground is explored by Ziba Mir-Hosseini in her article 'Islam, Women and Civil Rights: The Religious Debate in the Iran of the 1990s', which exposes the vitality of discussion on the status of women in 1990s Iran where ideas came to be hotly contested, albeit within a Muslim framework. By analysing the ways in which specialists in Islamic jurisprudence have confronted the changing social realities of Iranian women's lives, she highlights how far these shifts have led to change in jurisprudential constructions of gender. Some of the issues under discussion are specifically Islamic in that they are related closely to the lives of Muslim women in Iran, but others involve concerns which affect women in any society, Muslim or otherwise.

Another significant legacy of the 1979 revolution are the Iranian emigré communities now living in different parts of the western and non-western world. Large numbers of Iranians, for instance, have migrated to the United States where, in the process of settling, they have encountered very different ideas about the role of women to those that they left behind them in Iran. Akbar Mahdi in 'Perceptions of Gender Roles among Female Iranian Immigrants in the United States' investigates how far perceptions of gender roles among Iranian women living in the United States have evolved as a consequence of their migration, allowing women's voices to be heard in the process. As with the articles that examine developments in Iran since 1979, this study, by looking at Iranian emigrants' engagement with migration and American culture, defies many of the stereotypes of Iranian women found in western countries. Yet, whilst they hold views which might surprise many western onlookers, these women also seem to have been able to hold on to those cultural values which remain important to them as Iranian Muslims, in effect synthesizing the realities of their former and current lives in their own individual fashion. Indeed, trends towards globalization mean that women still living in Iran are now, whether they realize it or not, members of trans-national communities with shared interests and agendas. Asghar Fathi's 'Communities in Place and Communities in Space: Globalization and Feminism in Iran' attributes great weight to the technological developments which have permitted this process of globalization and which he suggests had positively contributed to improvements in the status of Iranian women by the 1990s. Despite what he perceives as significant setbacks caused by the policies of the post-1979 Iranian authorities, the realities and demands of a changing late twentieth-century society have intervened to help mitigate these disadvantages and encourage the Islamic state to review its approach towards women. At the same time, Fathi draws attention to the fact that most Iranian women share the same kinds of values as those of the majority of Iranian men, and so regard, like them, the policies of the Islamic state on women as legitimate and valid.

The articles in *Women, Religion and Culture in Iran* taken together clearly reinforce the argument that women can no longer be marginalized in any attempt to understand the ways in which societies such as Iran have coped with the complex challenges of the twentieth century. To paraphrase Paidar, understanding the position of Iranian women more than ever requires delving into both historical and contemporary social relations and political processes.[12] In addition, it means addressing the rigorously contested question of the impact of 'modernity', which lurks as a sub-text throughout this collection. But abandoning what now seems like the over-simplistic dichotomy of the 'traditional' versus the 'modern' in favour of less clear cut and more permeable boundaries between the two, as many of the contributors do, allows us to acknowledge that so-called 'traditional' cultures are very often no more 'static, monolithic, or misogynist' than their supposedly more dynamic and 'modern' counterparts. Processes of modernization, as the articles here suggest, can reinforce tradition as much as they challenge customs and beliefs. And, as Iran's recent past demonstrates, 'a view of culture as dynamic … can [also] help demythologise the concept of tradition'.[13] At the same time, 'twentieth century modernity', in the context of Iran, has assumed its own very specific character. When the modernizing state of the Pahlavi era sought to transform Iran along self-consciously western lines, its efforts were constrained by the particular nature and circumstances of Iranian society. Similarly, the Islamic state since 1979 has been unable to impose fully its vision of the correct place for women as a result of the structural changes which have occurred within Iranian society during this period.[14] Thus the lives of growing numbers of Iranian women at the beginning of the twenty-first century appear both significantly different from but also familiar to that of their mothers and grandmothers: with or without the chador, they look set to continue making a very significant and increasingly public impact on the nature of society and the state in Iran in future years.

Notes

1 For example, see Leslie P. Pierce (1993) *The Imperial Harem: Women and Sovereignty in the Ottoman Empire*, Oxford, and articles in Nikki Keddie and Beth Baron, (eds.) (1991), *Women in Middle Eastern History: Shifting Boundaries in Sex and Gender*, New Haven and London.

2 Barbara N. Ramusack and Sharon Sievers (1999) *Women in Asia: Restoring Women to History*, Bloomington, p. xxv.

3 Haideh Moghissi (1994) *Populism and Feminism in Iran: Women's Struggle in a Male-defined Revolutionary Movement*, London, p. 183.

4 Parvin Paidar (1995) *Women and the Political Process in Twentieth-Century Iran*, Cambridge; Janet Afary, 'On the Origins of Feminism in Early 20th-Century Iran', *Journal of Women's History*, Vol. 1, No. 2, Fall 1989; Joanna de Groot, 'The Dialectics of Gender: Women, Men and Political Discourses in Iran *c.* 1890–1930, *Gender and History*, Vol. 5, No. 2, Summer 1993; Valentine Moghadam, 'Women in the Islamic Republic of Iran: inequality, accommodation, resistance', in Valentine Moghadam (1993) *Modernising Women: Gender and Social Change in the Middle East*, Boulder, Colerado.

5 Haleh Afshar, 'Islam and feminism: an analysis of political strategies', in Mai Yamani, (ed.) (1996) *Feminism and Islam: Legal and Literary Perspectives*, Reading; Haleh Afshar (1998) *Islam and Feminisms: an Iranian case study* London; Haideh Moghissi (1999) *Feminism and Islamic Fundamentalism: The Limits of Postmodern Analysis*, London.

6 Afsaneh Najmabadi, 'Veiled Discourse-Unveiled Bodies', *Feminist Studies*, Vol. 19, No. 3, Fall 1993; Afsaneh Najmabadi, 'Feminism in an Islamic Republic: "Years of Hardship, Years of Growth"', in Yvonne Yazbeck Haddad and John L. Esposito, (eds.) (1998) *Islam, Gender and Social Change*, Oxford; Hisae Nakanishi, 'Power, Ideology and Women's Consciousness in Postrevolutionary Iran', in Herbert L. Bodman and Nayereh Tohidi, (eds.) (1998) *Women in Muslim Societies: Diversity within Unity*, Boulder, Colorado.

7 Ziba Mir-Hosseini (1993) *Marriage on Trial: A Study of Islamic Family Law*, London; Ziba Mir-Hosseini, 'Divorce, Veiling and Feminism in Post-Khomeini Iran', in Haleh Afshar, (ed.) (1996) London, *Women and Politics in the Third World*, London; Ziba Mir-Hosseini, 'Stretching the Limits: a feminist reading of the shariʿa in post-Khomeni Iran', in Mai Yamani, (ed.) (1996) *Feminism and Islam*, Reading; Azadeh Kian, 'Women and Politics in Post-Islamist Iran: the gender conscious drive to change', *British Journal of Middle Eastern Studies*, Vol. 24, No. 1, 1997.

8 For details on these kinds of debates in Egypt, see Margot Badran (1994) *Feminists, Islam and the Nation: Gender and the Making of Modern Egypt*, Princeton, and for developments in Muslim India, see Barbara Metcalf (1996), *Perfecting Women: Maulana Ashraf Ali Thanawi's Bihishti Zewar*, Berkeley, particularly the introduction.

9 For example, see Beth Baron (1994) *The Women's Awakening in Egypt: Culture, Society and the Press*, New Haven and London and Gail Minault (1998) *Secluded Scholars: Women's Education and Muslim Social Reform in Colonial India*, Oxford, especially Chapter 2 'A Suitable Literature' and Chapter 3 'Ladies' Home Journals: Women's Magazines in Urdu'.

10 For Egypt, see Badran, *Feminism, Islam and the Nation*, and for Pakistan, see Ayesha Jalal, 'The Convenience of Subservience: Women and the State of Pakistan', in Deniz Kandiyoti, (ed.) (1991) *Women, Islam and the State*, London.

11 For example, see articles in Farah Azari, (ed.) (1983) *Women of Iran: the Conflict with Fundamentalist Islam*, Reading.

12 Paidar, *Women and the Political Process*, p. 22.

13 Ramusack and Sievers, *Women in Asia*, p. xxv.

14 For discussion of the factors, such as the Iran–Iraq war, economic restructuring and women's own responses, which have constrained the power of the state to transform gender relations, see Maryam Poya (1999) *Women, Work and Islamism: Ideology and Resistance in Iran* London.

two

Women, Shi'ism and Cuisine in Iran

Shireen Mahdavi

The cuisine of Persia in its delicacy and intricacy resembles her other great arts: carpet weaving, miniature painting and poetry. This cuisine, which has been perfected through centuries of refinement, holds its own place with the most sophisticated cuisines of the world, such as the Chinese and the French. Persian cuisine in its present form has its origin in the Safavid period (1501–1722) when Shi'i Islam was declared the official religion of the country. One significant result of this declaration was the seclusion and confinement of women. Thus the affluent women of Persia were the only group with time and leisure to devote to the creation and development of the art of cooking.

The position of women within a social structure which isolated them and therefore kept them professionally idle produced the elaborate cuisine, one function of which was to keep the women busy at home. This chapter presents a hypothesis linking the evolution of Persian cuisine to the position of women, a relationship which has so far not been explored, and which merits further research.

Food and sex constitute the two basic needs of man and the foundation for the survival of the human race. The result of the one is production, and that of the other reproduction. Social and economic institutions have developed as a consequence of both necessities. Thus cooking is a social institution which cannot be viewed in isolation from the other institutions of a society and must be analysed within the totality of the social and economic context of the society itself.

More than any other discipline, anthropology has occupied itself with the subject of cuisine. The early anthropologists were interested in cooking from the supernatural and ritualistic point of view. Later the functionalist anthropologists, A.R. Radcliffe-Brown (1881–1955) and Bronlislaw Malinowski

(1884–1955), abandoned the religious explanation and emphasized the social function of food in creating, expressing and maintaining social relations.

The most well-known structuralist anthropologist who today is identified with the analysis of cooking is Claude Levi-Strauss. His primary objective and interest is to look at the spirit, *l'esprit humaine*, underlying various social structures, including cooking. He is concerned not only with the social structure itself, but with the structure of individual thought, particularly the unconscious one, underlying that structure. Society and culture are analysed in terms of language, and its various institutions in terms of the communications that take place between the individual and the group. Cooking is analysed in this manner as an unconscious form of language which expresses a structure.[1] However a comprehensive analysis should treat these approaches as complementary, rather than contradictory.

A recent comprehensive approach to cooking has been undertaken by the distinguished British anthropologist, Jack Goody. He compares traditional African cultures, which do not possess a *haute cuisine*, with Eurasian cultures, which do, and in answer to what conditions are necessary for the emergence of a high cuisine, he suggests that one major factor is the political and cultural stratification of society.[2] He considers the prerequisites for the emergence of a great cuisine like that of the Chinese.[3]

An elaborate cuisine is primarily related to a specific system of food production and distribution. In the first place a large number of ingredients should be available together with a wide range of recipes. The point here is that a great cuisine cannot develop if it is limited to the ingredients available in only one region. The second prerequisite is that there should be a large body of critical gourmet consumers. The court, courtiers and the aristocracy by themselves cannot provide this number: a broader elite of officials, civil servants and merchants are needed. Thirdly, there should exist in the society an attitude which gives priority to the pleasure of food consumption. A fourth very important prerequisite is the development of commerce and agriculture to create a foundation for the above three. Goody adds literacy as a further prerequisite for the development of an elaborate cuisine as it creates opportunities for learning and the transmission of recipes which can be passed on from one generation to another whilst being modified or elaborated upon.[4] A additional important prerequisite for a complex cuisine, is the availability of labour, domestic or otherwise.

Another important requirement for the formation of a great cuisine which is not touched upon in the literature but is perhaps assumed, is a settled population and urbanization: a mobile nomad population, which is engaged in neither trade nor agriculture, cannot develop a great cuisine. In the final analysis a *haute cuisine* is a feature of a hierarchical stratified society.

All social institutions evolve with time. Thus, in order to understand them more fully, the history of their evolution must be considered. The cuisine of any society today cannot be analysed without an historical examination of its evolution.

The origin of Persian cuisine lies in its ancient empires, particularly that of the Sassanids (226–651 AD), who ruled over most of the present day Middle East. As the empire expanded, major developments took place in the culture of food and cooking. Court cuisine reflected the grandeur and extravagances which were partially responsible for the downfall of the empire.[5] Many of the suggested prerequisites of a great cuisine existed in Sassanid society. The cuisines of the various conquered regions were brought together, as well as ingredients from far-off lands. The desire for luxury and the love of all pleasures, including that of good food, was prevalent in the court.

Christensen gives a vivid and detailed description of the court cuisine. The goat meat had to be that of a two month old goat, fed on its mother's milk plus cow milk. Amongst the different kinds of poultry the most preferred was an ordinary young chicken fed on hemp, olive oil and butter. After being killed and plucked, it was suspended for one day by foot, the second day by its neck and finally cooked in salted water. A recipe known as the 'King's Plate' consisted of hot and cold meats, rice jelly, stuffed vine leaves, marinated chicken and a sweet date purée. There were other recipes known by their regional names such as the 'Khorassanian Plate' and the 'Greek Plate'. A variety of jams, sweets and pastries are enumerated. The cuisine was highly complex and time consuming.[6]

After the conquest of Persia by the Arabs (636 AD), this life-style and cuisine were inherited and revived by the 'Abbasid caliphs (750–1258) who emulated most things Persian.[7] The banquets of the caliphs were renowned for their extravagances, variety and lavishness.[8] According to the Sassanid tradition, a court gentleman, in addition to his other accomplishments, was expected to have a practical as well as a literary acquaintance with cooking.[9] Essential elements of the royal banquet were erudition and the arts of poetry and conversation. For example the tenth-century Baghdad Caliph Mustakfi gave a banquet at which all the guests were expected to discuss the different varieties of food and the poetry that had been composed about them. Whilst the poetry was being recited, the food was being prepared in exactly the same manner.[10]

The cooking was cosmopolitan, the ingredients rare and expensive, from distant lands, and the procedure complex and lengthy. Multiple operations followed one another: roasting, boiling many times over and frying, whilst intricate sauces and ingredients such as minced meat with vegetables were being prepared for later addition. The names of many of the dishes and the flavourings, such as rose water from Fars and saffron from Isfahan in Iran, bear witness to the fact that their origin was Persian.[11]

The end of the 'Abbasid era (1258) brought about a change in the class of people interested in cooking. It was no longer the game of princes but the realm of scholars, who were interested in preserving for themselves and posterity the foods they liked. Thus the recipes which survive date from the thirteenth century, amongst them the famous *Kitab al-Tabikh* by Muammad b. al Katib al Baghdadi translated by A.J. Arberry as 'A Baghdad Cookery Book' written in 1226, that is 32 years before the fall of the 'Abbasids.[12]

There is a lacuna in our knowledge of Persian cuisine from the fall of the caliphate at the hands of the Mongols in 1258, and the rise of the Safavids in 1501. The advent of the Mongols and their subsequent conquest of Persia resulted, amongst many other things, in an interruption in the tradition of writing recipe books. Consequently our knowledge of the cuisine prevalent in Persia during the Il-Khanid period is limited, although there are detailed descriptions of the ingredients available through geography books, travel accounts and other writings of the time. The Mongols, probably due to their mobile nomadic nature, did not possess a *haute cuisine*. Their cuisine consisted of horse meat and fermented milk.[13] They possessed only one cooking utensil, a pot. According to the meagre sources available on cuisine during the Mongol period, not only did they not influence the cuisine of Persia, but they adopted and subsequently imported it to India. In Persian culture there exists only one dish, *shula*, the base of which is rice, the origin of which is attributed to the Mongols. In the Safavid cookbooks to be discussed below there are fifteen types of *shula*, but the most prevalent in Persia today is *shulizard*, a type of sweet rice pudding with saffron.[14] The fact that the Turko-Mongolian pastoral nomads roaming Persia in the Middle Ages did not possess a *haute cuisine* is further verified by the travel account of Ruy Gonzales de Clavijo, ambassador of Henry III of Castille to the court of Taymur in 1403. He describes many meals served en route by the local tribal notables or vassals of Taymur as well as feasts given by Taymur. According to his account, the principal meal of the elite was meat, both horse and sheep, either roasted or boiled, a whole roasted horse with its head on being the most special.[15] The food of the poorer members of the population also originated from their occupation of pastoral nomadism, namely a preserved dairy product, which appears to have been a cross between cheese and yogurt, and which could be kept for long periods.[16]

Our knowledge of the cuisine of the settled Persian population in the Timurid period stems from an unexpected quarter – the poet Bushaq (Abu Ishaq) At'ima, Fakhr al-Din Hallaj Shirazi. He was born in Shiraz in the early second half of the fourteenth-century and died in approximately 1423–27. The title 'Hallaj' indicates that he was a cotton carder by profession. Bushaq was a satirical poet whose *Divan*, using Persian culinary vocabulary and imagery, is a parody of the style of Firdusi, Khayam, Rumi, Hafiz, Sa'adi and other famous Persian poets whom he admired.[17] It is his work that provides evidence that Persian cuisine had either not disappeared during the 150 years of upheaval in the history of Persia or had once again found its way back into Persia. Due to a lack of sources only a hypothesis is possible. Primarily, this survival may be due to the fact that Shiraz was spared the onslaught of the Turko-Mongol hordes and in Fars, being the land of the Persians, much survived including the food. Alternatively it may be that the Muzaffarid dynasty (1313–93), who ruled Fars after the fall of the Il-Khanids and for the greater part of Bushaq's life, although claiming Arab descent, had been in Persia for six decades since the Muslim conquest and had been Persianized.[18] The survival of Persian cuisine may have been due to them and to other non Turko-Mongol dynasties and people.

The *Divan-i 'At'ima* is the only complete source available on the subject for the period under discussion, and contains numerous culinary terms of Persian cuisine up to the period of Bushaq's life. Not only are the names of various foods and ingredients given, but the festive occasions associated with them are spelled out, the eating habits of people described and even some brief recipes given.

The *Divan* consists of seven different parts. The longest and the most informative section of the *Divan* for culinary purposes is the first part, *Kanz al-Ishtiha* (Treasure of Appetite). It starts with an introductory section in prose followed by ten chapters in poetry. The sections are categorized according to different types of food and include sections on ready made food available in the bazaar, ingredients available in the grocery shop and food appropriate for the poor.

Although Bushaq frequented the court of the governor of Fars, the Timurid Prince Iskandar Mirza (1409–14), he was by profession a cotton carder and therefore moved in all social circles and was familiar with food consumed by different classes.[19] This is an interesting aspect of the *Divan* in comparison with the courtly Safavid recipes to be discussed below.

The foods named and discussed by Bushaq fall between those of *The Baghdad Cookery Book* and the following Safavid recipes, although many of them, at least in name if not by being the exact recipe, exist in present day Persian cuisine. Some in the process have acquired Arabic names, for instance *qaliya* which is the same as the Sassanian *khurish*, as it is known in today's Persia. Most of the ingredients mentioned are also used today. The major difference appears to be that the cooking takes place in one pot and there is a scarcity of rice recipes. In fact only four kinds of rice dishes are mentioned as opposed to eleven different kinds of *ash*. However the most important rice dish mentioned, *muz'affar* or yellow rice with saffron, appears to be similar to the present day *murgh pulau* particularly as it is sometimes mentioned with chicken.[20] The preponderance of rice dishes were to appear in the Safavid period.

The renaissance of Persian society after centuries of conquest and scattered dynasties took place under the Safavids (1501–1722). Many of the prerequisites cited for the emergence of a great cuisine existed in Safavid society. It was a hierarchial society both culturally and politically. At the top of the hierarchy was the Shah, and at the bottom the peasants in the rural areas and the artisans, shopkeepers and small merchants in the urban areas. Between these two poles was the aristocracy, both civil and military. Further a large, prominent and influential middle class in the form of the *'ulama* emerged during the Safavid period.

When the Safavids declared Shi'ism as the official religion of Iran, there was total ignorance of Shi'i theology in the country.[21] A new class, the *'ulama*, were needed, both for expounding the theology and for the imposition of the new religion. Prominent Shi'i *'ulama* had to be imported into Iran to establish this class. The head of the religious classes under the Safavids was known as the *Sadr* and was appointed politically.[22] By the end of Shah Isma'il's reign, when the conversion of the population to Shi'ism was almost completed, the *Sadr* and the religious classes devoted themselves mainly to the administration of religious institutions and the supervision of *vaqf* property, (land endowed to religious institutions). The management of the increasing amount of *vaqf* property created communal interests between the *'ulama* and the growing merchant classes and members of the *asnaf* (artisan guilds). A close alliance developed between the religious classes and the bazaar community.[23] These groups constituted a new culinary circle of consumers.

The Safavid economy was both agricultural and pastoral. Crops, mainly cereals were grown. There was an abundance of fruits of all kinds, especially grapes. Wine was produced by Jewish and Armenian communities and consumed in the royal court, an example of the strong influence of the pre-Islamic Persian past. At the zenith of Safavid reign under Shah 'Abbas I (1587–1628) international trade flourished. Thus all the prerequisites for the emergence of a *haute cuisine* were present and the Safavid cooking manuals bear witness to the appearance of such a cuisine.

There are few historical manuals of cooking in Persian. Two manuals dating from the Safavid period have recently been published. The first, called *Karnama*, was written in 1523 by a cook named Muammad 'Ali Bavarchi to an unknown aristocrat during the reign of Shah Isma'il (1501–24). The second, called *Maddat al-Hayat* was written 76 years later in 1599 by Nurallah who was cook to Shah 'Abbas I.[24]

A comparison of the two manuals throws a considerable amount of light on the development of cooking during the Safavid period. Bavarchi, the earlier cook, mentions 26 different kinds of *pulau* (rice cooked in the Persian manner containing ingredients) and eighteen kinds of *ash* (a thick soup containing herbs, cereals and rice). By the time we get to Nurallah's manual there are 54 kinds of *pulau* and 32 types of *ash*. The variety has almost doubled. Bavarchi does not give any recipes for *dulma* (stuffed vegetables or stuffed vine leaves), whereas Nurallah gives two *dulma* recipes. They both mention only one type of *kuku* (an egg-based dish, a cross between a quiche and an omelette).

Another cooking manual in Persian has come down from the Qajar period (1796–1925). It is called *Sufra-yi At'ima* and was written in 1883 by Mirza 'Ali Akbar Khan Ashpaz Bashi, cook to Nasir al-Din Shah Qajar (1848–96).[25] A comparison of the three manuals is most illuminating. The Qajar recipes are much more elaborate, refined and time consuming, containing dishes which did not exist in the Safavid period. A particular feature of the Safavid cooking in common with that of the 'Abbasid and the Timurid periods is one-pot cooking. Even the cooking of rice (*pulau*), which reaches the height of its refinement during the Qajar period, goes through a one-pot process during the Safavid period. In contrast Mirza 'Ali Akbar Khan describes in detail the four-fold process of washing, soaking, boiling and baking which goes into the final production of the rice.

Figure 2.1 Still life in front of palace garden with birds and a rabbit. Artist unknown, early to mid 19th century.

By courtesy of the Hashem Khosrovani Qajar Collection

A particular feature of Persian cuisine, the finely chopped herbs which go into many dishes, are missing from the Safavid recipes, although there is evidence that they were in existence during the period as John Fryer, who visited Persia in 1672, cites 25 different kinds of herbs and vegetables.[26] The elaborate *khurish*, or ragouts for plain rice (*chilau*), of which Mirza 'Ali Akbar Khan cites 16 major types and then further subdivisions within each type, are also missing from the Safavid recipes. For instance, within the major type of *fisinjan* there are ten sub-types. In contrast to one type of *kuku* and two types of *dulma* during the Safavid period, Mirza 'Ali Akbar Khan cites 13 different types of *kuku* and six different types of *dulma*. In point of fact, aside from the preponderance of the many rice dishes, the Safavid cuisine resembles more that of the 'Abbasids and the Timurid period in Persia than that of the Qajars. Three centuries separate the end of the 'Abbasids from the Safavids; similarly there are three centuries between the recipes of Muammad 'Ali Bavarchi and Mirza 'Ali Akbar Khan Ashpaz Bashi. The question arises as to what major institutional changes took place in Persian society between 1500 and 1800 AD to affect the nature of the cuisine.

In 1501 Shi'ism was declared the official religion of Persia by Shah Isma'il Safavid. The change in religion had two direct effects on Persian society: first the creation of a new influential class of Shi'i *'ulama*, and second the absolute seclusion of urban women. Rural and tribal women, due to their economic role in society, have never been secluded and there is some evidence that before the advent of the Safavids most women were neither secluded nor veiled.

The religious beliefs and reigning ideology of any society determine the fate of the masses, including women, and Iran has been no exception to this rule. At every stage of its history the position of women has been defined by the religion in practice at the time.

Zoroastrianism was the religion of the ancient Iranians. The story of the creation according to an off-shoot of this religion, Zurvanisim, specifies its views on the position of the female *vis-à-vis* the male in the world at large. According to this myth, man and woman were created simultaneously and equally out of plant life, as opposed to the Biblical story of creation in which Eve was created out of Adam's rib to assuage his need.[27] Not only did the female hold an honourable position in Zoroastrian mythology, but she also had well-defined civil rights in the society of the time.[28] There are documented examples of female rulers in ancient Iran. In the Sassanian period (AD 226–650) two of the daughters of Khusru Parviz, Purandukht and Azarmidukht, also reigned as queens. Purandukht is considered to have been an able queen who signed a peace treaty with Heraklius, the Byzantine emperor, returning to Jerusalem the wood of the cross on which Christ was crucified. Thus on the eve of the Arab invasion of Iran, not only were there female rulers, but women owned property, could become the guardians of disinherited sons, and could go to court both on behalf of and against their husbands.[29]

The Islamic position on women provided women in Arabia with certain legal rights, absent prior to Islam. These contained specific safeguards for the protection of women's property rights. These rights are considered revolutionary for their time and place of origin. However, the importation of this ideology into Iran after the Islamic conquest did not elevate the position of women with respect to the conditions held previously, but in fact it eliminated some of the existing rights and customs to the detriment of women. After the Islamic conquest, women in Iran never participated in politics officially nor ruled directly.

When in 1501 the Safavids declared Shi'ism the state religion of Persia the majority of the population were still Sunnis and many of the customs and institutions of the Timurid and Aqquyunlu periods still prevailed including

Figure 2.2 Still life in front of palace garden with cat. Artist unknown, early to mid 19th century.

By courtesy of the Hashem Khosrovani Qajar Collection

those related to the position of women. These Turkic dynasties shared many tribal ways in common with the Mongols including the high status of women. Women held a higher social position in the Turkic societies than within orthodox Islamic communities.[30] In her work on women during the Mongol period (1258–1335) Shireen Bayani notes that women held a prominent position both politically and socially.[31] The author attributes their high position to the predominance of tribal customs. She maintains that the Mongol success in putting these customs into practice was due to the fact that for two and a half centuries prior to the Mongol invasion, Iran had been ruled by Turks who shared many essential tribal ways in common with the Mongols. In considering this view it is interesting to note that women in Iran entered a period of relative obscurity and seclusion under two dynasties of Turkish origin: the Safavids and the Qajars. The question arises as to what ideology distinguished these two reigning dynasties from previous Turkish dynasties to the extent of changing their tribal customs. Beyond a certain amount of urbanization and great sedentarization, the most striking difference is the Safavid 1501 proclamation of Shi'ism as the official religion of Iran.

The tribal customs were still prevailing at the beginning of the reign of the Safavids. There is some evidence of the relative freedom, independence and influence of women in the early Safavid period.[32] Contemporary reports by Italian travellers and merchants indicate that, at the beginning of the Safavid reign, women were neither veiled nor secluded. In his account of the Battle of Chaldiran in 1514 between the Ottoman Sultan Selim (1512–20) and the first Safavid Shah Isma'il (1501–24), Caterino Zeno says: 'The Persian ladies themselves follow in arms the same fortunes as their husbands, and fight like men, in the same way as those ancient Amazons who performed such feats of arms in their time.'[33] There is further evidence of the physical prowess of the early Safavid women and their participation in the Battle of Chaldiran in the popular Safavid histories. Tajlu Khanum, one of Shah Isma'il's wives and the mother of Shah Tahmasb is reputed to have been an able fencer and wrestler who participated in the battle of Chaldiran.[34] Another royal woman who actually led an army in 1578–79 against the Ottomans in the battle of Shirvan was Khayr al-Nisa Bigum, the wife of Shah Muhammad Khudabanda.[35] An Italian merchant travelling in Persia during the same period, in discussing taxes, reports the abundance of prostitution, which seems to have been officially recognized and even encouraged. He says: 'Also the harlots, who frequent the public places, are bound to pay according to their beauty, as the prettier they are the more they will have to pay.'[36]

The head-to-toe covering, which became the custom during the later Safavid period and continued through the Qajar era to their official unveiling in 1936 does not appear to have been prevalent in the early Safavid period. Vincentio d'Alessandri, Venetian ambassador to the court of Shah Tahmasb (1524–76) describes the women as follows: 'The women are mostly ugly, though of fine features and noble dispositions, their costumes not being so refined as those of the Turkish ladies. They wear robes of silk, veils on their heads and show their faces openly. They have pearls and other jewels on their head.'[37]

This is further confirmed by the Venetian Michele Membre who went on a mission to the court of Shah Tahmasb who says: 'the Shah's maidens pass on fine horses; and they ride like men and dress like men, except that on their heads they do not wear caps but white kerchiefs ... and they were beautiful'.[38] Although it appears that Membre and D'Alessandri disagree on the facial characteristics of the women, the important fact is that these Europeans were permitted to see the women's faces.

In the early Safavid period a number of royal women played important political roles. Tajlu Khanum the mother of Shah Tahmasb, mentioned earlier, was eventually banished by her son for her political activities. Pari Khan Khanum, the daughter of Shah Tahmasb, was not only an influential princess during her father's reign but was also involved in politics after her father's death. She was a kingmaker who was instrumental in the accession of two successive Safavid Shahs, Isma'il II and Muhammad Khudabanda, which eventually led to her murder.[39] Ironically it was another influential Safavid woman, Khayr al-Nisa Bigum, the wife of Muhammad Khudabanda, who was instrumental in her downfall, and who held the reigns of power after her death, and until her own assassination at the hands of the Qizilbash. [40]

The miniatures of the early Safavid period also bear witness to the fact that women were not veiled. This is well illustrated in a German study of women in Islam supported by examples from miniatures and other artefacts. There are examples in this work of distinguished women without veils meeting with free men who were not related to them, if not in public, but at least in their own domain. Although these miniatures are illustrations of literary texts it must be assumed that the artist based his work on existing conditions familiar to him.[41] This is further supported by one of the five miniatures of the Divan-i Hafiz painted for Sam Mirza, who was a younger son of Shah Isma'il born in 1517.[42] Sam Mirza was a prominent patron of the arts throughout his life until his imprisonment by Shah Tahmasb in 1561. The miniature shows a flowering garden shaded by a beautifully ornamental canopy. A cupbearer is serving wine and there are musicians sitting on either side. But the main figures appear to be two dancing girls, one in red, the other in orange, who stand out in stark contrast against the dark green of the grass, swaying towards one another playing castanets. They are dressed simply but colourfully in long robes which reveal their necks. Their faces can be seen openly and their hair is covered only by a transparent material which is obviously more ornamental than practical. The girl on the carpet is from a different social class as she not only wears a fine cloak but also a bejewelled diadem in her hair. There is clearly no impediment to her appearing thus in front of male musicians and the cupbearer.

Over 100 years later, during the reign of Shah Sulayman (1667–94), Sir John Chardin reports Iranian women to be totally secluded and veiled thus: 'Their head is very well cloath'd and over it they have a Vail that falls down to their Shoulders, and covers their Neck and Bosom before. When they go out, they put over all, a great White Vail, which covers them from head to Foot, not suffering anything to appear in several Countries but the Balls of their Eyes. The Women wear four Vails in all, two of which they wear at Home, and two more when they go Abroad.' [43]

There is thus a suggestion that, as the Safavids lost their revolutionary zeal and became religiously more orthodox, a parallel development took place with regards to the position of women. The development of orthodoxy under the Safavids was accompanied by the growing power of the *'ulama* who gradually gained more and more power culminating in the unprecedented political, social and religious power of 'Allama Muhammad Baqir Majlisi (1627?-1700?).[44] The last Safavid Shah, Sultan Husayn (deposed 1722), was very much under the influence of the *'ulama* in general and Majlisi in particular, as a result of which he enforced strict Shi'i orthodoxy. An aspect of the development of this orthodoxy was the fact that the Shi'i interpretations of the Islamic position on women superimposed itself completely upon all past customs and traditions. The seclusion of women under Shah Sultan Husayn reached such a degree that when women of the royal harem made public outings the royal route had to be cleared of all males including shopkeepers.[45]

The position of women within Shi'ism is linked to Shi'i ideology which claims to stem from the Qur'an and various interpretations of it. The Qur'an says a great deal about the position of women but most of it has been interpreted in such a way as to become socially restraining and to justify men's rights and superior position. Thus the position of women within Shi'ism is circumscribed by that of men. The authority and superiority of the male according to Qur'an IV: 34 and interpreted by the Shi'i *'ulama* determined his position in the household and society.[46] The interpretation of Qur'an XXIV: 31 ordained the veiling and segregation of women and the interpretations of other suras, her rights within society.[47] Subsequently the role of women became essentially that of housekeeper, bringing up their children and providing the husband with sexual and culinary pleasure.

Shi'ism, as proclaimed by the Safavids, was accepted and revived by the Qajar dynasty (1795–1925). Simultaneously the veiling and seclusion of women continued and strengthened under this dynasty.[48] Travellers to Iran during the Qajar dynasty, contrary to those during the early Safavid period, all commented on the seclusion and exclusion of urban women from the public domain.[49]

The seclusion of women had a great influence on the life-style of the Qajars, ranging from architecture and culinary arts to fashion and the aesthetics of female beauty. The influence was particularly noticeable on domestic architecture, which reflected in turn on public architecture and urban planning. Private houses had to be built in such a style as to ensure the seclusion of women. All houses were surrounded by high walls with no windows opening onto the street, so that no stranger could look inside the house. As a result the streets were narrow and there were no exterior facades to the buildings. Access to the house was through a metal door which was kept closed at all times. The house itself was divided into two sections: a *biruni* for the exclusive use of the master of the house and his visitors and an *andaruni* for the use of the female members of the household and males permitted to enter under religious law, such as fathers, sons and brothers. This form of separation and division varied according to the social status and wealth of the owner. The division could be a simple curtain, a courtyard or a very beautiful garden. Aside from rare exceptions, the women languished in idleness behind those walls and inside the *andarun*.

The occupations of upper-class women were limited. The Reverend Samuel Wilson describes a visit to some upper-class ladies who, when being asked how they spent their time, replied: 'we do nothing but sleep and eat and wonder what we will have for the next meal'. Embroidery and sewing they have some taste for, and they confessed to some skill in making certain dainties.'[50] About the same time another traveller, Henri René d'Allemagne confirmed Wilson's impressions as far as upper-class women were concerned, but stated that: 'Middle class women occupy themselves by preparing lunch and dinner. ... They have great expertise in making jams and pickles.'[51] This opinion is corroborated by Polak who was court doctor to Nasir al-Din Shah Qajar and spent nine years in Persia.[52]

By the Qajar period not only were all the prerequisites for the emergence of a great cuisine in evidence, but they had evolved further from the Safavid period. The society was culturally and politically stratified, with a large body of gourmet consumers.[53] The alliance between the merchant and religious classes consolidated and was strengthened through intermarriage establishing a notable middle class who enjoyed good food.[54] International trade with both the West and the East expanded, bringing into the country new ingredients. Labour was available in the form of unoccupied, secluded females joined by domestic helpers. Thus elaborate cooking evolved from being the realm of the court to encompass the new middle class.

Traditionally the court cooks were men, but certain factors contributed to the emergence of female cooks as well.[55] One of these was that the kitchens were usually adjacent to the *andarun* and that food for the *biruni* was ordered from the *andarun*.[56] Further, due to the seclusion of women and the fact that strange men cannot venture into the *andarun*, female cooks were required. Frequently black female slaves, brought back by families when they made the holy pilgrimage, *Hajj*, to Mecca were trained or in more modest houses the lady of the house trained the daughter-in-law.[57] These cooks, both mistress and servant, upper as well as middle class, took the court recipes and elaborated upon them both as an occupation and as an element of conspicuous consumption. For instance Lady Sheil, the wife of the British Minister, reported that cooking and its supervision were amongst the accomplishments of aristocratic women and that a princess used to send her dishes accompanied by a note stating that it had been prepared by her own hand.[58] Further the elaborate sweetmeats were always made by the lady of the house.[59]

The Safavid and Qajar eras reversed the tradition found under the 'Abbasids. During the 'Abbasids, the peasant recipes were taken by the male court cooks and elaborated upon, whereas with the rise of the new middle class and the seclusion of women the court recipes were taken and elaborated upon by women from all walks of life.

Persian cuisine in its present form is an historical heritage which has been refined through inventive minds seeking an occupation. This delicate cuisine could have only been created by women who had endless free hours to devote to it. Fresh herbs which need to be cleaned and chopped very finely are used in many dishes. There is no dish which can be produced on the spur of the moment, except for a sweet version of an omelette known as *khagina* and an onion soup with coriander known as *ishkana*. All the dishes require many hours of preparation followed by multiple cooking processes ranging from braising, and frying to boiling. The sweetmeats, which were a particular feature of *andarun* life, were produced in intricately fine shapes and minuscule forms which were extremely time consuming. The same applied to the jams and pickles which were an essential part of a Persian meal. The position of women within a social structure which isolated them and kept them idle produced this elaborate cuisine, the function of which was to keep them busily occupied at home.

The history and development of Persian cooking demonstrates that social institutions are interrelated, reinforcing each other, and that a change in one affects the others. Even though superficially the interrelationship between Shiʿism and cuisine may seem unlikely, an attempt has been made to show that, in practice, a definite relationship existed, demonstrating the value of comparative historical analysis in studying society.

Notes

1 Claude Levi-Strauss (1978) *The Origin of Table Manners: Introduction to a Science of Mythology*, 3 vols. trans. J. D. Weightman, New York.
2 Jack Goody, (1977) *The Domestication of the Savage Mind*, Cambridge, pp. 129–49.
3 Maurice Freeman (1977) 'Sung', in K. C. Chang (ed.) *Food in Chinese Culture*, New York, pp. 143–44 and Jack Goody (1982) *Cooking, Cuisine and Class: A Study in Comparative Sociology*, Cambridge.
4 *Ibid.*, p. 129 and Goody, *The Domestication*, pp. 129–45.
5 For details of the Sassanid court life, etiquette and repasts see Pierre Brillant (1996) *l'Histoire de l'Empire Perse*, Paris, pp. 266–414.
6 Arthur Christensen (1944) *L'Iran sous les Sassanides*, Copenhagen, pp. 477–79.
7 Muhammad M. Ahsan (1979) *Social Life under the ʿAbbasids*, London, pp. 77–164.
8 Maxime Rodinson, 'Recherche sur les documents arabes relatifs a la cuisine', *Revue des Etudes Islamiques*, 17 (1949), pp. 95–158.
9 *Ibid.*, p. 100.
10 A. J. Arberry, 'A Baghdad Cookery Book', *Islamic Culture* 13 (1939), pp. 21–47, 189–214. Also by the same author 'La Dolce Vita' in A. J. Arberry (1964) *Aspects of Islamic Civilization*, London, pp. 155–190.
11 Ahsan, *Social Life*, pp. 77–164.
12 See note 9 above. Rodinson also lists a number of other manuscripts in Arabic.
13 Paul D. Buell, 'Pleasing the Palate of the Qan: Changing Foodways of the Imperial Mongols', *Mongolian Studies* 13 (1990), pp. 57–82.
14 See Charles Perry, 'A Mongolian Dish', *Petits Propos Culinaires* 19, pp. 53–55.
15 Roy Gonzales de Clavijo (1859) *Narrative of the Embassy of Roy Gonzales de Clavijo to the Court of Timour at Samarcand, A. D. 1403–6* trans. Clements R. Markham, New York, pp. 98, 134–35, 139 and many other pages.
16 *Ibid.*, p. 113.
17 Maulana Bushaq Hallaj Shirazi, Atʿima (1954) *Divan*, Shiraz.
18 The great Persian poet Hafiz was patronized by one of the Muzaffarid rulers.

19 The profession of cotton carding consisted of a person with a card or a metal comb or wire brush with which he cleansed cotton and separated the good fibres from the bad ones. It was an itinerant profession in that the carder moved around neighbourhoods announcing his presence; households needing his services would call him in.

20 The *Divan-i At'ima* merits a complete paper if not volume devoted to it from a culinary point of view. To my knowledge, with one exception, all existing discussions concentrate on his poetical style rather than the nature of the cuisine of the period. See for instance *Encyclopaedia Iranica*, s.v. 'Bushaq, At'ema' by Heshmat Muayyaid. The exception is an article by Ayla Algar, 'Bushaq of Shiraz: Poet, Parasite and Gastronome'. *Petits Propos Culinaires* 31 (1989), pp. 9–20. Aside from the derogatory title referring to Bushaq as parasite because he frequented the houses of the great, the article is in many other ways misleading. Possibly due to the fact that it is not based on the original full text but on an anthology compiled by Abdulgani Mirzoyef published in Dushanbe, Tajikistan in 1971, various errors of fact and interpretation occur. These are undertaken to prove Algar's incorrect theory that not only most of the dishes in Bushaq's time originated from Central Asia but that they do not exist in present day Persia.

21 Michel M. Mazzaoui (1972) *The Origins of the Safavids: Shi'ism, Sufism and the Ghulat*, Wiesbaden.

22 On the position of *Sadr* in the Safavid period see: C. P. Turner in EI2 s. v. 'Sadr'. 'The *Sadr* was to remain one of the highest and most coveted positions in the Safavid administrative hierarchy until the demise of the dynasty.' (Turner, EI2, VIII: 751). See also Roger Savory (1980) *Iran under the Safavids*, Cambridge, in which he makes several useful remarks on the office of the *Sadr*.

23 *Encyclopaedia Iranica*, s.v. 'Bazar: iii Socioeconomic and Political Role' by Ahmad Ashraf.

24 Iraj Afshar (ed.) (1981) *Ashpaz-yi Dawra-yi Safaviyya: Matn-i Dau Risala az an Daura*, Tehran.

25 Mirza 'Ali Akbar Khan Ashpaz Bashi, (1974) *Sufra-yi At'ima* Tehran.

26 John Fryer (1912) *A New Account of East India and Persia*, London, Vol. 2, p. 310.

27 M. Boyce (1995) *A History of Zoroastrianism* 2 vols, Leiden, Vol. 1, p. 308. Also Ibrahim Purdavud, 'Zan dar Iran-i Bastan', *Ayanda* 3 (1944), pp. 355–60, 510–14.

28 Christian Bartholomae (1958) *Die Frau im Sasanidischen Recht*, trans. M. H. N. Sahib Zamani, Tehran: 'Ata'i Press, pp. 48–9, 55, 63.

29 Christensen, *L'Iran*, p. 330.

30 For the high position of women within Turkic societies see: Maria Szuppe, 'La Participation des femmes de la famille royal à l'exercice du pouvoir in Iran Safavid au xvie Siècle', *Studia Iranica* 23 (1994), pp. 211–58; 24 (1995), pp. 61–122, pp. 212–13 in which she holds that not only were women active politically but that they actually participated in battle as warriors and received war booty.

31 Shireen Bayani (1973) *Zan dar 'Asr-i Mughul*, Tehran, p. 8.

32 See Szuppe, 'La participation des femmes de la famille royal'.

33 Charles Grey (ed. and trans.) (1873) *A Narrative of Italian Travels in Persia in the Fifteenth and Sixteenth Centuries*, New York, pp. 59, 223, 173.

34 See n.a. *Alam-ara-yi Shah Isma'il*, A. Montazer-Sahib ed. (Tehran, 1349/1970), pp. 80–1. For more on Tajlu Khanum see Szuppe, 'La participation des femmes de la famille royal', pp. 71–2.

35 *Ibid.* p. 65. See also Anthony Jenkinson (1886) *Early Voyages and Travels to Russia and Persia*, E. Delmar Morgan and C.H. Coote, (eds), London, pp. 447–8.

36 Grey, 'The Travels of a Merchant in Persia', p. 173.

37 *Ibid.* 'Most Noble Vincentio d'Alessandri', p. 223.

38 Michele Membre, *Relazione di Persia*, Naples, 1967, trans. Alexander H. Morton (1993) *Mission to the Lord Sophy of Persia (1539–1542)*, London, p. 25.

39 Shohreh Gholsorkhi, 'Pari Khan Khanum: A Masterful Safavid Princess', *Iranian Studies* 28 (1995), pp. 143–56. There is a disagreement in the Persian sources as to whether she was the daughter of Shah Isma'il and therefore the sister of Shah Tahmasb or his daughter. See E. G. Browne (1969) *A Literary History of Persia* 4 vols, Cambridge, Vol. 4, pp. 101–02. This confusion is due to the fact that Shah Isma'il also had a daughter called Pari Khan Khanum. For both Pari Khan Khanums see Szuppe, 'La Participation des femme de la famille royal', pp. 72–6, 79–89.

40 For more on Khayr al-Nisa Bigum see *ibid.*, pp. 90–100.

41 Wiebke Walter (1981) *Women in Islam*, trans. C. S. V. Salt, London.

42 Basil Gray (1961) *Persian Painting*, Cleveland, p. 137.

43 Sir John Chardin (1988) *Travels in Persia* 1724, Reprint, New York, pp. 215, 76, 193.

44 See Shireen Mahdavi, 'Muhammad Baqir Majlisi and Family Values' in Proceedings of a symposium in 1998 'Safavid Iran and her neighbours'. Forthcoming, University of Utah Press.

45 Muhammad Hashim Asif (Rustam al-Hukama) (1969) *Rustam al-Tavarikh*, ed. Muhammad Mushiri, Tehran, pp. 106–8.

46 This verse begins with the following: 'Men are the maintainers of women (*qawwamun 'ala an-nisa*), ...'. Different translations and interpretations of this verse portray man as manager, superior or simply preferred by God. The above translation has been taken from that of Maulana Muhammad 'Ali (1951) *The Holy Qur'an: Arabic Text, Translation and Commentary*, rev edn, Lahore, but in Marmaduke Pickthall's translation, *The Glorious Koran* the words 'maintainers of women' are rendered 'in charge of women'.

47 Sura XXIV: 31 in Maulana Muhammad 'Ali's translation reads as follows: 'And say to the believing women that they lower their gaze and restrain their sexual passions and do not display their adornment (*zinat*) except what appears thereof. And let them wear head coverings over their bosoms'. In the interpretation of this, there is a difference of opinion as to what the term 'adornment' (*zinat*) exactly means. Some interpreters maintain that it includes the beauty of the body, while according to some others it is exclusively applied to external adornment. For a further discussion of the interpretations of Qur'anic verses pertaining to women by the *'ulama* see: Shireen Mahdavi, 'The Position of Women in Shi'a Iran: Views of the 'Ulama' in Elizabeth Warnock Fernea (ed.) (1985) *Women and the Family in the Middle East: New Voices of Change* Austin, pp. 255–68.

48 Shireen Mahdavi, 'Women and Ideas in Qajar Iran', *Asian and African Studies* 19 (1985), pp. 187–97.

49 For some of these accounts see the following: Sir John Malcolm (1829) *The History of Persia* 2 vols, London; Lady M. L. Sheil (1973) *Glimpses of Life and Manners in Persia* (1856 original (1883) edn), London; Carla Serena, *Homme et Chose en Perse*, Paris; Jane Dieulafoy (1887) *La Perse, La Chaldee, La Susiane, relation de voyage*, Paris.

50 S. G. Wilson (1900) *Persian Life and Customs*, New York, p. 259.

51 H. R. d'Allemagne (1955) *Du Khorassan au Pays des Backhtiaris: Trois Mois de Voyage en Perse*, 1911 trans. M. H. Farahvashi, Tehran, p. 445.

52 J. E. Polak (1982) *Persien das Land und seine Bewohner*. 2 Vols. Leipzig 1865 trans. K. Jahandari *Safarnama-yi Polak*, Tehran, pp. 155–9.

53 *Encyclopaedia Iranica* s.v. 'Class System: v. Classes in the Qajar Period', by Ahmad Ashraf.

54 W. M. Floor, 'The Merchants (*tujjar*) in Qajar Iran', *Zeitschrift der Deutschen Morgenlandischen Gesellschaft* 126 (1976), pp. 101–35.

55 C. Colliver Rice (1976) *Persian Women and their Ways* 1923 reprint edn, Tehran, p. 186.

56 *Encyclopaedia Iranica*, s.v. 'Biruni' by M.A. Jamalzadeh and H. Javadi.
57 *Encyclopaedia Iranica* s.v. 'Aspaz-Kana' by E. Elahi.
58 Sheil, *Glimpses of Life*, p. 146.
59 Rice, *Persian Women*, p. 198.

three

CMS Women Missionaries in Iran, 1891–1934

Attitudes Towards Islam and Muslim Women

Gulnar Eleanor Francis-Dehqani

Introduction

During the course of the nineteenth century Christian missionary organizations, such as the British based Church Missionary Society (CMS), came to rely increasingly on the membership of female as well as male workers. Discovering the advantages of influencing indigenous women through female missionaries, the CMS began encouraging women's participation and was soon dependent upon their involvement. In Iran, where CMS established itself in 1869, wives were present from the earliest times. However, it was from 1882, and more particularly from the 1890s, that single women's involvement became a major part of the missionary endeavour that led to the founding of the Anglican Church in Iran.

In this chapter the role of CMS women missionaries in Iran is analysed with specific reference to their theological views regarding Islam and Muslims. In order to root the material within its own historical context it is necessary to begin by briefly considering the general attitude of Victorian missionaries towards inter-faith issues at that time. Having set the backdrop in this way, the remainder of the chapter will be dedicated to an examination of theological attitudes shown by CMS women in Iran towards Islam, and their work amongst Muslim women. A concluding section provides a general appraisal of the CMS women's views, indicating something of the inherent complexities and ambiguities involved.

Contextualizing the views of the CMS women in Iran

The World Missionary Conference (WMC), held in Edinburgh in 1910, was undoubtedly the most significant international missionary gathering during the late Victorian-early Edwardian era. In particular the report of Commission IV, 'The Missionary Message in Relation to Non-Christian Religions', is a useful barometer for better understanding of the general attitude of missionaries towards other faiths and their adherents.

Recent studies, such as Kenneth Cracknell's *Justice, Courtesy and Love*, have shown that despite mistakes and a lack of consensus, Christianity's dialogical approach to other religions, usually thought of as an invention of the 1970s onwards, did exist in embryonic form as early as 1910.[1] Cracknell, amongst others, justifies this assertion through an examination of views expressed in responses to the missionary questionnaire sent out by Commission IV prior to the WMC.[2] The report of Commission IV, compiled in time for the Edinburgh conference, was based largely on the results of these questionnaires, and reflected a remarkably positive mood amongst missionaries at the time concerning the world faiths.

Though convincingly argued, Cracknell's case is based primarily on sources provided by missionaries from working environments that were not Islamic but represented other non-Christian religions. Of those responding to the questionnaire, only a small proportion wrote from their experiences in Muslim countries and of these most expressed negative views about Islam and the interfaith question. Moreover, the prevalent anti-Islamic missionary stance was particularly strong within the CMS, which was influenced by powerful personalities with fixed negative views on Islam. Amongst them were William St. Clair Tisdall working in Iran, and the society's General Secretary, Eugene Stock, whose views set the tone during that period.

Only five women were amongst the 149 missionaries who responded to the WMC questionnaire and none were working in Iran. Consequently, it remains impossible to undertake a gendered analysis of the CMS women in Iran by comparing them with other female respondents of the questionnaire. However, understanding the international context and the environment within the CMS at the time remains important, as these provide the setting in which the women worked. Indeed, it is within this specific context that the women in Iran should be studied. For ultimately their contribution must be judged against their own contextual norm rather than against some arbitrary late twentieth century yardstick, randomly directed towards them.

CMS women, Islam and the Muslims of Iran

In *Justice, Courtesy and Love*, Cracknell suggests various approaches which may have aided missionaries offering positive responses towards other religions in their Commission IV questionnaires.[3] Two of these prove especially useful as a means of structuring the data about the women in Iran. First, there was a sense of the replies being couched in terms of people rather than whole religious systems.[4] Many showed an instinct for the personal – the individuals they knew – rather than the abstract. This meant regarding other faiths experientially, not according to their past history. Secondly, most positive respondents were unwilling to judge other religions on the basis of unacceptable social manifestations, though these were acknowledged and frequently criticized.

Muslims and Islam, or the particular versus the general

Edward Said has written extensively about the orientalist tendency to incorporate generally accepted views about Islam, with a more personal experience of it.[5] He evinces a distinction between the 'particular' and the 'general' in a Western approach to the East, arguing that people learn 'to separate a general apprehension of the Orient from a specific experience of it', whilst allowing both to coexist.[6] This paradox allowed westerners during the age of empire to relate warmly towards individual Muslims whilst condemning Islam by means of unqualified generalizations. It was precisely the ability to overcome this, through emphasizing individual friendships over and above entire religious systems, which enabled many respondents of the WMC questionnaire to have a more generous spirit towards other faiths. An inspection of the CMS archives, however, reveals the women in Persia wrote more in terms of 'Islam' as an institution than 'Muslims' as people with whom they formed relationships. Accordingly, it was relatively easy for them to denounce the whole nation without personally involving individuals whom they encountered.

Two themes emerge in this context, namely, 'the land' *en masse,* which they considered was in darkness, and 'the people' as a unit, whom they believed to be lost. In 1892 Mary Bird expressed hopes of building up house visiting so she could be used for God's service 'in this dark land'.[7] Out of this developed a call for 'the evangelisation of the land'[8] as the means by which God's spirit would become active in Iran. This rather abstract idea of 'the land' found its reflection in the notion of a 'thirsty perishing *people*', for which missionaries laboured to 'gather many souls out of the darkness into His marvellous light'.[9] Occasionally, 'the land' and 'the people' were ambiguously combined, in references such as the 'evangelisation of *Persia*' or 'the salvation of this erring *nation*'.[10] In either case, both land and people were regarded as residing in darkness, and the missionary hope and belief was that God would 'answer the many prayers for these lands *speedily*'.[11]

Though 'land' and 'people' formed the most comprehensive units, the CMS women's efforts directed their attention more towards the female population of Persia. It is hardly surprising that they too were usually mentioned in terms of a distinct, definable category, often referred to simply as 'Muhammedan women'.

Three themes in particular run through missionary attitudes towards this unified group. First, personal contact was essential, for Persian women had to be *reached* if the missionary endeavour was to be successful. Secondly, they were on the whole regarded as uninformed and ignorant. Finally, the missionaries expressed pity towards Persian women, convinced they could only be helped by means of the gospel message.

The common belief that to change a nation, its women needed to be reached was central to the missionary ethos by the late nineteenth century. Certainly, from the earliest days of CMS's presence in Persia, contact with women was regarded as essential. Soon after her arrival in 1891, Mary Bird wrote that her time was occupied in learning Persian so she could take best advantage of any opening among the Muslim women.[12] The following year she affirmed the importance of visiting women 'where ever I can gain admittance, so as to win their confidence, and get opportunities of hearing and speaking, and thus paving the way for future work'.[13] For prior to the growth in educational and medical work, home visiting was regarded as the most effective means of encountering women whose lives revolved around the private world of domesticity.

Having made contact with Muslim women, missionaries were quick to express generalized opinions about them as a group, regarding them, on the whole, as ignorant and uninformed. However, during the early period when Persia was part of the Turkish-Arabia mission, a distinction appeared between views postulated by CMS women in Iran compared with those in Iraq.[14] For the former, any ignorance they perceived as a trait of Persian women was usually considered an environmental fault within a society where female education was not encouraged, whereas for the latter, Arabian women of Baghdad were reproached due to their apparently inherent limitations from a very young age.

Emmeline Stuart, for example, commenting on high levels of female illiteracy and lack of educational opportunities, concluded that these were due to mistaken assumptions within Iranian thinking that women lacked the capacity for learning.[15] By contrast, Arrabella Wilson writing from Baghdad in 1890 was much more critical of Arabian women and girls:

> I have begun an infants class on Sunday afternoon just to teach them to repeat and, as far as I can, to understand verses of the Bible. It is work I dearly love, but they need an immense amount of patience for *thinking* is not in them and you may tell them a thing again and again without their taking it in, even the simplest thing … [16]

The missionaries in Iran were equally fond of generalizations, many of which were far from flattering. However, their comments about Persian women's ignorance were based more on sociological observations concerning society's treatment of women, whereas in Baghdad unqualified remarks were presented as innate truths.

By far the most common feeling expressed by CMS women towards Iranians was one of pity. This is distinguishable from sympathy or compassion, also a

Figure 3.1 Staff at the Julfa Mission hospital including several Armenians, 1894. Missionaries seated, from left, Mrs Agnes Carr, Dr Donald Carr, Miss Henrietta Conner (nurse), Miss Mary Bird

Figure 3.2 Patients waiting outside the Julfa general hospital in 1895

Photographs from the Thompson family archives

Figure 3.3 Dr Emmeline Stuart with a hubble-bubble pipe, dressed in Bakhtiari tribal cloths, 1902

Figure 3.4 A group of patients waiting to be treated at the Jubareh dispensary in Isfahan, c. 1905

Photographs from the Thompson family archives

typical missionary response, but one that usually developed over a longer period of time and grew from personal contact. By contrast, pity was a sentiment many expressed in broad terms and with little knowledge of particular circumstances. Its corollary was unequivocal assurance that missionaries themselves, as channels for the Christian message, could help relieve the misery of Persian life. Thus, pathetic, pitiable life-styles were often assumed for 'the people' of Iran even by the most recent missionary recruits. Laura Stubbs, soon after reaching Julfa, recalled her journey across Persia:

> As we passed through the villages one felt so sorry for the people. We longed to be able to speak to them and to tell them the 'Old, old Story'. They looked so like 'sheep having no Shepherd'. [17]

These observations were based not on knowledge of Iran, but on theological suppositions and confident evangelical theories, buried deep in the subconscious and stubbornly immutable. Ten years later, Stubbs' sentiments persisted as she sadly recalled passing through villages near Yezd, knowing they were in utter darkness without a single missionary: 'Oh that God may make us [Mary Bird and herself] channels of life to these dying souls'.[18] Not surprisingly, such generalized comments were frequently directed towards Iranian *women* specifically. Philippa Braine-Hartnell first went to Persia in 1892 as helper to the Tisdalls whilst also doing missionary work in an unofficial capacity. Three years later she was eager to be taken on as a full CMS missionary. In her letter of application she expressed a desire to work 'among the poor downtrodden women of Persia'.[19]

This emphasis on missionary help as a necessity for compensating the supposedly lamentable circumstances of Persian lives was essentially an expression of theological significance. The tiny band of missionaries was in no position to solve the problems arising from socio-political and economic structures within Qajar Iran. Whilst they recognized their human limitations, however, most believed the religious conversion of Iranian individuals and the nation as a whole could alleviate much of the suffering. This hypothesis was based on the commonly held evangelical belief in personal salvation as the antidote for all societal problems. Ultimately, it provided the CMS women with a resolute motivation to work for the achievement of their goals.

Inevitably, the desire to palliate the ills of society by redemption through personal conversion, was accompanied by a condescending demeanour, at its worst, intimating arrogance. The patronizing attitude to which so many missionaries adhered was a typical feature of Victorian evangelicalism's overly enthusiastic approach. It originated from a deeply held belief in Christian superiority placing a burden of responsibility upon all who accepted it. In the militaristic terms common at the time, the gospel was used as a weapon in the battle to win souls. For many believed conversion, followed by personal salvation, would lay the foundations for a new spiritual and physical community. As deliverers of the Christian message, missionaries were convinced they possessed the necessary solution to ensure a positive future for Iranians. Their motivation was genuine, as was the desire to alleviate suffering. However, the figurative generalizations to which they clung in order to express their ideas, together with deeply embedded assumptions of superiority, meant a patronizing tone remained inevitable.

It should be noted that the contact missionaries had with ordinary people in Iran was a rare experience for Europeans at the turn of the century. They are, therefore, amongst the most reliable social commentators from that period and it is incumbent upon us to take their comments seriously.[20] They witnessed hardship and suffering in the lives of many and elucidated this by means of the familiar linguistic framework of Victorian evangelicalism. The oppressive structures of their language should not, however, diminish from the underlying reality of their words. To acknowledge the poor condition of Iranian society, especially with regard to the position of women, is not to discriminate against Islam or condemn all that is Persian. Rather, it is a rejection of that particular brand of distorted orientalism which, losing impetus in the search for truth, fails to understand the nineteenth century within its true context.[21]

There are two exceptions to the CMS women's widespread classification of Persian Muslim women as a single homogeneous group. The first is more general, regarding the distinction often made between rich and poor. The second, concerns those occasions when missionaries did move beyond generalizations, and related to *individual* Persian women.

From the earliest days, CMS was aware of profound implications for its work in the social chasm between Iran's rich and poor. Access to wealthy women was generally more difficult, allowing the mission fewer opportunities to influence this group. The conventions of Islamic segregation were adhered to more strictly for wealthy urban women compared with their poorer and/or rural counterparts. Furthermore, rich townswomen were not required to work but had regular staff to carry out household duties. This, according to Bird, created a superficiality which made wealthy women 'so frivolous, so taken up with their gorgeous dresses and ornaments, their endless cups of tea and pipes, and so self-satisfied'.[22]

The difference between rich and poor was frequently expressed in terms of a typically English fascination with class. For eagerness to influence the upper echelons of Iranian society was based upon a transferral of the British class-based ideology, in which middle- and upper-class women were regarded as affecting change for their supposedly helpless working-class sisters. This theory extended to the Persian context, developing into a belief that only gentlewomen could forge real change within the country.

This did not mean the social and religious requirements of poorer women were neglected, but simply that they were considered entirely differently. Jessie Biggs, for example, was concerned about educating various classes of women separately so that each could be taught according to their needs. English, French and science were of little use to poorer girls who needed to be 'taught to earn their own living ... according to the customs of the country'.[23] Whilst this was an articulation of characteristically class-based superiority, it also arose from practical requirements. Poorer women with no other means of income were given appropriate skills for earning money at a time when Persian society had little use for developing intellectuals amongst such women.

In contrast to general remarks about the women of Iran and the distinction recognized between rich and poor, there are countless examples of detailed narratives concerning the lives of individuals. What these accounts have in common is that the majority refer to people who, under the influence of the mission, were either showing keen interest in Christianity or had already been baptised. There are, for example, detailed descriptions of faithfulness and courage displayed by a number of female converts. Likewise, enquirers not yet ready to commit themselves to the Christian way of life were entrusted to the prayers of missionary supporters at home in the hope that conversion would soon follow.[24]

The CMS women's capacity for referring to individual Persians who were of a professional interest, whilst continuing their tendency to generalize about the people as a whole, may be interpreted in a variety of ways. It is possible to argue that they were only willing to develop relationships with those from whom they had something to gain. Accordingly, their association with Persian women was based on a power balance in which they had something to offer, but nothing to receive in return. Alternatively, the women they met through work were obviously also those with whom they formed relationships and it was natural, therefore, that these should be the people about whom they wrote as individuals. The pertinent point is that developing personal friendships did not eliminate the generalizations but co-existed alongside them. Whilst an attitude of superiority seeps through the missionary letters, it is balanced by authentic warmth and friendship.

To be sure, CMS letters were aimed at a specific audience eager to hear positive results about missionary efforts in Iran. The language and tone of much of the material is designed to satisfy these requirements and adumbrates a pattern within which the CMS women felt secure. However, the archives also include expressions of humility and admiration for the strength and courage shown by converts experiencing persecution. While the language conforms to expected norms, there remains a real sense in which the missionaries regarded Persian Christians as fellow pilgrims along the journey of faith. For many years they continued insisting that the growing indigenous church needed nurturing and developing through seasoned missionary expertise. However, they also acknowledged their need to learn from the Persian experience, particularly in accepting the burden of suffering.

The CMS women are typical of Said's orientalists whose individual and general approach to the East and its people co-existed, each apparently unencumbered by the other. Inevitably, this resulted in a complex relationship between missionary and Persian women. An inability to recognize inappropriate universalized assumptions resulted in an air of superiority underlying the mission's presence in Iran. Furthermore, the appropriation of the early stages of a positive theology of religions, in the way expressed by many missionaries at the 1910 WMC, is not possible. The generalized approach employed by CMS women persistently suggested the mission had something to offer the people of Iran for which nothing could be given in return.

Nevertheless, analysing missionary attitudes towards individuals introduces a variant approach indicating the composite nature of their relationship with Iranians. Friendships undoubtedly developed and many missionaries were profoundly influenced by the Persians whom they knew. They remained unwilling or unable to supersede the theological framework in which they operated, never displaying radical change from the traditional CMS approach. However, this should not lead to the assumption that their relationships were all one way. Many were aware of gaining more than they had given, and learning more than they had taught. The majority developed a deep love for the people of Iran, growing primarily from experiences of personal friendship. Their shortcoming was the inability to recognize the paralysing effect of generalized assumptions with regard to the people of Iran and the indigenous church community.

Despite this, their writings act as a kind of counterbalance to much contemporary post-imperialist literature, which, with its fiercely anti-mission stance, refuses to concede the right of non-western individuals to choose Christianity for themselves. There is a tendency to assume that all who converted as a consequence of missionary efforts did so merely in the face of coercion and intimidation, and that subsequent generations have followed suit because of the overwhelming power of western cultural imperialism. This neo-paternalistic hypothesis inverts the arrogance of nineteenth century orientalism, but still maintains an attitude of superiority by defining what is best for peoples of the East.

By contrast, admiration for the courage of converts enabled the CMS women in Iran to reveal their faith in a Christianity that transcends cultural and national boundaries and adapts to its new environment. For despite the contours of their orientalist mindset, and the limitations of its accompanying vocabulary, essentially they were eager not to westernize Persian society, but to Christianize it. Today we may be unable to detect the difference, yet for the missionaries the distinction was self-evident. For some, the benefits of Christianity were inexplicably linked with the influence of western civilization. Generally, however, the Persia mission made an early and conscious effort to separate these two dimensions, believing it was both possible and desirable. Annie Gauntlett, for example, argued that 'the need for the Gospel and *the Gospel only* in Persia, has grown with the facilities for preaching it'.[25] Yet, as explained by Dr Winifred Westlake, this was not synonymous with a case for westernization:

We don't want to Anglicise the Persian women, do we? No, if we may be used to set them free from the trammels of Mohammedanism, placing them in the light of the Gospel of Christ, they will develop as God wills, and who can tell what they may do in His honour and glory.[26]

Whilst we may reject many of their sentiments and the manner in which they were expressed, amidst the rhetoric it is possible to hear missionary voices carrying across the generations, challenging us to respect personal conscience in the quest for religious wholeness. Since western global ascendancy and the age of empire in particular, choosing Christianity can all too easily be regarded as alignment with the superiority of strength and power. For, at the very least, being a Christian is a symbolic association with the force of western domination. The CMS women's insights, however, challenge this often subconscious assumption, presenting the possibility of a faith that does not restrict new cultural expression, but encompasses the richness of human experience.

Islam and its unacceptable social manifestations

Cracknell's second proposition concerning the positive respondents to the WMC questionnaire is that they showed an unwillingness to judge other faiths on the basis of unacceptable social manifestations, though these were both acknowledged and criticized.[27]

The CMS archives include much material linking missionary assessments about Islam to perceptions of its Iranian social reality. A deep rooted and widespread interpretation was one based on a straightforward cause and effect relationship between religion and social degradation. Accordingly, the very existence of Islam was posited as the direct source of Iran's social problems, engendering belief that if the former were destroyed the latter would automatically improve. This negative appraisal of Islam based on a particular interpretation of its cultural manifestation appears to have been imbued in the CMS women before they arrived in Persia.[28] However, contrary to many respondents of the WMC questionnaire,[29] the experience of living in a community with a different faith seems to have intensified rather than changed their views.

In England one realizes to a certain degree the great need of these people who do not know Christ as their Saviour; but I think this realization becomes far deeper and stronger to those who come out amongst them. I can truly say my missionary zeal and prayer have become intensified since I came to Persia.[30]

The reasons for an intensification of such preconceptions were essentially social. Missionaries who remained in Iran for long periods persisted in constructing Islam as the theological foundation for the ills of society, interpreting many events in Persia as indicative of the 'horrors of a religion of man's making'.[31]

After ten years experience, Stubbs still found that, 'Daily the wrongs and sins and sorrows of this land of Islam dawn upon me'.[32]

The harmful impact of Islam was delineated not only in vague terms on the basis of its overriding presence as an institution. More specific examples were also proffered by the missionaries. Dr Emmeline Stuart, in writing about one of her trips to a village near Julfa, used the episode as an opportunity to explicate the dubious effect of Islam upon the behavioural patterns of Persian women.[33] She describes the arrival of a woman paid by the mullahs to agitate a gathering of villagers through reciting the death narrative of the martyr Hassan. The wild gesticulations, loud hoarse tones, wailing and beating of chests that followed were, for Stuart, indicative of how ignorant people could be stirred up by fanatics to participate in deeds of violence.

The appalling state of Iran's medical care was further regarded as an implicit consequence of Islam. According to Stuart, almost every patient seen by the mission was 'a sufferer from the ignorant treatment of Persian doctors'.[34] Whilst missionaries recognized this was partly due to lack of education and technology, they also considered it the result of a corrupt system. Mary Bird, for example, wrote about a baby, first misdiagnosed by a Persian doctor and then refused treatment due to the family's shortage of funds. In the brief article, emotively titled 'A Baby Murdered', Bird explains that by the time the child was brought to the mission there was nothing they could do to save his life. [35]

The forms of social degradation that most concerned the female missionaries were those impacting upon Iranian women. Indeed, it was a woman's status that represented the most unacceptable face of Islam's social reality, proving it was a false religion. This common theme was adhered to by many missionary organizations at the time.[36] Amongst the missionaries in Iran, Dr Stuart was one of the most passionate on the subject, believing the scandal of Islam's treatment of women was manifested most strongly through polygamy, divorce and child marriages.[37] She was not alone, however, and the archives are littered with similar references by many of her colleagues.

Missionary analysis of the Iranian situation was based upon an understanding of the natural link between a false religion and its resulting social degradation. By extension, Christianity was regarded as the solution to this problem and the means of breaking the destructive cycle. In an uncomplicated way the CMS women passionately believed the national embracing of Christianity would establish the necessary theological structures from which alleviation of Iran's social problems would flow. Accordingly, they perceived themselves as requisite catalysts for bringing about the necessary transformation. For, by proclaiming the gospel message, they could lead the nation and its people out of darkness, into the light of Christ. Writing about potential converts, Dr Stuart explained: 'they are seekers after truth and *we* intend to give them the opportunity of finding it'.[38] Similarly, Jessie Biggs was pleased to be 'the messenger of glad tidings to very many, who humanly speaking would otherwise have no one to lead them to the Truth'.[39]

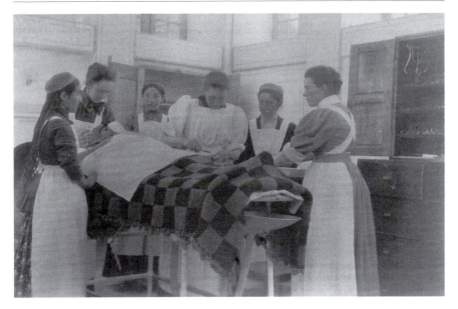

Figure 3.5 Dr Emmeline Stuart (Centre) operating in the Julfa women's Hospital, c. 1899

Figure 3.6 Miss Lily Buncher, missionary in Persia 1898–1908, using a ladder to get into a kajaveh, c. 1903

Figure 3.7 Miss Jane Moore, missionary in Persia 1908–38, mounting a mule by stepping on a man's back, c. 1907

Photographs from the Thompson family archives

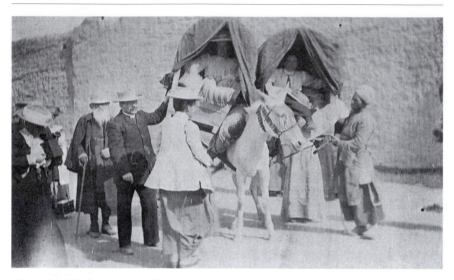

Figure 3.8 Missionaries travelling in kajavehs, c. 1907

Figure 3.9 Miss Zoë Parry, (CMS Missionary in Persia 1909–13) on mule back, c. 1910

Photographs from the Thompson family archives

By proclaiming their vocation and delineating its objective in this way, the British women were doing more than participating in fanciful power games. They were, rather, defining themselves and discovering their identity as Christian missionaries and western women, freer to participate in the church's mission abroad than at home. Through this process, however, they concurrently defined Iranian women according to their own perception of reality. Persian women – regarded as those who needed what the missionaries offered – became the 'other', thereby giving credence to the CMS women's developing notion of 'self' as autonomous human beings with a valid and justifiable religious calling. In thus defining Iranian women, the CMS missionaries created and defended their own identity whilst denying their Persian sisters the freedom to do likewise.

The resulting reality for the CMS women was a dualism in which they co-operated in the imperialist agenda, whilst at the same time participating in the progress of the western feminist movement. As they legitimized their role in working alongside male colleagues, they united with growing numbers of their western sisters in proclaiming the right of all women to define themselves, and participate in the public arena of work. Meanwhile, their self-definition was achieved at the expense of Persian women, cast in the role of 'other' and used as justification for the female missionary purpose. In short, the perceived need of Persian women for the emancipatory Christian gospel became the apology for CMS women's public vocation. Thus, the prevailing imperialist agenda, together with its underlying evangelical tenets persisted, whilst the widespread western gender assumptions, separating the private and public world of men and women began to crumble.[40]

Furthermore, through willingness to attribute the problems of Persian society wholly to the Islamic way of life, the CMS women exposed a significant rupture in their comprehension of Victorian Britain's social reality. Extremely critical of the unacceptable social manifestations of Iranian Islam, they continually displayed stubborn resistance in the face of problems emanating from their home society with its hypocrisy and oppression of women. Rationalizing the Persian situation was straightforward, for adherence to a false religion produced poor social conditions (especially for women), ultimately resulting in a corrupt and immoral society. However, a comprehensive understanding of the British scene necessitated a certain amount of ideological gymnastics based on ambiguous, even paradoxical interpretations of social reality.

Theoretically, the CMS women distinguished and, therefore, separated Christianity from its wider cultural and social environment. However, on a deeper more subconscious level, they accorded the benefits of western civilization – especially its affluence and the high position they claimed it offered women – to the influence of Christianity. Therefore, just as they interpreted the religion of Islam as directly associated with their perceptions of Iranian social reality, so too they coupled their judgements of British society with prevalent views about Christianity. Whereas a wholly negative relationship was transposed onto the socio-religious connection in Iran, an unrealistically positive gloss was employed in describing the Western/Christian correlation in Britain. Several factors combined to enable this generous portrayal of the home environment that had restricted them so definitively until they had chosen to leave.

First, by physically removing themselves from Britain, the CMS women effectively freed themselves from the shackles of impeding home conventions and strict gender confines. Their purpose was described in terms of responding to the call of vocation and the Christian duty to follow God's will. However, many were probably aware of the greater opportunities available to them through participation in missionary work. Certainly, once abroad they were released to be more fully themselves in a way that British society, and the church in particular, would not allow at home. Finding scope to develop their talents and utilize their skills in new and stimulating ways, they mistakenly came to regard this freedom as reflecting the situation of all British women. These feelings were compounded by long periods away from home, obscuring memories and concealing the multifarious socio-economic problems facing Britain at the time. Such an apotheosis of British society presented a distorted image of Victorian England and a false representation of the position of women within it.

Secondly, based on the writings of Adrienne Rich, Nancy Paxton has referred to the problem of loyalty facing late nineteenth and early twentieth-century British women abroad.[41] The pressures of imperialism and pride in the homeland led to many inconsistencies within the feminist movement, often compelling women to choose between the extreme poles of allegiance or infidelity towards the country they had left behind. The matter was considered straightforward and, ultimately, women were forced to regard themselves either 'loyal or disloyal to [British] civilization'.[42] While many, in Iran and elsewhere, would have preferred to maintain a critical stance, under severe pressure to conform they ultimately gave in to total allegiance, impeding any possibility for captious analysis. The imperialist agenda was internalized so effectively that rebellion was seldom achieved, for resisting complicity threatened the fragile position which women were beginning to create for themselves.

Overall, the CMS women in Iran reveal mixed responses in their negotiation of the gender, imperialist and religious questions facing them. Conditioned to accept the basic gender assumptions of their day, they began challenging these by claiming the autonomy to define themselves, travel abroad and take up more public responsibilities within the mission structures. Encumbered by fewer restrictions they tentatively experimented with their new-found liberty. By stretching the ideological boundaries, they participated in improving the future for British women, yet all their efforts remained contained within the non-controversial confines of standard evangelical and orientalist frameworks. Islam was vilified with both religious and social justification, whilst the position of women provided the main motif in undermining the theological and societal structures of Iran. Therefore, the language used to describe their work presents an entirely negative evaluation of Islam, providing no indication that the CMS women participated in the formative advancement of a Christian theology of religions.

Contextualizing and reinterpreting missionary opinions

Thus far there appears to be little that is positive in terms of openness and sympathy shown by the CMS women towards Islam. Their views, whilst broadly in line with the general CMS ethos, conflict with many of those expressed by the respondents of the WMC questionnaire and the report of Commission IV. However, in order not to judge them too hastily or discard them as irrelevant historical relics, several qualifications should be noted. These help to contextualize the women both within their period and according to their particular circumstances in Iran.

The pressure of conforming to expected linguistic models, writing for an evangelical audience, and working in what was considered a more hostile Islamic environment, all compounded to restrict significantly the expression of views presented by CMS women in Iran. To properly appreciate them, it is vital to look beyond the obvious and superficial, searching for more subtle means of understanding deeper perceptions and emotions. For the most part the missionaries remained bound by theological and orientalist conventions undergirding Victorian language. However, it is possible to look beneath their words, scrutinizing the experiences and events that altered their lives. Indeed, it is through the very act of stripping back the descriptive material which survives, that glimpses of their deepest feelings – which supersede language and touch the very core of humanity – become apparent.

The superficial elements undoubtedly conformed to expected norms, for these women knew nothing of post-imperialist insights and were unaware of the subtleties of gendered language or the intricacies of religious pluralism. Nevertheless, they had embarked on a journey that took them beyond the familiar and kept them there for many years. To survive without becoming despondent, and continue despite constant failure, implies that the substance of what they experienced was deeper than hitherto suggested.[43] It indicates that their life's work was not so much a concern about ideas but a passion for people. That despite their writings, their deepest motives were nourished through relationships with individuals and the love affair many enjoyed with the country as a whole. The women remained unable to express these experiences and were perhaps even unaware of them. Yet without the forming of mutual relationships, the palpable depth of love and concern shown towards Iran and its people would have been impossible to sustain.

A broad interpretation of CMS's archival material generally helps delineate the notion of developing mutuality in the relationship between missionary women, Iran and its people. Two issues arise in particular. First, though the women often wrote about Persia and its populace in abstract and detached tones, this should not undermine the real warmth and love felt towards the country. Secondly, as the years progressed they remained in Iran because they believed the people wanted them. The missionaries clearly acted on the conviction that they were responding to a need expressed by those amongst whom they lived and worked. A survey of their writings helps depict these themes.

Due for home-leave in 1907, Biggs was clearly not looking forward to her departure and wrote, 'This land and people have won my heart and I am very reluctant to leave'.[44] In Kerman, Mary Bird was delighted to witness Muslim children read and write during a prize-giving ceremony at a Zoroastrian school. Despite feeling an opportunity for Christian instruction had been lost, her pleasure in seeing the young students fulfil their potential is unmistakable:

> It really was wonderful to hear the girls reading the Koran, and Persian history and ... answering questions in geography, doing arithmetic and writing, and reciting a long Moslem catechism.[45]

Yezd seems to have had a particular impact on the missionaries, with many revealing immense fondness for the place and its people. Reflecting on her first trip to the city, Biggs remarked, 'the people, I think, no one could help liking'.[46] Similarly, Dr Elsie Taylor expressed great sadness at the prospect of leaving Yezd after her marriage: 'I *love* it, and the people – and I shall leave a great many friends behind'.[47] A number of references show the missionaries regarded Yezd, in some way, as being 'home'. During the period of British evacuations in the First World War, Annie Stirling wrote from Tehran, thankful to be safe but constantly 'wishing and praying for the day to come when we may return to our Yezd homes and our Yezd work'.[48] Likewise, returning from England in 1923, Ellen Brighty wrote: 'Here I am at last safely back in Persia – though I am not to go back to my 'home' in Yezd just yet', and although busy training hospital assistants in Isfahan, she admitted, 'my heart goes out to my own dear people in Yezd'.[49]

The sadness often expressed by those approaching retirement or leaving the country for other reasons was usually a result of their depth of feeling for Iran. After 31 years as a missionary, Philippa Braine-Hartnell wrote: 'Such as I love Persia, I suppose it must be retirement now', and Stirling, approaching her fortieth year in Iran, admitted deliberate delay in sending her letter of retirement: 'I suppose having been allowed to be in dear Yezd for so many years makes it all the harder to settle down at home'.[50] In 1929 Frances McKitterick, preparing to depart from the mission, expressed great sadness upon leaving Iran: 'I am very sorry to give up my work amongst a people I have learnt to love, and am very glad that I have had an opportunity of helping them, even if it has only been in a very small way'.[51]

Notably, the affection expressed by missionaries was not exclusively one-sided. Records provide evidence of the love extended by many Persians towards the British women and indicate the high esteem in which they were held. Mary Bird is perhaps the most outstanding example, though letters of gratitude were sent about several individuals, and others were implored to stay in Persia after retirement.[52] For example, His Britannic Majesty's Consulate (HBM Consul) wrote to CMS expressing the appreciation of Parsees in Kerman for the work of Dr Catherine Ironside who later died in Iran:

> The Parsees said that never before have they received such skilled and sympathetic treatment and especially appreciate the work done by Dr Ironside among their women.[53]

Episodes such as these intensified the feeling amongst missionaries that their work and presence, far from being an unwanted intrusion, was welcomed by many Persians. Countless examples show they continued work because of a belief that they were responding to the will of local people. Travelling in Iran as early as 1897, Annie Stuart was 'cordially welcomed by the ladies of the anderoon at all [the] central resorts, and pressed to come again'.[54] Delighted by any warm reception, the missionaries were always eager to stress that they did not force themselves upon the people. Mabel Ward, writing about two girls adopted by missionaries, informed CMS of their recent baptism, carefully emphasizing that the decision was entirely their own.[55] The overriding sense that the CMS women were responding to an expressed need is perhaps best encapsulated by Biggs:

> It is not us thrusting ourselves upon people but that they go home disappointed for we have not enough workers to do all the visits people would like us to do. .... It would be easier if they did not want us but when they ask for us to visit them it makes it double hard to refuse.[56]

It is possible, of course, that Persians were merely captivated by the novelty and unfamiliarity of foreign ways and beliefs. For notwithstanding the benefits of CMS's medical and educational establishments, missionaries were also a source of diversion – a kind of amusement in the otherwise ordinary lives of many Iranians. Indeed, the missionaries themselves were not unaware of this, though their analysis was usually optimistic. Soon after beginning work in Yezd, Mary Bird commented that homes were opening up, not just for medical work or out of curiosity to see a foreigner but for teaching and prayer also.[57]

An appropriate contextualization of CMS women in Iran between 1891–1934 should include recognition that complete mutuality between those representing British and Persian cultures was extremely unlikely, if not impossible. At the time, East and West were almost total strangers to one another. Contact between the two worlds was relatively recent and the way towards common understanding and sympathy had barely begun. Indeed, if we are critical of orientalist attitudes common amongst westerners, we should not forget the scorn with which foreigners were often treated by peoples of the East. With specific reference to Qajar Iran, Wright correctly points out that whilst the

CMS missionaries represented a motley group, 'some broad-minded and tolerant, others ... bigoted and narrow-minded', so also, 'arrogance and contempt for the foreigner were not an exclusive British monopoly', for linguistic, religious and cultural differences created misunderstanding and resentment on both sides.[58]

Conclusion: An assessment of missionary attitudes towards Islam and Iran

My eagerness to emphasize context and search beneath the superficiality of historical records underlies the notion that researchers should neither expect nor seek out neatly packaged resolution or straightforward analysis. Human nature, adapting to a new environment or set of circumstances, seldom responds in simple patterns that remain conveniently identifiable after the passage of time. Victorian missionary methods and motives, particularly concerning women, involved a complex reaction to an array of theological, socio-political and economic factors. Moreover, any contemporary evaluation is itself reacting to similar ingredients whose emphasis and priorities, however, have changed considerably.

It would be unsatisfactory to judge the CMS women in a simplistic or uncomplicated manner. For the truth is they represent an amalgam of mixed motives and diverse results. Understanding themselves as participators in God's mission for the world, they believed in what they did as worthy and good. Within the context of Victorian evangelicalism, where salvation was only considered possible through Christ, their longing to convert the Iranian people was based essentially on admirable motives. And their desire to alleviate poor social conditions in Persia was a human response to the suffering encountered. Nevertheless, compared with other missionaries of their day, as represented by the WMC questionnaire, their theological views were conservatively exclusive. The generosity shown by many of their colleagues and the positive mood reflected in the Commission IV report does not reverberate in the writings of CMS women active in Persia.

Problems in relating to individual Muslims and linguistic constraints restricting expressions of friendship, were probably less detrimental to their overall views than criticisms of Iranian society directly attributed to Islam. It is notable that the tendency towards generalizations *vis-à-vis* the country and people of Iran is more typical of the earlier years. There are few such references beyond 1903, and by 1913 they have virtually disappeared. This is most likely a result of developing friendships and deepening love for the nation leading to an unwillingness for universalized condemnation. The same is not true, however, of writings concerning the social ills of Iranian society based on the theological imperfections of Islam. Here, early feelings, expressed through strong language, recur time and again, persisting into the late 1920s.

It seems that as the years progressed, increased contact with Iranian people and developing relationships did impact on preconceived missionary opinions. Subconsciously, a depth of understanding was cultivated and natural affection for the country surfaced. Meanwhile, however, the women remained unable, or unwilling, to express this change in the essence of their writings. They were either incapable of discovering the necessary framework for expressing the shift, or remained cautious about causing controversy amongst their supporters in England. Concurrently, the reality of Iran's social problems constantly troubled them, reinforcing negative views about Islam and the need to work for its destruction. Equally important was the religious assurance of evangelical Christianity with its bold confidence in providing the theological structures for social change. The missionary women's use of religious language and imagery remains consistent throughout the period, reflecting the uncompromising certainty with which they viewed their faith.

They were, on the whole, concerned not to force themselves or their views onto people, believing that in most instances they were responding to a call from the indigenous population. Moreover, where their letters indicate anti-Islamic views, it should be remembered they were designed for a specific audience. In conversation with Iranians efforts were made to avoid offensive or insulting remarks in favour of polite and courteous discussion. This, however, did not diminish personal theological convictions. Today, in an environment of liberalism, this trait makes many Christians uneasy. For mutuality and inclusivity are frequently hailed as the best approaches to co-operation. Regardless of how inappropriate their theological and sociological agenda may now seem, the missionary women's love for those amongst whom they lived and worked remains authentic. To be sure, it often began as a love they were duty-bound to feel as Christians responding to their Lord's command. But for many, this blossomed into genuine and deep affection, upon which were built relationships of mutual friendship.

There is little in the archives to suggest widespread and rational appreciation of Islam or sympathy towards its theological integrity. However, whilst CMS women remained convinced that religious change and disconti-nuity were vital for Iran, their overall contribution to the growth of understanding between East and West should not be diminished. Amongst the earliest western women to live for long periods in an eastern environment, the CMS missionaries experienced unprecedented contact with the indigenous population. They operated within the dominant theological and orientalist restrictions of their day, often conforming to, rather than challenging, basic negative assumptions. Nevertheless, through early efforts such as theirs barriers began to break down and eventually the Christian world started to wake up to the need for more open understanding of its Muslim counterpart. Historically the CMS women were part of a movement promoting greater contact between the peoples of the world, bringing closer together those who had once been total strangers.

Contemporary ideas in interfaith dialogue and global ecumenism are possible largely because of the nineteenth century missionary movement that participated in a move towards globalization. As a result, the world has become a smaller place and its inhabitants are more aware of their intrinsic relationality. The CMS women in Iran played a less explicit role in the development of religious tolerance than some of their colleagues elsewhere. This should not, however, undermine their implicit participation – through a presence amongst, and contact with, the local people – in laying foundations for a more open and sympathetic future.

Notes

A fuller version of this chapter is available in Gulnar Francis-Dehqani, *Religious Feminism in an Age of Empire: CMS Women Missionaries in Iran, 1869–1934*, University of Bristol: PhD Thesis, pp. 70–99; also published under the same title by CCSRG, University of Bristol (2000). Unpublished sources referred to in this chapter include CMS archives and journals; *Annual Letters*. London: Church Missionary House (Held in the Mission Studies Library at Partnership House, London); G2/PE/O – Original Papers and letters sent to CMS headquarters. Reference followed by the year and record number (held in the Heslop Room, Birmingham University Library); *Mercy and Truth: A Record of CMS Medical Missions*. CMS: London (held in the Heslop Room, Birmingham University Library); Stuart, Emmeline (1909), 'The Social Condition of Women in Muslim Lands', *Church Missionary Review* (August), pp. 458–64.

1 Kenneth Cracknell (1995) *Justice, Courtesy and Love: Theologians and Missionaries Encountering World Religions, 1846–1914*, London.
2 Detailed forms were sent to 149 active missionaries, representing different denominations and geographical regions, to assess their opinions and approaches towards other religions and their adherents.
3 Cracknell, *Justice, Courtesy and Love.*, pp. 202, 219, 285.
4 *Ibid.*, p. 202.
5 Edward Said (1987) *Orientalism: Western Conceptions of the Orient*, London (1995 reprint), pp. 95–103.
6 *Ibid.*, p. 101.
7 G2/PE/O 1892: 53.
8 Bird, G2/PE/O 1898: 28.
9 Bird, G2/PE/O 1893: 87 (my emphasis), and Ethel Stuart, G2/PE/O 1903: 36.
10 Included in a joint letter from 'the missionaries of the C.M.S. labouring in Persia' to the Home Committee in London registering a complaint at the decision not to 'occupy Isfahan' but continue 'concentrating their forces in Julfa'. Laura Stubbs and Mary Bird were among the five to sign. G2/PE/O 1893: 105 (my emphasis); and Mary Bird, *Annual Letters* (1895) p. 12 (my emphasis).
11 Wilkes, G2/PE/O 1895: 57.
12 G2/PE/O 1891: 85.
13 G2/PE/O 1892: 53.
14 There were many similarities between the situation of CMS women in Iran and their counterparts in Iraq. However, there is also a need for caution as it would be wrong to assume too many generalized similarities. This issue about the cause of indigenous women's ignorance is an example of the diversity about which one should be aware.
15 'The Social Condition of Women in Muslim Lands', *Church Missionary Review,* August 1909, p. 462.

16 G2/PE/O 1890: 136.

17 G2/PE/O 1891: 90.

18 G2/PE/O 1901: 143.

19 G2/PE/O 1895: 77.

20 For a useful discussion of missionaries as social commentators with specific relevance to the Indian situation see Geoffrey Oddie (1996) 'Missionaries as Social Commentators: The Indian Case' in Robert Bickers and Rosemary Seton (eds.), *Missionary Encounters: Sources and Issues*, Surrey, pp. 197–210.

21 Rodinson uses the phrase 'distorted orientalism' in referring to a classification of the orient which, rather than rendering it diabolic, goes to the other extreme and through an extraordinary ideological about-face practically sanctifies Islam and the east. This form of Muslim apologetics, she argues, through its refusal to be critical of Islam in any way, loses its analytical advantage and becomes little more than indulgent description. See Maxine Rodinson (1991) *Europe and the Mystique of Islam*, Seattle & London, pp. 78, 106, 127.

22 Mary Bird, *Annual Letters* (1895) p. 11.

23 G2/PE/O 1919: 67.

24 See, for example, Emmeline Stuart, *Annual Letters* (1899) pp. 77–8; and (1900) pp. 262–3; Mary Bird, *Annual Letters* (1895) pp. 10–12; and (1896) pp. 20–24.

25 G2/PE/O 1916: 72, (my emphasis).

26 Westlake, G2/PE/O 1903: 140.

27 Cracknell, *Justice, Courtesy and Love*, p. 285.

28 It is ultimately impossible to know whether the views of the CMS women were in accord with their own instincts or a result of indoctrination through training which brought them in line with the conservative CMS ethos.

29 Cracknell, *Justice, Courtesy and Love*, p. 260.

30 Martha Adamson, G2/PE/O 1906: 123.

31 Biggs, G2/PE/O 1903: 120; writing in connection with the recent persecution of Babis, in which one man had been killed by Muslim fanatics.

32 G2/PE/O 1901: 143.

33 'In Persian Villages', *Mercy and Truth* (1898), ii, pp. 7–10.

34 Emmeline Stuart, 'New Hospital for Women in Julfa', *Mercy and Truth* (1899), iii, p. 150.

35 In *Mercy and Truth* (1899), iii, p. 263.

36 Writing in 1910 from an American perspective, Helen Barrett Montgomery expressed the then uncontroversial sentiment that 'the darkest blot upon the prophet Muhammad is the low appreciation of womanhood'. See, Helen Barrett Montgomery (1910) *Western Women in Eastern Lands: An Outline Study of Fifty Years of Woman's Work in Foreign Missions*, New York, p. 52.

37 For a detailed analysis of Emmeline Stuart's views on Islam's treatment of women see Francis-Dehqani, *Religious Feminism in an Age of Empire*, CCSRG, pp 168ff.

38 Emmeline Stuart, *Annual Letters* (1900), p. 263, (my emphasis).

39 G2/PE/O 1909: 73.

40 The arguments in this section have been based upon a modified form of Foucault's theory of power discourses and reverse discourses, and Said's notion of 'self' based upon some 'other' in binary opposition. See Said, *Orientalism*, pp. 1–2. See also Michel Foucault (1978) *The History of Sexuality, Vol. I: An Introduction*, New York: Pantheon, esp. pp. 26 and 101. For more detail see, Francis-Dehqani, *Religious Feminism in an Age of Empire*, CCSRG, pp. 18–19.

41 Nancy Paxton (1990) 'Feminism Under the Raj: Complicity and Resistance in the Writings of Flora Annie Steel and Annie Besant', *Women's Studies International Forum*, 13:4, p. 338.

42 Adrienne Rich quoted in Paxton, '*Feninism under the Raj*', p. 338.

43 In human terms the mission was undoubtedly a failure for the number of converts remained very small and the large-scale changes which the missionaries intended for the Iranian nation were never realized.

44 G2/PE/O 1907: 109.

45 G2/PE/O 1914: 48.

46 'First Impressions', *Mercy and Truth* (1903), vii, p. 266.

47 G2/PE/O 1904: 41.

48 G2/PE/O 1916: 32.

49 G2/PE/O 1923: 57.

50 G2/PE/O 1928: 1 and 1933: 17.

51 G2/PE/O 1929: 96.

52 For a full analysis of Mary Bird's life and work in Iran see Francis-Dehqani, *Religious Feminism in an Age of Empire*, CCSRG, pp. 84–113.

53 G2/PE/O 1920: 76.

54 Bishop Stuart, G2/PE/O 1897: 170.

55 G2/PE/O 1907: 188.

56 'First Impressions', *Mercy and Truth* (1903), vii, pp. 267–8. See also G2/PE/O 1905: 84.

57 'Work Among Women in Yezd', *Mercy and Truth* (1901), v, p. 135.

58 Denis Wright (1977) *The English Amongst the Persians*, London, pp. 119, 155.

four

A Presbyterian Vocation to Reform Gender Relations in Iran

The Career of Annie Stocking Boyce

Michael Zirinsky

American missionary activity in Iran began in 1829 when Eli Smith and Timothy Dwight explored Azerbaijan for the Boston-based American Board of Commissioners for Foreign Missions. This exploration was 'part of a broad American religious phenomenon, the 'Second Great Awakening,' which impelled American Protestants to preach the Gospel of Jesus Christ to all mankind. On Smith and Dwight's recommendation, the American Board appointed Justin Perkins to establish a mission at Urmia to work with the Assyrian Christians of the region. After a generation during which schools, hospitals and an Evangelical Church were established in western Azerbaijan, in 1871 the American Board transferred the mission to the New York-based Presbyterian Board of Foreign Missions.

The Presbyterians officially renamed the enterprise 'The Mission to Persia', and they sought to minister to Muslims and Jews as well as Armenian and Assyrian Christians in Iran. Under the authority of the Iranian government, the Presbyterian Board expanded their mission throughout the north of the country, opening new stations at Tehran, Tabriz, Hamadan, Rasht, Qazvin, Kermanshah, and Mashhad before World War I. This expansion was carried out in rivalry with French Roman Catholic and Russian Orthodox missions, and in collaboration with the Anglican Church Missionary Society. Presbyterian missionaries, two-thirds of whom were women, spent their lives in Christian service to Iranians, operating schools and hospitals and engaging in social work as well as organizing an Iranian Evangelical Church. Until the vast expansion of US activity which began with World War II, the Presbyterian Mission was the most important American interest in Iran. After 1945, under the dual impetus of ecumenicism, which changed the Church's emphasis from evangelism to assisting local religious and charitable organizations, and ebbing Church finances, the mission

Figure 4.1 Annie Stocking Boyce, 1906

By courtesy of Presbyterian Historical Society, Presbyterian Church, Philadelphia (USA)

declined in importance. Nevertheless, it remained in Iran until after the 1978–79 Islamic Revolution.

Presbyterian missionaries came to Iran with a social agenda.[1] Because their explicit purpose was to preach the Gospel of Jesus Christ, and it was for this reason that American churches funded their lives, they usually framed their objectives in terms of Christianity. Yet it seems clear from studying their records[2] that, in terms of social conditions, they were as critical of Iranian Christians as they were of Muslims and Jews. To a secular observer it is apparent that they wished to promote in Iran a way of life which was American, although they called it Christian.

If I may anticipate my conclusions, what American Presbyterian missionaries wished to establish for Iranians was a life-style which might be expressed in the following way.

- All boys and girls should be educated in modern schools.
- There should be adequate, modern housing and clothing for all.
- Modern medicine should ease pain and suffering.
- Gender relationships should be modernized:
  - there should be no child marriage, no polygamy, no easy divorce;
  - marriage should be by 'romance', that is, by choice of the marriage partners, not simply arranged by families;
  - women should have the possibility of remaining single and following careers;
  - in marriage the role of the wife was to be a partner and help-mate of her husband and the mother of their children.
- A major role for educated, modern women was to keep house, for the benefit of all society.

This programme amounted to 'a campaign to advance the freedom' of Iranians, especially Iranian women whom the missionaries saw as held in subjugation.

This subject marks the intersection of several important topics. These include American social history (especially the history of religion and the history of gender relations), Iranian social history (especially the impact of the west on Iran and the development of Iranian society into twentieth-century realities), and international relations (especially the complex and bedeviled relationship of Iran and the USA).

In order to explore the question of American missionaries and gender reform in Iran, I will discuss the life of Annie Stocking Boyce. Her missionary career in Iran began during the 1906–11 Constitutional Revolution and did not end until after World War II. She was a pioneering educator and journalist. At various times she served as teacher and principal of the American Girls' School in Tehran, as teacher and house-mother at the American (Alborz) College of Tehran, where her husband served as Dean and Professor of Education, and as founder, manager and editor of *Alam-i-Nesvan*, a durable and influential magazine dedicated to uplifting Iranian women. On the basis of written records, she was an extraordinary personality, whose role in twentieth-century Iranian history seems comparable to that of her colleague and older contemporary, Dr Samuel Martin Jordan, founder of Alborz College.[3]

Annie Woodman Stocking Boyce

Born in Wiscasset, Maine, on 7 January 1880, Annie Woodman Stocking ('Nan') Boyce worked as a Presbyterian missionary in Iran from 1906 until her retirement in 1949. She was a third-generation Iran missionary; her grand-parents (William Redfield Stocking and Jerusha Emily Gilbert Stocking) served at Urmia, 1837–54, where her father, William Redfield Stocking II was born in 1844. The younger William Stocking himself served as a missionary at Urmia, 1871–79, burying a wife (Harriet E. Lyman) there in 1872 and marrying Annie's mother (Isabella C. Baker) on the field, before withdrawing to accept a Congregational pulpit at Williamstown, Massachusetts. There, in the town dominated by Williams College, one of America's elite institutions of higher education for men, Annie Woodman Stocking grew up.[4]

After her education at Williamstown High School and Wellesley College (AB, 1902) – a university for women comparable in quality to Williams – and several years working as a secretary in Albany, New York, Annie Stocking felt a strong call to become a missionary in Iran. She wrote in her letter of application to the Presbyterian Board on 8 February 1906, 'missionary work in Persia is a family inheritance, a privilege and a responsibility to which I have fallen heir.'[5]

She came to Tehran in September 1906 and was assigned to teach in the Iran Bethel school for girls. Iran Bethel had been founded in 1874, two years after the opening of the Tehran Station, and its curriculum for girls was intended to be 'similar to that given in the boys' school'. Although it had long educated Armenians, in the early twentieth century increasing numbers of Muslims sent their daughters there. Annie Stocking was directed to learn Persian in order to work with these girls. In 1906–07 the school had 41 Muslims enrolled, out of a total student body of 124.[6]

Annie Stocking's arrival in Iran coincided with Iran's Constitutional Revolution. The spirit of Constitutional reform excited her and helped to shape her subsequent career. Writing to New York early in 1907, she observed that,

> No westerner could live in Persia the past few months without feeling intensely interested in the recent movement toward a more liberal and representative government. That the [Iranian] nation is groping after better things politically, and awakening to a consciousness of the justice and advantages of popular representation in making laws, is very evident.[7]

In her own mind, she seemed to mix the political events which she observed with her mission to educate Iranians. Writing on 8 March 1907 to Mission Secretary Robert Speer in New York, she wondered, what our friends at home are reading about Persia these days. We hear all sorts of rumors and there is much unrest in the country. An open rupture between the Shah and the Parliament seems almost inevitable but we hope all these things will work out in some way for the best interests of the work. The educational awakening among the Moslems seems wonderful.[8]

She was an engaged observer of the Revolution. Writing to New York at the end of the summer of 1908 about fighting in Tabriz, she declared,

The last word we had was that the Revolutionists were victorious. I hope so for *I can't bear to have the Shah have everything his own way and it does my American blood good to know that there are Persians who are willing to fight to the bitter end for liberty* [emphasis added].[9]

This attitude, mixing Christian and educational vocation with advocacy of fundamental reform, continued throughout her career as a missionary in Iran.

During her first years in Tehran she, 'led morning chapel for the Persian-speaking group [in Iran Bethel School] … taught Bible to all grades in Persian … taught a great variety of subjects in English and … had a small class in Physics in the boys school.'[10] During her first term she met Arthur Boyce, a short-term (1907–10) teacher at the boys' school. Their relationship continued when he returned to the States to complete a doctorate, and 'while on furlough, in March, 1914', she married him,

our romance [emphasis added] having started while he was a short-termer in the Teheran Boys School. After our return to Teheran in April, 1915, I continued to have some classes in the Girls School, giving much time to working out a course in Home Economics. Often I brought the girls of the class to our home and gave them practical demonstration of the lessons I was teaching. My chief aim was to make the girls feel that household management was an art – not merely servant's work as many believed, and was worthy of the best efforts of educated girls.[11]

In other words, despite her excitement by and approval of the political events of the Constitutional Revolution, she chose to focus her efforts to transform Iran on the *private* lives of women. She clearly saw her own life as one she needed to make a model worthy of Iranians to emulate.

Alam-i-Nesvan

Annie Stocking Boyce also threw herself into public work to transform the lives of women. Writing retrospectively about her career in about 1948 she declared:

One of my chief interests was acting as sponsor, manager and editor of *Alam-i-Nesvan*, a magazine published in the name of the alumnae of the

Girls School and devoted to the interests of women – health, care of children, food, dress, news of the progress of women, etc. ... In the twelve years of the magazine's life [from 1920] it is a big satisfaction to believe that it had a real influence in advancing the cause of the freedom of the women of Iran.[12]

How did she come to this work? Papers preserved in the Presbyterian Historical Society suggest some of the factors.

Annie Stocking Boyce planned *Alam-i-Nesvan* during Iran's post-World War I chaos, when violence made it seem possible that the Bolshevik revolution might force the evacuation of westerners from the country. In July 1920 she wrote in a letter:

I think I told you about the magazine for Persian women our Alumnae Ass'n has undertaken. I am intensely interested in it and see wonderful possibilities in it. We expect the first number to come out Sept 1st. *It is very much my child* [emphasis added].

There are so many worthwhile things to do out here. If only we can stay and keep on with the work! It is an awful thought to consider that it *might* have to be abandoned. Another complicating factor is the troubles in Baghdad.[13]

Referring to the magazine as 'my child' is an interesting metaphor, especially in view of a letter she had written in 1917 to her sister Ethel, almost three years after her marriage to Arthur Boyce, when she was already 37 years old.

Arthur is always his sweet, sunny self and his patience and endurance never seem to fail. He is a very good sort of person to live with and grows better all the time! You are wondering if we have any hopes of a family. How I wish I could say we had for we want a baby very much. The doctors say there is no reason why we should not have children, but somehow they do not come and I am getting older all the time. It has been [such] a perpetual disappointment to me that I made up my mind last month that I must try not to think of it any more or even *hope* for a little one, but just give myself up to other things and try to forget about children. This is not easy and sometimes I feel as if someone had died, but since I made this decision and told the Lord I would give it all up and leave it in His hands and not even ask Him anymore, my life has had much more peace in it and I feel much steadier and stronger for the future.[14]

Thus it seems that Annie Boyce strongly wished to be a mother as well as a wife. When children were denied her, she transferred much of her energy into a campaign to improve the lives of Iranian women and *their* children.

Details of her campaign to advance 'the cause of the freedom of the women of Iran' can be seen in her annual 'Personal Reports', made to the Presbyterian Mission and her supporting churches.[15]

In her first report as a married woman, for example, in 1916 she noted that, 'My work for the year might be divided into Home Work and Outside Work.'[16] Under the heading of Home, she included entertaining – 'on some of [which] occasions I wore my wedding dress to make it seem as if [my guests] had a part in my wedding' – relief work for poor Persian women ['we distributed over half a ton of charcoal, some rice and a little sugar and tea, [and] many pairs of shoes ... for cold feet'], and supervising a 'needlework industry ... . Four women supported or helped to support their families by this work'. Her Outside Work included teaching, holding evangelical meetings, and going to Iranian women's homes: 'Calling is always an important part of a woman's work'.[17] In her own mind, and that of the Mission, her work was clearly 'Christian'. Yet when viewed from a secular perspective, it seems a combination of religious and social work, with the focus being on relief of distress and uplift, that is, education for women and building female self-reliance.

In 1918 Boyce wrote that: 'This year it was my turn to be President of the Alumnae Association of Iran Bethel School', and she began to use this organization as a forum for transforming Iranian women's lives.

> In January [1918, while Tehran was suffering high mortality from famine and epidemic disease] under the auspices of the Association, Dr. Neligan of the British Legation gave four Friday afternoon lectures on Practical Hygiene. These were given in Persian and the average attendance was over eighty, mostly Persian ladies. In March we asked a well-known graduate of the Boys' School to give a lecture, for ladies only, on The Persian Press, for the benefit of the Relief Fund ... we cleared fifty tomans.[18]

Her 1921 report is especially interesting for two reasons. First, she recorded economic conditions in the year of Reza Khan's coup.

> Most of the year we paid over 30 cents a pound for granulated sugar but it has recently gone down to 24 cents. It seems a good deal to us to pay, as we did part of the year, 24 cents a pound for a poor grade of mutton, 50 cents a dozen for eggs and 18 cents a quart for milk, and this in a city where a day laborer is paid well at forty cents a day.[19]

This high cost of living was associated with increased mortality; 'there have been many deaths among our friends in the church and outside'. Combined with the 'bright times', it made for

> all the round of human joys and sorrows to share as a friend. [Consequently,] This year in all the contacts there has seemed to be more opportunity than ever to talk of the deeper things of life and the power of Christ to satisfy the needs of all men everywhere.[20]

Despite, or rather *because* of her religious consciousness, she began to throw herself into a secular work of profound influence. Under the aegis of the Iran Bethel Alumnae Association, which she continued to serve as president, she began 'the publication of *Alam-i-Nesvan*, or *Woman's World*, a magazine for Persian women'.[21]

> The Editorial Board [Boyce wrote in 1921] consists of six Persian girls, one Armenian who has done part of the work of Business Manager, and myself. We have published one number every two months or six during the year. Five hundred copies of the first number were printed, four hundred of succeeding numbers. At the close of the year we had 190 subscribers and the sale of single copies was so large that few copies of the first three numbers are on hand. *Alam-i-Nesvan* is a 40 page magazine, with departments of Hygiene, Care of Children, Housekeeping, Dress, News of the Progress of Women, literary and general articles. Physicians of the city have provided the health articles, Mrs McDowell and Miss [Grace] Taillie [R.N.] have written those on Care and Training of Children and we are indebted to others for suggestions, ideas and money. The girls have been enthusiastic and some of them have worked hard. Lacking experience they have naturally required very careful leadership and I have given a large amount of time to the magazine. I find that one sixth of the total number of pages printed I first prepared in English and this includes editorials, articles on Household Management and the life story of Mary Lyon and Frances Willard. With three Moslems on the Editorial Board and no religious liberty in the country we cannot hope to make the paper a religious magazine. And yet I am sure it is exerting a vital Christian influence. One of the girls on the Board is so strict a Moslem that she will not take a cup of tea in my house and yet in her heart I believe she joins in the prayer offered at every Board meeting, and offered in the name of Christ, that *Alam-i-Nesvan* may be a blessing to the women of Persia.[22]

Subsequent personal reports showed the progress of the magazine. In 1922 Annie Boyce noted that:

> *Alam-i-Nesvan* ... closed its second year in June with all bills paid. We had 251 subscribers ... not a large number actually but comparatively very large. I doubt whether any publication other than ours could count so many for the reason that so many newspapers and magazines are suppressed that people are afraid to pay a year's subscription and prefer to buy single numbers. ... the most powerful factor in getting prestige for a paper here, seems to be to keep the paper going – and we must keep *Alam-i-Nesvan* going at any cost. No other publication attempts to give the informing, and I trust, inspiring material which we aim to print and the magazine is bound to exert a quiet, steady influence in the uplift of Persian womanhood. Grace Khanum, who is by far the most capable girl on the Magazine Board, expects to go to America in the fall for study and I do not know how we can get on without her. I quite approve of her going to America, however, for unless some Persian girls go to other countries, how are they to get the

vision of what is possible for the womanhood of their own country? I expect
Grace to come back and exert a wide influence in journalism and help lead
in the woman's movement which some day will sweep Persia.[23]

That the magazine's bills were paid owed something to innovative fund-raising.
In April, 1922, two lectures were sponsored for mothers, by 'Dr. Neligan of the
British Legation' on 'the "Hygiene of the Baby"' and by Mrs McDowell on
'Teaching Obedience to Children'; 'about a hundred women were present each
time'. Also:

> The last week of school we had 'movies' for two nights in the large
> assembly room of the boys' school – for Persian ladies only. The profits
> (92 tomans, about 92 dollars) went to *Alam-i-Nesvan*. But the profits were
> not as significant as the fact that this was the first entertainment of its kind
> ever given for Persian women ... Moslem women are never allowed to
> attend the public moving-picture places on Lalezar.

Boyce understood that such revolutionary activity presented danger, and she
prayed, 'May God make us worthy of the trust of the people and help us always
to keep the name of the American School above reproach.'[24]

Yet as Reza Khan tightened his grip on the country, the magazine had to
contend with careful supervision by the Iranian authorities. In 1925 – after her
return from her second furlough in the States – she noted that,

> The problem of the *Alam-i-Nesvan* magazine for Persian women is to get
> enough of the right kind of material. Original articles are at a low ebb. The
> few women who used to contribute have mostly left the city; the censor of
> the police department has been most rigid in his inspection and has
> forbidden the publication of two articles by our most popular contributors,
> one Dilshad Khanum. People say that the magazine does not have the *flavor*
> it used to have. On the other hand we are getting an excellent grade of
> translated work. A friend at home subscribes to several magazines which we
> scan most eagerly with the hope of finding suitable material for translation.
> The Popular Science Monthly has furnished most in this connection and is
> responsible for the Science Questions and Answers which have met with
> much appreciation. Although our magazine is intended for women we feel
> that its most loyal supporters are men. And it would seem as if the magazine
> met with a warmer welcome outside of Teheran than in this city. The palm
> goes to Miss Bryan of Hamadan who has sent us forty-five subscriptions. A
> very neat sum was netted for the magazine through two motion picture
> shows given in the large room of the boys' school in April. This is the fourth
> year that we have had these 'cinemas' for Persian women and there is
> something laughable in the fact that the Chief of Police felt he could not take
> the heavy responsibility of giving permission without referring the request
> to His Highness, the Prime Minister [Reza Khan].[25]

In the spring of 1926 Annie Boyce found another outlet for her maternal feelings. She and her husband took into their lives a

> dear little Persian lad, Parviz, ... in whose life and education we hope to
> have an ever-deepening influence, whether he remains in our home or
> whether we place him with a Persian family. To see the world anew
> through the clear brown eyes of a little village boy five and a half years old
> has been one of the precious experiences of life.[26]

In subsequent years the Boyces seem to have adopted Parviz, who had been baptised in the winter of 1922, 'when his father, a simple village man, brought his little boy to the city and dedicated the year old baby to God in baptism.'[27] However, they had him live much of the time in the Boys' School dormitory, so that he could have a more Iranian environment than in their home.[28]

Still, she focused her work heavily on *Alam-i-Nesvan*, which expanded in 1927. The magazine 'began publishing monthly beginning with January, 1927, and ... circulation in the provinces is greatly increased. We jump from 400 to 600 copies of each issue.' One of the new subscriptions 'to our humble magazine [was] from the household of the Crown Prince of Persia', and there were also 'one addressed to the Queen of Afghanistan and another to the Sister of the King of Afghanistan. ... After this,' Boyce wrote, 'we must take into consideration our influence on royalty.' All was not rosy, however, as

> the last of May, the Dept. of Education [found] fault with us for
> publishing an item translated from an American paper to the effect that
> the women of Trebizond have cast aside the veil. We are told that the Shah
> has been annoyed by a telegram from Tabriz referring to the item and
> asking why His Majesty permits the publication of such injurious
> information! We feel like both laughing and crying over such an
> exasperatingly silly situation.[29]

In 1928, the journal returned to its bi-monthly format, but its circulation increased.

> We are publishing 650 copies of each issue. ... Our subscription list in
> Teheran is 200. We send 300 to thirty-one cities of Persia – Barfarush
> leading this year with 31 subscribers; Resht, Kerman, [and] Sultanabad are
> close seconds. If we are safe in assuming that on the average five people
> read each copy in circulation, the magazine can count its reading public as
> numbering perhaps 2500 people all over the country.[30]

Annie Stocking Boyce's 1929 report suggests that the difficulties with the Iranian government had been worked out. She wrote, 'One of the best articles contributed this year was written by a young man who is one of the secretaries of the Shah's court. ... He wrote an article, largely historical, on the position of woman in society.'[31]

Her next report (1930) suggests that she believed her work to be both increasingly popular and successful in its efforts to raise Iranian consciousness.

> The magazine *Alam-i-Nesvan* (*World of Women*) has been booming in this its tenth year (1930). Last year the maximum output was 750 copies. After the first two issues this year an edition of 1000 proved too small and now we are printing 1200. Credit for the advance is due to the great energy and even greater enthusiasm of Abbas Aryanpur, our Managing Editor, and also to the fact that we took on a paid office assistant whose work Abbas Khan has directed. As a feature, in the January number, we asked our women readers to write us about their Ideal Husband. Numerous letters were received, more than we could print in the March magazine, the burden of many being, 'What's the use of our describing the man we would like to marry when we never have any choice in the matter, anyway?' In the May number we printed replies to the question, 'What are the qualities of your Ideal Wife?' Before we proposed these questions, a man sent us an article discussing the relative desirability of city and village girls as wives and declaring himself in favor of a village girl. This is a different matter from what it would be in America for here village girls are universally ignorant and untrained. His article called forth several spirited replies and the discussion was carried over into the local dailies. Now we are trying to set on foot a movement whereby within a year 5000 women and girls will promise each to teach one other woman or girl not in school, to read. If we attain our goal this year we hope it will be but the beginning of a popular education movement which will help to wipe out the terrible percentage of illiteracy, especially among women.[32]

In 1931 circulation of *Alam-i-Nesvan* grew to 1300, and Mrs Boyce took pleasure in 'the wide-spread influence of the magazine. When Mrs McDowell prepares her excellent articles on the Care and Training of Children, she knows that they will be read by mothers (and doubtless fathers) in all the large cities of Persia and many smaller towns.' Also in 1931, *Alam-i-Nesvan*, completed publication of a translation of *Pollyanna* by Abbas Khan Aryanpur 'with Mr. [William] Wysham in consultation,' and began:

> running as a serial the translation of *Charm by Choice*, a little book written by a woman physician at home and published by The Woman's Press. In the book the emphasis is on health as a basis of charm and Persian women are at a stage in their development when they welcome information on correct diet (including reducing!), exercise, the care of the skin and even 'the correct use of cosmetics.' This translation is being made by Moluk Khanum Jalalee, a graduate of our girls school, who does excellent work along this line. Her father has recently become governor of Isfahan and she is to continue the work from that city.

Also, 'in the March, 1931, issue Dr. Blair contributed a very helpful article on First Aid.'[33]

Alam-i-Nesvan ceased to exist during the Great Depression, apparently for financial reasons. Annie Stocking Boyce's 1932 and 1933 reports have not been found in the archives, perhaps because she did not write them; she was on furlough in the USA in these years. Before she departed, however, she wrote in an April 1932 letter that she had,

> been giving much time lately to work connected with the magazine for women. ... Our finances are in bad shape and I have been trying to increase our circulation among people who will pay in advance. That sounds queer but it is no joke, I assure you. ... About three weeks ago the Board cabled that there was to be a cut of 10 per cent on all appropriations. ... We are very much troubled over this.[34]

In view of Reza Shah's increasing sensitivity to criticism and increasingly tight control over the Iranian press, however, one wonders if there might have been reasons other than financial for the closing of *Alam-i-Nesvan*. According to the centennial history of the mission, in whose writing Annie Stocking Boyce participated, 'During the last year of its existence it was deemed best to turn the paper over to a Persian woman editor, it steadily lost ground and was discontinued in 1934.'[35] In any case, Annie Boyce seems to have ended her supervision of it on her departure from Tehran in 1932.

Other work

On her return to Tehran in 1933, Annie Boyce threw herself into the full spectrum of the life of a married missionary woman, working and praying 'for the time Persia shall be a garden-spot in the Kingdom of God'. She taught English and ethics to boys and girls, and had 'a good deal of miscellaneous work', including renewing acquaintances, setting up a new household, and actually living with her now thirteen year-old adopted boy, Parviz.[36]

But reading the reports she wrote following her return from furlough in 1933, in comparison with earlier reports, leads a reader to suspect that something vital had gone out of her life. The loss of *Alam-i-Nesvan* must have hurt deeply. Yet she sought, for the remainder of her career in Iran, to achieve the same ends by other means.

Looking backward at the mid-1930s, from the end of her career, she was proud that:

> At the time the veil was abandoned, Agha Hekmat who was then Minister of Education asked me to give a series of lectures at Kanun-i-Banuan [the Woman's Center] on proper social relations of men and women – 'Adabiat-i-Moasherat'. These were especially for women school teachers who were much interested in wanting to know the right customs.[37]

Her contemporary account of this event bubbles with enthusiasm, although it also makes clear how small was the scale on which she operated. In the summer of 1936 she wrote,

> Ever since I came to Iran I have always hoped that I would live to see the unveiling of Moslem women. In the early days such a possibility seemed very remote, far, far in the very dim future. Eight years ago it seemed imminent, right at our doors, but failed to come to pass. For at least six years it has been possible for women to abandon the veil if they wished, but so few took advantage of the situation that the response was discouraging. But this year, my thirtieth in Iran, unveiling has come, achieved with almost incredible swiftness, when once started, and with amazing thoroughness. Iranian women are at last entering into their own and I rejoice to have lived to see it! ... Three different evenings at *Kanun-i-Banuan*, the Women's Center, proved most interesting and made me feel in touch with the forward movement in some of its new aspects. A very real thrill in the realization of what it all meant, came to me as Miss [Jane] Doolittle and I met with two Moslem women who were a committee of the Women's Center to prepare a little manual on proper dress and social procedure for the guidance of the newly emancipated, and who asked our criticism on what they had written.[38]

From the vantage point of the late 1990s, perhaps Annie Boyce's enthusiasm appears misplaced. 'Unveiling' was resisted by many Iranians in the 1930s, women especially, and it appears to have been seen as a sign of the increasing tyranny of Reza Shah. Also, in the 1970s, young university women's wearing the chador was an important sign of dissatisfaction with the regime, a prelude to the Islamic Revolution. Today, when wearing *hijab* is a legal requirement for all women in the Islamic Republic, foreigners as well as Iranian Muslims, the issue appears to be of more interest to foreigners than to Iranian women.[39] Yet I believe that Annie Boyce stood with her colleague Mary Park Jordan who, on the eve of the royal edict banning the chador, cautioned her colleagues not to confuse external signs with internal realities.

> In late years this outdoor covering has been no hindrance to education or progress, though resented by some, both men and women, as a badge of ignorance and servitude and an insult to the men of Persia. One of the leaders of what might be called the feminist movement in Persia has frequently said: 'We are working for the lifting of the veil of ignorance and superstition. The removal of the *chuddar* is of no great importance.'[40]

Yet clearly Annie Boyce believed she had a role to play in the new world created by Reza Shah's edict. In 1938 she wrote of her efforts in co-operation with the Iranian government,

'What can one do when a man with whom she does not wish to have any association, comes up to a woman on the street, insists on shaking hands with her and walking along beside her?' This question was put by a woman who came forward to speak to me after my first lesson on Etiquette at the Woman's Club (*Kanun-i-Banuan*). On thursday afternoons the teachers of the government elementary schools for girls are required to attend lectures arranged for them at the Woman's club. The Minister of Education asked me to give four lessons, one a month during the spring on the 'Politeness of Intercourse.' This was an opportunity to be of service in an unusual way, for since the unveiling of women two and a half years ago, Moslem women are very anxious to understand foreign ways of doing things, especially correct social procedure. It was fun to play the role of Emily Post of Iran to an audience of from 200 to 400 women who were keenly interested in the subjects discussed. There was opportunity to stress sincerity and the spirit of kindliness and thoughtfulness as the foundation of true politeness.

It was [also] in the great hall of the Woman's Club one evening in February that we heard a lecture on Marriage by Madame Sadigeh Daulatabadee, president of the club. The lecture was of course in Persian and the Moslem audience was large but Khanum Daulatabadee spoke openly against polygamy and free love and her lecture was printed in the paper next day.[41]

Annie Stocking Boyce also worked at the American College of Tehran [later Alborz College], which had grown out of the Boys' School. There she taught, acted as a 'house mother' (dormitory supervisor), and was as important a school personality as were ACT's founder, Dr Samuel M. Jordan, his wife, Mary Park Jordan, and her own husband, Arthur C. Boyce. In 1948 she wrote,

> Although I did some teaching in Alborz I felt that my main work in helping my husband was in making our home a place where students, alumni and friends were welcome. We did much entertaining of students and whenever possible, their mothers. I also kept my friendships with the graduates of Iran Bethel of my time, calling on them and arranging class reunions in our home.[42]

Her 1936 Personal Report gives a contemporary view of her work helping her husband.

> We have felt that knowing the boys personally was even more important than looking after their physical wants. ... two evenings a week we had dinner with the boys in the big dining room, sitting in turn at the different tables. On Saturday evenings for most of the year there was a social time after dinner with songs, games, etc. ... On Tuesday nights after dinner we had the boys come in groups, to our living room, for tea and cakes, then games, radio, conversation – as fitted the mood. In this way practically every boy was entertained three times during the year.[43]

Then, in 1940, all mission schools were ended by Reza Shah.[44] This was neither the end of the Boyces' careers in Iran nor the end of missionary efforts to reform gender relations. However, it was a prelude to Reza Shah's removal from the scene by the intervention of Great Britain and the Soviet Union, in the midst of World War II. Annie Boyce commented on these events in her 1942 Personal Report.

> More amazing than the coming of the British and the Russians was the going of the Pahlavi on September 16th. People were prepared for this by a series of broadcasts in Persian from London for a week preceding the abdication. Never can we forget the sensation of sitting in our living room and listening to the accusations against the Shah, each night growing in boldness and intensity until we could scarcely believe that we were hearing such declarations in the Persian language. There was nothing new in the statements but heretofore these things had been said only in whispers. There was universal rejoicing when the dictator left and the atmosphere of freedom which resulted was truly thrilling. One event of prime importance was the liberation of several hundred political prisoners, among them several of our personal friends one of whom had been sentenced for life. However, the mood of exaltation was rather short-lived, and restless uncertainty took its place. Prices of all commodities continued their upward trend and now, nine months later, the peak seems still unreached.[45]

Since 1941 thus marks a watershed in twentieth-century Iranian history, this is an appropriate juncture to end this exploration.

Conclusions

I believe we should see Annie Stocking Boyce's career as an essential aspect of an American Presbyterian campaign to reform gender relations in Iran.

By upbringing, education, and Church affiliation she was part of the American elite. Williams College was – and is – one of America's best regarded universities. It was founded by the Congregational Church, and Annie Boyce's father's position as Congregational minister in this small College town surely kept the family in close contact with Williams faculty and students. Certainly her own education at Wellesley continued her development as a member of the American elite, and by joining the Presbyterian Church (which had taken over the Iran mission field from the Congregationalists in the 1870s) she joined the Church associated with President Woodrow Wilson, Wilson's Secretary of State Robert Lansing, President Coolidge's Vice President Charles Dawes, President Dwight Eisenhower, and Eisenhower's Secretary of State, John Foster Dulles, and Director of Central Intelligence, Allan Dulles.

Throughout her youth Annie Stocking absorbed ideas of American messianism, a mission to enlighten humanity and to participate in a history whose manifest purpose was the progressive liberation of humanity. This liberal, Protestant view of history assumed that humankind rose, beginning with the Reformation, from monarchical tyranny toward democratic, parliamentary self-government. America was thus 'a city on a hill', meant by divine providence to lead humanity toward a better life. Consequently, Annie Stocking (like her contemporary Howard Baskerville) seems to have seen the Iranian Constitutional Revolution as the work of God, consistent with the earlier revolutions in England, America and France.

When the Iranian revolution was 'strangled' in 1911, it was natural for Annie Stocking to transform her enthusiasm into a campaign to liberate Iranian women. This was 'safe' in the eyes of Russia, Britain and many Iranian conservatives. Also, it was consistent both with the long-standing missionary impulse to foster 'Woman's Work for Women' and with the contemporary campaign for women's suffrage, which became law after World War I in America, as well as in Great Britain, Germany and other western countries.

Annie Boyce was part of a large and powerful bureaucratic organization, the Presbyterian Church in the United States of America. She did not act alone. The Board of Foreign Missions supported her financially, but it also required that she make regular reports and that her work be a disciplined part of the overall activity of the Board. Thus, although I have focused here on her particular life and career, I think it is reasonable to regard her work as an aspect of co-operative activity. She was part of a missionary community including both her colleagues in Iran and the Church at home. She acted in Iran as an agent of her Church. Missionaries who did not do so were sent home.

There is no question but that Annie Boyce and her colleagues believed that what they were doing was God's will, that it was living the Gospel of Jesus Christ. Yet a non-Christian observer understands that in content much of what they did was secular. It spread an American way-of-life at least as much as it spread Christianity. Of course many Americans, even today, do not make a fine distinction between Church and State, as efforts to reintroduce prayer into public schools and the constant repetition of the cliché 'America is a Christian country' make clear. But the content of American missionary education in Iran, including the content of the magazine *Alam-i-Nesvan*, appealed powerfully, in logic and modernity, even to non-Americans and non-Christians.

Did this campaign to advance freedom have influence in Iran? That is difficult to prove. But surely the progress made by Iranians, in standards of living, literacy, higher education, sanitation, life expectancy, opportunities for women's education and careers outside the home, and constitutional, parliamentary self-government, is largely consistent with what the Presbyterian missionaries were trying to inculcate.

Notes

1 See Frederick J. Heuser, Jr., 'Culture, Feminism, and the Gospel: American Presbyterian Women and Foreign Missions, 1870–1923', Ph.D. dissertation, Temple University, 1991; Kristin L. Gleeson, 'Healers Abroad: Presbyterian Women Physicians in the Foreign Mission Field', Ph.D. dissertation, Temple University, 1996; Arthur Judson Brown (1936) *One Hundred Years: A History of the Foreign Missionary Work of the Presbyterian Church in the U.S.A.*, New York; John K. Fairbanks (1974) *The Missionary Enterprise in China and America*, Cambridge; Patricia Hill (1986) *The World Their Household: The American Women's Foreign Mission Movement and Cultural Transformation, 1870–1920*, Ann Arbor. John Hersey (1985) *The Call*, New York, is an excellent fictional account of the American missionary experience in China which was his own upbringing. I have written extensively on the subject of Presbyterian missionaries in Iran; see 'Render Therefore unto Caesar That Which is Caesar's; American Presbyterian Educators and Reza Shah,' *Iranian Studies*, 1993, pp. 337–56; 'A Panacea for the Ills of the Country: American Presbyterian Education in Inter-War Iran', *Iranian Studies*, 1993, pp. 119–37; 'Harbingers of Change: Presbyterian Women in Iran, 1883–1949', *American Presbyterians; Journal of Presbyterian History*, 1992, pp. 173–86; and 'Presbyterian Missionaries and American Relations with Pahlavi Iran', *The Iranian Journal of International Affairs*, 1989, pp. 71–86.
2 These records are preserved at the Presbyterian Historical Society (PHS), Philadelphia, Pennsylvania. This paper is primarily based on these records, and I am deeply indebted to the entire PHS staff for their efficiency and helpfulness. Presbyterians believe that history is the record of God working on earth; historical records consequently are conserved by the Church as an act of faith, so that human beings can study the past in order to know God.
3 To my knowledge, no systematic description of *Alam-i-Nesvan* has yet been written. Yahya Armajani was of the opinion that *Alam-i-Nesvan* was 'a real force in the uplift of the women of the country ... in any study of the progress of women in Iran it is essential to study the pages of *World of Women*', 'Sam Jordan and the Evangelical Ethic in Iran', in Robert J. Miller (ed.) (1974) *Religious Ferment in Asia*, Lawrence, Kansas, p. 32. In recent years I have had enquiries about Presbyterian records of this journal from Janet Afary (Purdue University) and from students of Nikki Keddie (UCLA) and Mansoureh Ettehadieh (Tehran University); this paper is in part a response to these enquiries. Under the Shah, an Avenue was named after Dr Jordan. The Islamic Republic has renamed the Avenue 'Africa', but to get there by taxi in 1997, one still must ask for 'Khiaban-i-Jordan'.
4 Presbyterian Historical Society [PHS], Personnel file [H-5].
5 *Ibid.*
6 A. W. Stocking, Tehran Station Quarterly Letter, 26 January 1907, PHS, MF10, F761a, r.272; Arthur Judson Brown (1936) *One Hundred Years*, New York, pp. 498–9; annual report of school principal Jane E. Doolittle, 1929–1930, PHS, RG 91–20–12.
7 A. W. Stocking, Tehran Station Quarterly Letter, 26 January 1907, PHS, MF10, F761a, r.272.
8 A. W. Stocking, Tehran, to Robert Speer, New York, 8 March 1907, PHS, MF10, F761a, r.272.
9 A. W. Stocking, Tehran, to R. W. Speer, New York, 15 September 1908.
10 'Memoranda re Work of Mrs Arthur C. Boyce in Iran (Compiled by herself),' n.d., PHS, RG 91–18–11.
11 *Ibid.*
12 *Ibid.*

13 Ms letter to an unknown addressee, July 1920, signed 'Fondest Love, Annie', PHS, RG 91–18–11; 'troubles in Baghdad' refers to the Arab revolt against the British mandate in Iraq.

14 Annie Stocking Boyce ('Your ever affectionate Nan') to 'Dearest Ethel', Tehran, 9 February 1917, PHS, RG 91–18–11.

15 I have reviewed her reports for the years ending June 30th 1916, 1918, 1921, 1922, 1925, 1926, 1927, 1928, 1929, 1930, 1931, 1934, 1935, 1936, 1937, 1938 and 1942. These reports always ended with thanks to God, as in her 1928 report, 'And so at the end of another stretch of the pilgrim way, I pile my stones of remembrance and the largest stone of all is gratitude to Him who has led all along the road', PHS, RG 91–1–10. As I write, it seems to me that there is a certain correlation between such explicit missionary piety and the conventional contemporary commencement of public proceedings in the Islamic Republic of Iran with the formula, *Bismillah al-Rahman al-Rahim*, 'In the name of God, the Merciful and Compassionate'.

16 I find this phrasing a fascinating parallel to Iranian division of society into *Anderun* (inside) and *Birun* (outside).

17 Personal Report of Annie Stocking Boyce, 'written for the State Street Presbyterian Church Sunday School, Albany, N.Y.', Tehran, 1916, PHS, RG 91–1–7.

18 Personal Report of Annie Stocking Boyce, 'written for the State Street Church Sunday School, Albany, N.Y.', Tehran, 1918, PHS, RG 91–1–7.

19 Personal Report of Annie Stocking Boyce, 'written for the Westminster Church of Albany, N.Y.', Tehran, 1921.

20 *Ibid.*

21 *Ibid.*

22 *Ibid.*

23 Personal Report of Annie Stocking Boyce, Tehran, 1922, PHS, RG 91–1–7.

24 *Ibid.*

25 Personal Report of Annie Stocking Boyce, 'Written especially for the Westminster Church Sunday School, Albany, N.Y.', Tehran, 1925.

26 Personal Report of Annie Stocking Boyce, Tehran, 1926, PHS, RG 91–1–9.

27 Personal Report of Annie Stocking Boyce, Tehran, 1935, PHS, RG 91–7.

28 Personal Report of Annie Stocking Boyce, Tehran, 1930, PHS, RG 91–18–11.

29 'Ups and Downs', Personal Report of Annie Stocking Boyce, Tehran, 1927, PHS, RG 91–1–10.

30 Personal Report of Annie Stocking Boyce, Tehran, 1928, PHS, RG 91–1–10.

31 Personal Report of Annie Stocking Boyce, Tehran, 1929, PHS, RG 91–1–11.

32 Personal Report of Annie Stocking Boyce, Tehran, 1930, PHS, RG 91–18–11.

33 Report of *Alam-i-Nesvan* for the Year ending June 30, 1931, PHS, RG 91–18–11.

34 Annie Stocking Boyce, The American College of Tehran, 14 April 1932, to 'Dear Friends in Albany', PHS, RG 91–18–12.

35 *A Century of Mission Work in Iran (Persia), 1834–1934,* 'Printed for private circulation', Beirut (The American Press), n.d. (1934), 134 [I am indebted to Margaret Hoffman for lending me a copy of this rare work]; Personal Report of Annie Stocking Boyce, Tehran, 1935, PHS, RG 91–7–3.

36 Personal Report of Annie Stocking Boyce, Tehran, 1934, PHS RG 91–7–2.

37 'Memoranda re Work of Mrs Arthur C. Boyce in Iran (Compiled by herself)', n.d., PHS, RG 91–18–11.

38 Personal Report of Annie Stocking Boyce, Tehran, 1936, PHS, RG 91–7–3.

39 This is a *very* tentative conclusion. On my 1997 travels in Iran, this is a subject I never raised and which no woman volunteered to discuss with me. Still, as Elaine Sciolino observed in *The New York Times Magazine*, 'The Chanel Under the Chador', 4 May 1997, pp. 44–51, Iranian women 'may cloak themselves in the black robes of Shi'ite

fundamentalism, but underneath [they] are wearing power suits and carefully forging an Islamic women's agenda.' And this is the sort of real liberation for which Annie Stocking Boyce and her Presbyterian colleagues were working in early twentieth-century Iran.

40 Mary Park Jordan in *Women and Missions*, reprinted in *The Moslem World*, 1935, 301.
41 Personal Report of Annie Stocking Boyce, Tehran, 1938, PHS, RG 91–7–4.
42 'Memoranda re Work of Mrs Arthur C. Boyce in Iran (Compiled by herself)', n.d., PHS, RG 91–18–11.
43 Personal Report of Annie Stocking Boyce, Tehran, 1936, PHS, RG 91–7–3.
44 For details of this event, see Zirinsky, 'Render Unto Caesar That Which Is Caesar's'.
45 Personal Report of Annie Stocking Boyce, Tehran, 1942, PHS, RG 91–7–6.

five

Women and Journalism in Iran

Hossein Shahidi

This chapter reviews Iranian women's involvement in journalism from the emergence of the first newspaper published by an Iranian woman in 1910, to 1997 when hundreds of women were working on dozens of female-oriented periodicals as well as on other newspapers. The article considers the involvement of Iranian women in journalism in the context of the country's increasing urbanization, the rise in literacy and women's enhanced social, political and economic participation. Having analysed the content of the range of journalism produced by Iranian women, the chapter concludes that they demonstrate a considerable interest in specific issues rather than generalizations, and a sharp eye for detail and the personal touch – qualities which are vital to attracting and maintaining the attention of the readers.

The first Iranian newspaper specifically to address women was published in 1910 – 73 years after the first Persian language newspaper had appeared in the country – but only four years after the Constitutional Revolution, during which Iranian women had participated in mass political action.

The paper, a weekly called *Danish,* or Knowledge, was published by a female optician,[1] Dr Kahhal, who had studied medicine with the American missionaries working in Iran.[2] An announcement on the front page of the first issue described the paper as 'a newspaper dealing with moral issues, childcare and house-keeping, useful for girls and women, which will not in any way discuss *politiques* or the country's policies'.

The pledge not to discuss politics – which had been one of the commitments made in the publisher's application for a licence[3] – did not appear again later on. The second issue was described as 'a moral and literary newspaper which is directly aimed at ladies' and maiden's education and women's moral purification', and the third and later issues did set out a wider agenda, albeit rather vaguely, by adding the words 'etc., etc.' to the list. None the less, *Danish* persevered along a non-political path, offering advice on the importance of 'feeding one's husband on time', 'keeping his room warm', using make-up to secure his affection and, hence, ensuring 'a blissful family life'. There were articles on health and child-care; tips on how to be kind to one's servant, cook or nanny, without 'being fooled' by them and spending more than one can afford; as well as fiction, and reports on girls schools,[4] which, for the muslim majority, were still a great novelty.

Less than a year after its launch, *Danish* had closed down, as its costs could not be met by its inevitably small circulation.[5] At the time, not many Iranian women were able to read and write, hence an appeal in the first issue of *Danish* which said: 'As for ladies who are not literate, it is the duty of the respectable gentlemen to read the magazine to them every week, so that they may not be deprived of this bounty. Maybe this in itself would encourage them to acquire literacy'.[6] Hard as they may have tried, the respectable gentlemen could not have done very much. Their own literacy rate, although many times greater than women's, was only about 5 per cent.[7] Also, with the country still in the throes of the revolution which sought to limit the power of the Qajar autocracy, they had dozens of other newspapers to read, political meetings to attend and battles to fight. And all of this must be seen in the context of a poor nation of just over 10 million, most of whom lived in small, more or less isolated villages.[8] Since the birth of *Danish*, Iranian women's journalism – as indeed the entire profession – has gone through four phases of expansion, most recently after the end of the Iran-Iraq War in 1988. Each of the first three phases was followed by a period of suppression. These peaks and troughs correspond with the following periods of rise and fall in political activity in the country:

1 Rapid growth of newspaper publication from the Constitutional Revolution in 1906 to the overthrow of the Qajar dynasty and the assumption of power by Reza Shah Pahlavi in 1926.
2 Fifteen years of suppression of the press by Reza Shah until his fall in 1941.
3 Expansion of journalism from the fall of Reza Shah and his replacement by his son, Muhammad Reza, to the 1953 American–British-backed coup which toppled the nationalist Musaddiq government and consolidated Muhammad Reza Shah's rule.
4 Suppression of political journalism and the gradual rise of a commercial press under Muhammad Reza Shah until his fall as a result of the 1979 Revolution.
5 Explosive growth of political journalism from 1979 until the closure of hundreds of political newspapers in 1982–83.
6 The absence of opposition political journalism, and the gradual emergence of specialist, technical and trade journals (including some published by and for women) until the end of the Iran–Iraq War in 1988.
7 A re-emergence of political, albeit disguised as social or cultural, journalism since the end of the war, and the acceleration of the process under the Islamic Republic's reformist President Ali Akbar Rafsanjani.

The early Iranian women's journals, which appeared between the publication of *Danish* in 1910 and Reza Shah's coronation in 1926, initially dealt only with education, health, child-care and house-keeping. Faced with the common notion that journalism, as well as politics, was a man's world, some women's newspapers must have felt it necessary to offer a rationale as to why they should be published at all. A proclamation on the front page of *Nama-yi Banuvan* (Ladies' Letter) said: 'Women are men's first teachers'.[9]

As the Constitutionalist Movement took root, women's journals expanded the range of their subjects to include the discussion of 'politiques and the country's policies'. The most openly political women's journal of the time, and the first women's newspaper to use the word 'woman' in its title, was the bi-weekly *Zaban-i Zanan* (Women's Tongue), which was published in 1919 in the central Iranian city of Isfahan, a deeply religious city, where, in the words of the Isfahan-born historian, Muhammad Sadr-i Hashimi, 'the clergy, and especially the pseudo-clergy were at the peak of their influence and importance'.[10]

Zaban-i Zanan soon turned into a 'controversial newspaper, which engaged in polemics with men and focused its debates on freedom and autocracy, rather than on men and women and the specific women's issues'.[11] During its second year of operation, the newspaper's offices came under attack by stone-throwers, who also fired shots at the police.[12] Shortly afterwards, the publication of an article against the so-called '1919 Agreement' – signed by the Iranian government with Britain to secure loans and employ British military and civilian advisors for re-organizing Iran's army and civil service – led to the closure of *Zaban-i Zanan*.[13]

The publisher of *Zaban-i Zanan*, Sadiqa Daulatabadi, was among the pioneers of the Iranian women's movement. She was born in 1882 to a landed family, the youngest and only daughter of her mother's seven children. Both her parents came from leading clerical families and her father was the religious and civilian authority in the village of Daulatabad, which he owned, as well as in the surrounding district of Barkhar, north of Isfahan.[14] Her second eldest brother, Yahya Daulatabadi, was among the leading figures of the Constitutional Revolution and was several times elected as member of parliament for Isfahan. While still a child, Sadiqa studied Persian and Arabic and later had tutors who helped her complete her secondary education at home. Before launching her newspaper, she had already set up Isfahan's first girls'school and an association for women's education under the name of *Shirkat-i Khavatin-i Isfahan* (Isfahan Women's Company).[15]

After the closure of *Zaban-i Zanan*, Sadiqa Daulatabadi moved to Tehran and re-launched the paper as a monthly, established a school for girls from poor families, and also took part in a campaign to discourage the use of imported goods. In 1922, she travelled to Berlin to attend the International Women's Congress, and then to Paris, where she studied education at the Sorbonne. Upon returning to Iran in 1927, Daulatabadi took a prominent role in women's education, as well as in promoting the 16 policies adopted by Reza Shah to end the use of the Islamic dress code, the *hijab*.[16]

Figure 5.1 Front cover – *Zanan*, No 34, Ordibehesth 1376 (April-May 1997), with the picture of the would-be President Khatami

By courtesy of Ms Shahla Sherkat

Figure 5.2 Front cover – the sewing monthly, *Burish* (Cut), No 41, Urdibihisht 1376 (April-May 1997)

By courtesy of Ms Shahla Sherkat

Iran's occupation by the Allied powers in 1941 and Reza Shah's abdication in favour of his son, Muhammad Reza ushered in the second stage of expansion of the Iranian press, which lasted until August 1953, when Dr Muhammad Musaddiq's government was overthrown in a coup backed by the United States and Britain. During this period, nearly 2700 new newspapers were published in the country, that is 39 times as many as had appeared in the first 70 years of the history of journalism in Iran.[17] Among these were women's magazines with openly political titles such as *Zanan-i Pishrau*, or Progressive Women, *Qiyam-i Zan*, or Women's Uprising, and *Huquq-i Zanan* or Women's Rights.[18] Social and political issues, including women's suffrage also found their way into other, less militant sounding women's periodicals. In 1946, the monthly *Banu* (Lady), carried an article by the leading academic and women's rights campaigner, Dr Fatima Sayyah, responding to the question: 'Madam, what would you do if you were to go to the National Consulatative Assembly (parliament)?'

Dr Sayyah argued that as voters would show greater concern with the female candidates' moral rectitude and their knowledge and expertise, 'the first woman members of parliament should possess an indefatigable will and total integrity'. Pointing out that in the first elections, women deputies would form a very small minority, Dr Sayyah advised the would-be women parliamentarians to 'create a united league' to deal with issues which are strictly related to the interests of women and children. Such a league would be then have the task of forcing the parliament to reconsider the country's social legislation and compensate for the injustices which Iranian women had suffered for centuries in respect of their rights as mothers, wives and heirs'.[19]

In another newspaper article the previous year, Dr Sayyah had already discussed the need for electoral reform and women's suffrage, 'at least for literate women although we see no reason why an illiterate woman should not be able to enjoy her electoral rights.' She also called for 'equality of rights in marriage and divorce', and for the 'enforcement of the compulsory education law, especially with respect to girls, because official statistics show that out of every 100 elementary school graduates, 60 are boys and 40 are girls, and that among the adults, there are many more illiterate women and illiterate men.'[20] However, Iranian women were not to enter parliament until the mid-1960s.

In spite of the suppression of the radical press after the 1953 coup, non-political professional journalism survived. Iranian newspapers had traditionally relied on a variety of funding: the publishers' personal fortunes; subsidies from individuals or groups seeking to expand their influence; advertisements placed by the government; and, to a much lesser extent, commercial advertising. In the 1950s and 1960s, population growth, increased urbanization, and the oil-driven rise in the standards of living had enabled the press to rely much more heavily on commercial advertising.

The year of 1956 saw the launch of Iran's first commercial women's newspaper, the weekly *Ittila'at-i Banuvan* (Information for Ladies), published by one of the country's two main newspaper groups, *Ittila'at*. Eight years later, when

Ittila'at's rival, *Kayhan*, had launched its weekly, *Zan-i Ruz* (Modern Woman), Iran had a population of 24 million, 40 per cent of whom lived in cities. The literacy rate had reached 30 per cent, and women made up 30 per cent of the literate population.[21]

Although in the domain of family life, sexual equality was far from accomplished, there were many more women working in education, medical care and the civil service and Muhammad Reza Shah's White Revolution had brought about women's suffrage. In 1971, Iranian women journalists had formed a union, *Anjuman-i Zanan-i Ruznama-nigar-i Iran* (Association of Iranian Women Journalists). By the mid-1970s, the *Anjuman* had 38 permanent members and 50 associated members.[22]

With the 1979 Revolution, Iranian journalism entered its third 'Spring of Freedom'. More than 500 newspapers were launched in the first year after the Revolution, about 30 of them published or edited by women. Some were Islamic, including: *Nahzat-i Zanan-i Mussalman,* or The Muslim Women's Movement; *Zan-i Mussalman,* or The Muslim Woman; *Rah-i Zaynab,* or The Path of Zaynab, named after the Prophet Muhammad's grand-daughter; and – the only one still being published – *Payam-i Hajar,* or Hagar's Message, named after the Prophet Abraham's wife.[23]

Most, however, were tied to left-wing organizations – with titles such as *Bidari-i Zan,* or Woman's Awakening; *Paykar-i Zan,* or Woman's Struggle; *Rahai-yi Zan,* or Woman's Emancipation; and *Sipida-yi Surkh,* or The Red Dawn. In addition to articles about the conditions of the Iranian – especially working-class – women, these magazines had articles on Rosa Luxemburg, Alexandra Kollontai and Nadezhda Krupskaya. In the case of the latter, sometimes there would also be a debate on her life with her husband, Lenin, and the exact nature of his relationship with the French-born socialist, Inessa Armand.

In their personal lives, many left-wing activists had to deal with a conflict between sexual attraction and ideological compatibility. The problem may not have arisen, at least not very rapidly, within the traditional male-dominated framework of marriage. But in revolutionary circumstances, with almost all political groups advocating gender equality, ideological differences could easily lead to personal tension between a couple, and possibly even impact on their social relations and the political organization to which they belonged.

Anxious to prevent insubordination and the collapse of their hierarchies, organizations with underground para-military structures, issued instructions on managing their activists' personal relationships. Whilst religious groups offered their own interpretations of Islamic rules of matrimony, one left-wing group published a pamphlet called 'Guidelines for Choosing Your Partner', originally issued by the Communist Party of the Philippines.

For the third time since the 1906 Constitutional Revolution, the question of women's rights was being discussed by Iranian society, this time with an astoundingly wide basis. On the one hand, street demonstrations in protest

Figure 5.3 Front page – *Zan* (Women) daily, No 173, 27 Esfand 1377 (18 March 1999)
By courtesy of Ms Faizeh Hashemi-Rafsanjani

Figure 5.4 Front cover – *Danish* (Knowledge), the first women's newspaper in Iran, No 1, 16 September 1910. The sentence in the box reads: 'This is a newspaper dealing with moral issues, childcare and house-keeping, useful for girls and women, which will not in any way discuss politiques or the country's policies'.

By courtesy of Shukufa and Danish, the first Iranian women's newspaper; published by the National Library of the Islamic Republic of Iran, Tehran, 1998 against the imposition of the Islamic dress code would come under attack by groups of club-wielders who shouted: 'Ya rusari ya tusari', (either a scarf on your head, or a punch in your head). At the other end of the spectrum, on state radio, a spokeswoman for a socialist group announced an election manifesto which included women's right to use their bodies as they wished.

One can only speculate how the debate over women's rights and other post-revolutionary issues would have developed had the country not been engulfed in an eight-year war with Iraq. In the event, by the early 1980s, almost all opposition groups had been suppressed, their newspapers had been banned, and Iranian journalism had begun a decade of sluggish growth, with a very high content of specialist, technical and trade subjects. The 1988 cease-fire was shortly followed by a rise in the numbers of new newspapers, and a steady move towards sports, entertainment, youth, families and women.

Today, about 30 Iranian periodicals address women and families, or are owned or edited by women.[24] Several are quarterlies published by universities, including the journals of the colleges of nursing and midwifery, and those of the women-only Al-Zahra University which cover subjects as diverse as basic sciences, painting, sculpture, literature, psychology and politics. Most of these journals are managed, edited and produced exclusively by women.

Iran's six-year old specialist sewing monthly – *Burish* or Cut – is owned, edited and written by women, who also design its dozens of colourful – but loose fitting and modest – women's outfits, worn by attractive, ink-drawn models, whose hair is hidden behind ballooning, ghost-like white scarves.

The Islamic Seminary in the city of Qum publishes the monthly *Payam-i Zan* or Woman's Message which is managed and edited by men, but many of its articles are written by women. Other Islamic women's journals published or edited by women include the official, Arabic language monthly, *al-Tahira* (The Pure Woman), its English language sister, *Mahjuba* (The Covered Woman), and the Spanish-language quarterly *Kausar* (named after a heavenly spring mentioned in the Qur'an).

Whilst these specialist women's periodicals address a select audience, two other groups, news-and-entertainment and news-and-current affairs for women have the highest circulation. The first group includes four bi-weeklies which have appeared in the 1990s: *Khanavada* (Family), *Khana va Khanavada* (House and Family), *Ruzha-yi Zindigi* , (The Days of Our Lives), and *Rah-i Zindigi* (The Path of Life). Although the first three are either owned or edited by men, most of their bylines are female. The fourth, and youngest, *Rah-i Zindigi*, is owned, managed and edited by a woman (Mitra Suhail).

In contrast to most women's magazines in the west which carry front cover photographs of glamorous – sometimes scantily clad – women, the four women-and-family oriented Iranian magazines have cover pictures of beautiful children, mostly little girls. Inside, there are many more colour pictures of children sent in by their parents, sometimes along with a work of art by the child, or because the child has done well at school. With parents apparently eager to have their children's pictures printed in the papers, the magazines not only do not have to incur any expense to fill a substantial part of their pages, but can also run competitions to chose the best pictures.

All four magazines offer medical advice, as well as counselling and legal guidance on emotional and personal problems, such as failure in romance, being forced into divorce or ending up in a polygamous marriage. All four magazines also carry classified ads for make-up and hair-dressing, classes in anything from cooking to foreign languages and preparation for university entrance exams. Many ads offer services such as losing or gaining weight, hair repair (for men) and drugs rehabilitation.

The pages of these popular papers seem to have been declared a politics-free zone, even during the presidential elections in May 1997, when political activity in Iran was more intense than any time since the 1979 Revolution. There is no shortage of politics in the two high-circulation news-and-current affairs women's journals: the *Kayhan* group's weekly, *Zan-i Ruz*, or The Modern Woman, which unlike its rival *Ittila'at-i Banuvan*, has survived the Revolution, albeit after several changes of editors; the more outspoken monthly, *Zanan*, or Women, which grew out of a dispute between the editorial board of *Zan-i Ruz* and the *Kayhan* group's conservative management in 1991.

In the oil-rich 1960s and 1970s, *Zan-i Ruz* carried many pages with titles such as 'Love', 'Make Up' and 'Movie Stars', and serialized novels with romantic, sometimes thinly-veiled erotic, themes. The picture on the front cover would often be that of a glamorous entertainer, or some other minor celebrity. Advertisements took up around one-third of the pages.[25]

The front cover of the 1990s *Zan-i Ruz* usually deals with the current political issues. Instead of glamour, there are news reports and commentaries on domestic and international developments affecting the Muslim world. There are still pages of advice on marital disputes and other family problems; sewing, aided by patterns copied from foreign publications, but with ink-drawn head and limbs superimposed on the pictures of the original models. And there are cooking and child-care items and serialized novels.

In the run-up to the 1997 presidential election, the lead story in *Zan-i Ruz* denounced a German court which had implicated the Iranian leadership in the assassination of four Iranian opposition activists in Berlin in 1992. One picture on the front cover was of Iranian women covered head-to-toe in black chadors, the most strict version of the Islamic dress code in Iran, during a demonstration against the German court's ruling. Another was of women from a nomadic tribe in western Iran, dressed in their more colourful, but equally virtuous, traditional clothes, tending a flock of goats.

There were two pages on the presidential election, covering the views of the three main candidates' on women and other issues, and the news that one political group, the Women's Association of the Islamic Republic, was backing the moderate candidate, Muhammad Khatami. There were also news stories on legislation to reduce the working hours of female civil servants; the restrictions imposed on Afghan women by the Taleban authorities; and the marketing of Sara and Dara dolls – Iranian counterparts to Barbie and Ken.

The same issue of *Zan-i Ruz* carried a detailed and well-written report on clan vendettas and other aspects of tribal life in western Iran. There was the personal account of a woman's failed marriage with a severely disabled war veteran; a serialized love story set against the background of the Iran–Iraq war; pages on first aid and child-care; recipes for deep fried prawns and spicy pancakes, which by the standards of most Iranian families can only be considered exotic; and 16 pages of patterns for dresses, curtains and lampshades in lively colours – and knitted egg covers in the shape of animals, including mice.[26]

The 1990's *Zan-i Ruz* still addresses a middle-class readership, but one with much more limited means than the pre-revolutionary days. This is one of the factors behind the fall of advertising to around a quarter of the pages of the weekly. Another reason is the fact that the paper is now owned by the state and can rely on public funds to cover some of its costs.

Zanan is a much better produced journal, to some extent because, unlike *Zan-i Ruz,* it has as a monthly deadline. It is also much more political. In its pre-election issue, *Zanan*[27] devoted 10 pages to the presidential election, leading with an interview with Mr Khatami, who was to win in a landslide, largely thanks to the votes of the women and the youth. Another interviewee was Ms Azam Taliqani, the publisher of the oldest post- revolutionary women's magazine in Iran, *Payam-i Hajar,* and the first woman to run for the presidency in Iran.

In her interview with *Zanan*, Ms Taliqani said she had nominated herself primarily in order to seek clarification of Article 115 in the Islamic Republic's Constitution which prescribes that the President should be elected from amongst '*rijal* of religion and politics'. Persian speakers often use the Arabic word *rijal* or its singular, *rajul*, as synonyms for the Persian words *mardan* (men) and *mard* (man) respectively. However, at the time of the 1997 Presidential elections, some supporters of women's rights in Iran argued that when used in political or social discourse, *rajul* or *rijal* could simply mean personality or personalities. Whether the use of the word *rijal* in the Constitution could be seen in the latter context, would have been a matter for the constitutional supervisors, the Council of Guardians, to decide. In the interview, Ms Taliqani also pointed out that other Islamic countries, such as Pakistan and Bangladesh, had had women heads of state or government. In the event, the Council of Guardians rejected Ms Taliqani's nomination, along with those of 233 other candidates, using its prerogative not to specify the reasons why. Four men, three of them clerics, were allowed to run.

Mr Khatami, who had been the Minister of Culture and Islamic Guidance in President Rafsanjani's administration, said in his interview with *Zanan* that many experts believed that women could reach the presidency in Iran, 'but the esteemed Council of Guardians are the official interpreters of the Constitution'.

He also said that he saw no problem with women joining the cabinet, but that he disagreed with the idea that there should be a ministry for women's affairs, arguing that 'the growth of non-governmental organisations' would be more effective in improving the conditions of the Iranian women. He also warned of a crisis among the youth, due to the widening gap between the ages of puberty and marriage, and expressed disappointment that because of what he described as the reluctance to observe Islamic tolerance, the way had been left open to a catastrophe.

In the same issue, *Zanan* also printed a set of questions for the other main contender for the presidency, the conservative speaker of Parliament, Mr Natiq Nuri – whom the magazine had not been able to interview. Most of the questions were identical to to those put to Mr Khatami, but a few were not.

Whereas Mr Khatami had been asked to comment on his reputation as a well-dressed and charismatic person, Mr Natiq Nuri was being asked to explain whether his recent habit of wearing a smart pair of glasses had been due to medical reasons or, in the words of the magazine, had had to do with 'some people's belief in a correlation between eye-glasses and literacy'.

In a rephrasing of the infamous question, 'when did you stop beating your wife', Mr Natiq Nuri was asked whether he had ever punished his wife, and if so, how. Finally, the Speaker of Parliament was asked to confirm or deny the suggestion that should he be elected, he would close down *Zanan* for having posed these questions.

The questions were printed underneath a stern-looking photograph of Mr Natiq Nuri – without glasses – while the interview with Mr Khatami – who had been wearing smart glasses for a long time – was accompanied by pictures which showed him alternately as animated, thoughtful or amused. *Zanan*'s front cover picture of a smiling Mr Khatami led his opponents to say that the public would not be taken in by smiles alone, but would be looking for substance.

While the other women's journals carry stories about or interviews with the stars of Iranian cinema and television, *Zanan* usually criticizes the way women are portrayed on the screen. It runs fiction, by Iranian and other writers, as well as poetry by both men and women, and a column by a woman lawyer (Mehrangiz Kar) on legal matters affecting women.

Zanan is not in the habit of running recipes, clothes patterns or beauty tips, although in the same election issue, there are three pages of instructions for skin care and facial exercises aimed at delaying the onset of old age. It carries slightly fewer ads than the other women's magazines, but is unique among them for running advertisements for professional photo-copiers, a firm of stock-brokers, a lady piano teacher and courses in several European languages, as well as in Chinese, Japanese and Hebrew.[28]

Using a rather wide definition of print journalism to include its audience as well as the communicators, the Iranian women's press accounts for about 5 per cent of the country's newspapers. In 1995, an official seminar on 'Women and the Media' heard that 'only about 3 per cent of the news carried by newspapers is related to women'.[29] The speaker (Minu Badi'i), herself a reporter with the daily *Kayhan*, commented that 'while the western media present a very sinister and unreal picture of women', the Iranian press, and the media in general, had 'marginalised the women'. 'Setting aside news related to the President's Office for Women's Issues,' the speaker said, 'the newspapers have little news concerning women other than stories on scientific or medical developments.'

Another woman reporter from *Kayhan* (Humaira Hussaini-Yigana) suggested that 'since newspapers reflect the views of the authorities' and that few women are in senior management or political leadership, one of the main reasons why women's issues are not raised across the society – and indirectly in the press – may be the fact that women are not involved in news-making activities.

The same speaker also said that the managers and editors-in-chief have the greatest effect on how news and information is presented, but in spite of the high quality of women journalists' work, no woman is the editor-in-chief or desk editor of any daily newspaper. There were newspapers, she said, without any female political journalists, and the managers of one daily believed that there was 'no need to leave to a women what could be done by a man'.

Addressing the seminar, President Rafsanjani's Advisor on Women's issues, Shahla Habibi called for more reporters, producers and directors with expertise in women's issues, arguing that 'just as economics needs to be covered by a journalist who knows about economics, journalists covering women's issues should be aware of women's mentality, language, literature, and their desirable status from the point of view of religion and tradition.' In practical terms, Ms Habibi said journalists had to be educated about women's issues, and special women's groups had to be set up within the various media organizations.

Having moved beyond the barriers to entry into the profession, women journalists come across new difficulties. Some of these – such as inadequate training, relatively poor pay and job insecurity – are shared by men too. Others are peculiar to women, such as the possibility of attracting unwanted personal attention merely for having asked a male interviewee for his first name.

However, recent data indicate that Iranian journalism is likely to witness a growth in women's contributions, and consequently an increase in the coverage of issues related to women, as well as coverage and analysis of other subjects from the female point of view. In 1972, the first detailed directory of the Iranian press listed only about 50 women journalists.[30] In 1997, there were some 400 women journalists in the country, indicating an annual rate of growth of 28 per cent. Meanwhile the total number of journalists had risen at an annual rate of less than 12 per cent.[31]

On average, Iranian women journalists are five years younger and two years less experienced than their male colleagues, but they are considerably better educated – with 50 per cent at graduate level, while the average for the entire profession is 35 per cent.[32] Whereas less than 33 per cent of all Iranian journalists are full-time professionals, the ratio among women journalists is higher than 40 per cent.[33] In other words, female journalists are not only likely to be more thorough and systematic in their approach to their work than their male colleagues, but they may also be more committed to the profession.

Only a small proportion of Iranian journalists have studied journalism. In 1993, out of a grand total of approximately 1000 men and women who had graduated in the various branches of communication up to that year, only 60 were still working in the press.[34] None the less, the dissertations of the graduates could provide an insight into the intellectual mindset of the working journalists.

A recent catalogue of journalism college dissertations demonstrates that men, who constitute 40 per cent of the graduates, tend to be more interested in the political, economic and general historical aspects of the media – subjects which are more likely to appeal to specialists. Woman graduates, on the other hand, appear much more inclined towards content analysis and examining the social impact of the media. The few listed dissertations which deal with the personalities and professional styles of prominent Iranian journalists are all written by women.[35]

These same tendencies towards personalized and detailed journalism could be seen at work in the Iranian press at large. Of the four popular family-oriented magazines already mentioned, the female-run *Rah-i Zindigi* has a more elegant layout, and a softer tone, with far fewer crime stories in particular. At the annual Iranian Press Festival, which is organized by the Ministry of Islamic Guidance, several women have won awards, sometimes for their coverage of potentially sensational issues, such as the incidence of AIDS in Iran,[36] or the many cases of murder, mutilation and rape which are examined at the Tehran Coroner's Office during a working day.[37]

But women journalists' contributions have not been limited to individual or family matters or the purely social and cultural issues. In many dailies, as well as in the specialist monthlies, women have been writing on a whole range of subjects – among them Iran's international relations, parliamentary debates, the state of the economy, and the causes of and possible remedies for the worsening problem of air pollution in Tehran. Women constitute all of the staff reporters on Iran's leading economics monthly, *Sanat-i Hami va Naghl* (Transport Industry).

Outside the editorial offices, computerized type-setting and design have opened the way for women's involvement in the technical side of journalism. One of the best books on the Iranian press law has been written by a woman lawyer;[38] and the publisher of one of the country's most recent and most controversial newspapers, *Jami'a* (Society) was defended by a women lawyer when he appeared before the special press court in June 1998 to face charges of publishing lies and libels.[39] At universities, where men heavily outnumber women in the sciences and engineering, during the academic year 1997–98, 337 women were studying journalism, 2.5 times as many as their male colleagues.[40] There has also been a steady rise in newspaper readership among Iranian women, with housewives moving up to the second highest rank, right behind the civil servants.[41]

Shortly after President Khatami's election in May 1997, the former President Rafsanjani's daughter, Faizeh Hashemi-Rafsanjani, obtained her long awaited permission to publish a daily newspaper, called *Zan* (Woman), and the paper was launched a year later. A second women's daily, planned by Mr Rafsanjani's Advisor on Women's Affairs, Ms Shahla Habibi, is yet to emerge, hampered, at least partly, by the enormous costs of publishing a daily newspaper.

Ms Hashemi-Rafsanjani's *Zan* quickly established itself as an innovative paper, both in form – tabloid size with a relatively simple and elegant layout – and in content – with a lively approach and a wide range of subjects, including, naturally, women's rights. Not surprisingly, the paper soon found itself confrontation with the conservative factions of the Islamic Republic establishment. In January 1999, barely six months after its launch, *Zan* was closed down for two weeks because the Press Court had found it guilty of insulting the Chief of Police Intelligence, Brigadier-General Muhammad Reza Naqdi, who had been accused, among other things, of illegal imprisonment and the torture of several reformist officials.

In April 1999, the paper was closed down again – this time by the Revolutionary Court – for having published excerpts from the Iranian New Year's message of the former Iranian Queen, Farah Diba, who has been living in exile since the 1979 Revolution. The Ministry of Islamic Guidance, which is in charge of supervising the activities of the press, declared the closure out of order, since the proper procedure for filing a suit against the paper had not been followed. Other critics of the court's decision argued that, in fact, *Zan*'s reformist politics had lead to its closure, because the former Queen's message had also been reported in a number of other papers, without the Court taking any action. These protests notwithstanding, *Zan* remained closed, a fate which later befell a number of other reformist newspapers later that year.

None the less, even before the launch of a daily newspaper dedicated to women, by the late 1990s, women journalists in Iran had already made their mark on the society at large and journalism in particular. In 1936, some 240 years after the appearance in Britain of the first newspaper devoted to women, the British journalist Emilie Peacocke wrote: 'The story of modern journalism is that of the rise of the Woman's Story'.[42] Some 60 years on, the same could perhaps be said of women journalists in Iran.

Notes

1 Some historians have identified Dr Kahhal as the wife of the male optician Dr Hussain Khan Kahhal. However, ads for the optician's clinic in *Danish* itself make it clear that the doctor is a woman, see, for example, No. 2, 30 September 1910, p. 8, and No. 3, 15 October 1910, p.2.
2 G. Cohen, *Tarikh-i Tahlili-yi Matbuʻat-i Iran*, Vol. 2, Tehran 1981, pp. 696. On p. 697, there is a photograph of Doctor Kahhal and her son, Abbas at the offices of *Danish*.
3 *Ibid.,* p. 390.

4 M. Muhit-i Tabataba'i, *Tarikh-i Tahlili-yi Matbu'at-i Iran*, Tehran 1988, p. 173.

5 *Ibid.*

6 *Danish, ibid.*

7 J. Bharier (1984) *Economic Development in Iran (1900–1970)* (Persian Translation), Tehran, p. 51.

8 *Ibid.*, pp. 38–9.

9 M. Sadr-i Hashemi (1984) *Tarikh-i Jarayid va Majallat-i Iran*, Isfahan, Vol. 4, p. 262.

10 M. Sadr-i Hashimi, *Tarikh-i Jarayid*, Vol. 3, p.7.

11 Muhit-i Tabataba'i, *Tarikh-i Tahlili-yi*, p. 174.

12 Sadr-i Hashimi, *Tarikh-i Jarayid*, pp. 8–9.

13 Cohen, *Tarikh-i Tahlili-yi*, p. 702.

14 Y. Daulatabadi (1983) *Hayat-i Yahya*, Tehran, pp. 11–12.

15 M. San'ati (Daulatabadi), 'Sadiqa Daulatabadi: A Biography', in *Nima-yi Digar Persian Language Feminist Journal*, Vol. 17, Winter 1993, p. 64.

16 *Ibid.*, pp. 68–9.

17 M. Barzin (1991) *Statiscital Analysis of Persian Press (1836–1978)* (Persian), Tehran, p. 20.

18 P. Shaikhalislami (1973) *Zanan-i Ruznama-nigar va Andishmand-i Iran*, Tehran, p. 183–9.

19 *Banu*, Vol. 2, No. 12, December 1946, quoted in M. Gulbun (1975) *Naqd va Siyahat, Majmu'a-yi Maqalat va Taqrirat-i Duktur Fatima Sayyah*, Tehran, pp. 148–50.

20 *Ayanda*, Vol. 3, No. 10, September 1945, quoted in Gulbun, *Naqd va Siyahat*, pp. 143–7.

21 Iran Statistical Centre (1976) *Salnama-yi Amari-yi Kishvar*, Tehran.

22 M. Barzin, 'Anjumanha-yi Matbu'at-i dar Iran ta Sal 1357' (Press Associations in Iran until 1978–79) in *Rasana*, Vol. 2, No 3, Autumn 1991, pp. 59–60.

23 Author's calculations based on S.F. Qasimi (1993) *Rahnama-yi Matbu'at-i Iran*, Tehran.

24 *Salnama-yi Matbu'at-i Iran*, Tehran 1996.

25 M. Barzin (1976) *Matbu'at-i Iran 1964/74*, Tehran, pp. 90–1.

26 All examples from *Zan-i Ruz*, No. 1601, 19 March 1997.

27 *Zanan*, Vol. 6, No 34, April 1997.

28 *Zanan, ibid.*

29 This and all subsequent quotes from the Seminar from: *Rasana*, Vol. 5, No. 4, Winter 1995, pp. 92–4.

30 Gh. Salayar (1972) *Chihra-yi Matbu'at -i Mu'asir* (The Face of the Contemporary Press), Tehran.

31 In 1993, Dr Mihdi Muhsinian-Rad found that out of 2145 Iranian journalists, 13 per cent, or 279, were women. Since then, there has been a rise of about 50 per cent in the numbers of newspapers and magazines published in the country. Assuming a similar rise in the total numbers of journalists and a constant gender ratio, there should be 418 women journalists in Iran. However, as many journalists contribute to more than one publication, the total number may not have risen by 50 per cent. On the other hand, there seems to have been a faster rise in the numbers of women joining the profession in recent years. Therefore, in the absence of more detailed data, the figure of 400 appears to be a reasonable, if not conservative, estimate. See M. Muhsinian-Rad (1993), *Payam Afrinan-i Matbu'at* (The Message-Creators of the Press), Tehran, The Ministry of Culture and Islamic Guidance. Salayar, *Chihra-yi Matbu'at*, records the names of 800 journalists working in Iran in 1972. In 1986, this author estimated the total number of Iranian journalists at around 3000, i.e. an annual rate of growth of 11.46 per cent.

32 Muhsinian-Rad, *Payam Afrinan-i Matbu'at*, pp. 2–11, and in *Rasana*, Vol. 5, No. 4, Winter 1994, p. 93.

33 Muhsinian-Rad, *Rasana, ibid.*

34 Muhsinian-Rad, *et al.* (1994) *Ruznama Nigaran-i Iran va Amuzish-i Ruznama Nigari* (Iranian Journalists and Journalism Training), Tehran, p. 141.

35 F. Qasimi (1996) *Fihristigan-i Matbu'at-i Iran* (The Union Catalogue of Communication), Tehran, Vol. 11.

36 Zhila Bani-Ya'qub's report, 'AIDS: Disease or Crime?' in the *Hamshahri* daily, as reported by *Rasana*, Vol. 7, No. 1, Spring 1996, p. 93.

37 Lili Farhadpur's report, 'Passing Through the Customs of the Deceased', printed in the monthly *Daricha*, Vol. 1, No. 3, pp. 12–17.

38 S. Ebadi (1991) *Literary and Artistic Rights*, Tehran.

39 Fariba Tavakoli, defending Hamid-Reza Jalaie-pour, as reported by *Jami'a*, 13 June 1998.

40 *Rasana*, Vol. 9, No. 1, Spring 1998, p. 60.

41 *Rasana*, Vol. 7, No. 1, Spring 1996, p. 91.

42 D. Griffiths (ed.) (1992) *The Encyclopaedia of the British Press*, London, p. 688.

six

From the Royal Harem to a Post-modern Islamic Society

Some Considerations on Women Prose Writers in Iran from Qajar Times to the 1990s

Anna Vanzan

The first part of this chapter is a brief overview of the history of prose written by Iranian women from Qajar times up to the Iranian Revolution. The second part of the article focuses in particular on the literature written after the revolution of 1978–79, and analyses themes and styles expressed by the leading women prose writers of contemporary Iran. The chapter explores the relation 'woman-literature-society' in contemporary Iran, and aims to offer a new perspective on a model of post-modern Islamic society in which traditional and modern cultural models are intertwined by women.

Until the 1940s, women writers were virtually non-existent on the Persian literary scene. The country's culture, which developed in a patriarchal contest, did not allow female writers to emerge; therefore, in the literary history of Iran we find only sporadic female names. The single example in the classic epoch is that of the Seljuq princess and poetess Mahasti, after which we have to wait until the nineteenth-century, when women from the upper classes, especially the ones belonging to the ruling dynasty of the Qajars, began to get a better education than had been received previously.

The result was a modest poetic production, especially in the Sufi environment which gave birth to Sakina Begum, who signed her poems as 'Iffat (the Pure), and Bibi Hayati Kirmani who left an entire *divan*.[1] The other community which encouraged women's emancipation and literary expression was that of the newly founded Baha'i religion: the most outstanding female symbol was the famous Qurrat al-'Ain who left behind some scattered writings and poetry.[2] However, very little was actually printed and therefore handed down to posterity. In addition, the women cited above had an education and so a degree of knowledge most unusual among their female compatriots: in other words, they were not representative of the general situation of women in ninteenth-century Iran.

Very little prose was written, and the earliest signed sample seems to date from the late nineteenth-century: the *Ma'ayib al-Rijal* (Vices of Men),[3] composed in 1894–95 by Bibi Khanum Astarabadi as an answer to the anonymous and misogynous book *Ta'dib al-Nisvan* (How to Chastise Women), printed some years before. It is significant that at the outset, female prose was a text of protest, a tendency that was confirmed at the turn of the century when, after Muzaffar al-Din Shah's granting of the Constitution (1906), women found an arena for expression in the magazines and journals published by the numerous female associations, in which they voiced their discontent and manifested their struggle for emancipation.[4]

In the post-constitutional period, when women's activities were developing, the memories of the Qajar princess and feminist Taj al-Saltana, perhaps the longest piece of prose ever written by an Iranian woman, were written but not published. Taj al-Saltana's *Khatirat* is an interesting social document which gives insight into the institution of the harem while casting light on the change in the status of the women at the beginning of the twentieth-century. As literature, it is an example of an emerging body of modern Persian prose evolving from a flowery, convoluted style, to a simpler and more direct one. Stylistically, the author aspires to emulate the European, namely the French traditions, that is, (a) the memoirs and the moral essays of the seventeenth- and eighteenth-century authors, who, by giving the flavour and the atmosphere of the social milieu in which they lived, described their environment in detail; and (b) the psychological novel of the nineteenth-century, which studied human character. The narrative frame alternates between an autobiographical style modelled on Rousseau's *Confessions* and a narrative one characteristic of the picaresque novel. However, taken as a whole, the memoirs suffer from much repetition, historical mistakes, lapses, use of incorrect words, inconsistencies of opinion and irregularities of language. This is due to many factors (which cannot be analysed here), including the fact that the diary is unfinished, abandoned in the midst of its author's confession.[5]

Taj al-Saltana's experiment was not followed for decades: we can talk about female prose production again only in the 1930s, when Zahra Khanlari and her husband founded the famous literary review *Sukhan,* and she published the collection of short stories *Parvin u Parviz* (1933). Later, Zahra Khanlari dedicated herself more to didactic texts and the prose adaptations of Persian classics to be used as textbooks. In those years, Simin Danishvar, the future leader of female prose writers was studying literature at Tehran University, and in 1948 she published her first collection of short stories, *Atash-i Khamush* (The Dead Fire), followed by two other collections in 1959 (*Shahri chun Bihisht,* A City like Paradise) and 1962 (*Bih Ki Salam Kunam?* Whom Shall I Greet?). But for her and for Persian modern prose in general the decisive year was 1969, when her novel *Savushun* (Mourning) was published. The success was enormous both in Iran and abroad, where the book was translated into several languages, and it can now be considered the turning point for modern Persian prose.[6]

Westernization and specificity

As we know, the Persian literary tradition was extremely rich in poetry, much less in prose, and modern prose in Iran owes much to European models, especially in the matter of 'forms': however, it has often been erroneously assumed that twentieth-century Persian culture is a vassal to the west, at least in the field of prose. Rather than a mere imitation, modern Persian prose has often been the result of that typically Persian vocation which casts in alien frameworks autochthonous spirit and inspiration. Persian writers frequently adopted cultural syncretism, by capturing foreign motives during their sojourns abroad or by studying western classics which they translated into Persian.

The fact that women's prose in Iran did not develop until the 1940s necessarily raises the question of whether Persian women writers drew their inspiration from Western or 'universal' female-feminist literature or from the consolidated models of their male compatriots. If modern Persian prose was born with a tangible delay compared to the European one, we may conclude that Persian women's prose suffered from a double delay, as the product of acculturated authors who were, in addition, women. We said above that, at the beginning of the twentieth century, Persian women could count on numerous feminist organizations and on intense journalistic activity. This might lead to the conclusion that when women produce literature, be it a poem, a novel, an autobiography or a tale, it is a literature of protest in which they denounce their downtrodden rights and their marginalization. Obviously, some part of contemporary female prose in Persian presents motives connected to the emancipation of women – their rights, their life within the family and society. But we cannot speak exclusively of feminist literature, rather, only a small part of the recent works produced can be classified under this label.

In addition, these themes are not a novelty, as they go back to the Constitutional period; and in more recent times – the 1940s and 1950s – they have been developed by Iranian writers such as 'Ali Dashti Muhammad Hijazi, whose novels had, as their protagonists, women whose lives dealt with dramatic social situations (above all prostitution), which Hijazi depicted with compassionate realism.

Forms and themes

It has been written that:

> Persian prose and Persian women have one bitter experience in common:
> they have both been suppressed for many centuries, women by men, prose
> by poetry.[7]

However, it now seems that both women and prose are taking revenge: in post-revolutionary Iran, women's success over their male colleagues is undeniable as they are more innovative and prolific.[8] Prose has become an important medium for women's self-expression and the short story appears to be the favourite means of female narration.

It is too easy to relate Iranian women writers' predilection for short stories to Virginia Woolf's considerations on why many women choose to write short stories, that is a lack of time and of mental toughness.[9] It has also been argued that the short story is a sort of apprentice form, a prelude to a more mature form of literature, in other words the novel. However, in the case of Iranian women writers it can be argued that many of them wrote novels as well as short stories: and, in any case, the length of a story is not necessarily indicative of its quality or importance.

Rather, Iranian women writers' liking for short stories, on the one hand, puts them in the international stream of women's literature; on the other, it stresses another similitude they share with their male compatriots who very often take up the form of the short story. For both female and male writers of Iran, the short story maintains many connections to the oral mode of storytelling (folk tales, anecdotes, fables) which is deeply rooted in Persian culture.

As for themes, contemporary female prose – or should we say 'fiction'? –has a wide variety of motifs, not all necessarily concerning the female world and, above all, not all seen from a 'feminist' perspective.[10] For example, let us examine the common theme 'woman and the family' which develops into three main channels: marriage, the always menacing threat of a co-wife and divorce. The object of blame is often not the father/husband/tyrant, but rather women themselves, as the main cause of their own misfortune.

In *Hayvan* (The Animal) by Mihan Bahrami,[11] Anis, a lady belonging to the bourgeoisie, makes her son marry a poor peasant, so that he will not be sent to the front during the war against Iraq. However Anis despises the daughter-in-law so deeply that soon after this marriage she arranges another one for her son, this time with a bride of high social rank. This new wedding ceremony takes place while her first daughter-in-law is delivering a baby. In Muniru Ravanipur's novel *Dil-i Fulad* (Heart of Steel),[12] the protagonist Afsana falls in love with her tenants' son, Siyavush. The young man is a drug addict and has been left by his wife. At first, Siyavush's mother encourages the love between him and Afsana; but once Siyavush recovers from his addiction, she favours his separation from Afsana.

It could be noted that in the above cases the negative protagonists are two mothers-in-law, who are considered 'wicked' in many cultures. But mothers-in-law are not the only women to be blamed in this women's literature. In *Yik Sar u Yik Balin* (One Head on One Pillow) by Simin Danishvar[13] a poor tailor is cheated by a fascinating neighbour, Gul-i 'Anbar, who not only 'steals' her husband (who almost appears to be a victim of the woman's charm), but even her son. The tailor does not offer a successful resistance to defend her family and herself, though she is a woman who eventually achieves success in her professional life. The hidden message could be: can a woman who succeeds in her career really be successful as a wife and a mother? Perhaps the extreme example of this tendency is in the famous story *Buzurg banu-i ruh-i man* (The Great Lady of My Soul),[14] by Guli Taraqqi in which it is a woman who incarnates bigotry, lack of critical judgement and favours the restriction of women's rights.

These are only four out of the many samples which we could cite of women protagonists of contemporary Persian women's fiction who are culpable either for remaining silent and subdued, or for complicity in perpetuating patriarchal traditions. It should also be emphasized that when the 'feminist' critique prevails, especially in certain short stories, rhetoric suffocates the narrative energy and the prose loses its artistic connotation and literary value. Some short stories, and especially those written by exiled women, are more similar to chronicles, which, though they capture a historical moment, are too tied to that contingent occasion, and do not express lasting universal values.

We quote here, as samples, two short stories which have also been translated into English:[15] in the first one, A. Rahmani describes a trip to the mountains in northern Tehran which is disturbed by a quarrel she has with a *pasdar* after her veil has slipped from her head. As a result, the story turns into a vibrant protest against the violation of human (i.e., female) rights. The second one by Fereshteh Kuhi is centred on the description of a funeral for a *pasdar*, which evolves into a sharp critic of Shi'ite customs. The author continually calls attention to her discomfort caused by the heavy veil, which covers her and openly despises the women, who manifest their grief by crying and beating their chests. This important part of Iranian tradition and culture is mocked and rejected, while in the meantime the gap between the 'intellectual' and the others widens. It is hard to find in this narrative the 'sense of sisterhood and identification between the writer and other women [that] dominates this literature', according to Farzaneh Milani's authoritative opinion.[16] Rather, it focuses on the question of the veil, which has become the symbol of women's oppression for the west, for most of the Iranian Diaspora and for part of their compatriots who are still in Iran.

Female literature symbolized by the two samples above has often used the question 'to veil or not to veil' as a leitmotiv and has identified the veil with the fight for civilization, progress and women' rights. However, such symbolism often overpowers the narrative itself and transforms it into a sort of political pamphlet, or into a rhetoric allegory. Naturally, the allegory of the veil is burdened with many messages and it has often become central to literary analysis. I quote again Farzaneh Milani who, by discussing the genre of women's autobiography writes:

> no veiled woman has ever published the details of her personal life, let alone a novel or an autobiography, whereas unveiled women have published a substantial number of both genres. In the resolutely nonsexual and impersonal writings of such women, the authors remain almost inaccessible.[17]

This affirmation is challenged, for instance, by the veiled poetess Tahera Saffarzada who uses the veil as a symbol of woman's freedom and by the political activity of Zahrah Rahvanard who reveals her life publicly.

It is true, however, that all the Iranian women's autobiographies – all published, by the way, after the Islamic Revolution – have been written by unveiled women. If we examine their names, we easily come to the conclusion: unveiled women = emancipated women. We find in fact, two female ex-monarchs (Farah Banu, Soraya Esfandiyari); the twin sister of an ex-monarch (Ashraf Pahlavi); an enlightened and highly educated noble, Setareh Farman Farmayan; a jewellery designer belonging to the high bourgeoisie, Susan Azadi; and some revolutionaries fighting under various flags. Some of these women, especially the ones who belong to the former political establishment, use the events from their lives in order to justify themselves or to justify the deeds of the pre-revolution administrators. Their personal histories are mostly interesting because they were members of famous families – they were wives, sisters, daughters of men crucial to Iran. In addition, they are not professional writers, so much so that their names are usually accompanied by a professional one, or there are evident signs of a ghost writer's hand.

Most of these books were written in English, which indicates that the authors address not their compatriots who live in Iran, but western readers and exiled Iranians. In other words, this kind of narrative, though interesting as a historical phenomenon, is somewhat extraneous or only marginal to Persian literary life.

The foregoing discussion leads us to two considerations: that (a) generally speaking, Iranian professional women writers are not fond of the autobiographical genre, which is not very popular among males either;[18] and (b) the question of the *veil* is not a common denominator in the Iranian professional women writers' narrative. Rather, there are other subjects of social content, more consonant with Iranian literatis' consciousness, that characterize their production, as we will briefly see.

Social commitment and connotations

As we know, Persian prose has been socially committed since its very beginning: Muhammad Ali Jamalzada, in the preface to his *Yiki bud yiki nabud* (Once upon a Time, 1921) had clearly stressed the importance of Persian fiction as a way to achieve social progress. If we look at the women writer's biographies, we can see that they experience a social commitment even before expressing it in their writings: in fact, they are teachers, professional translators, editors of literary journals and they often lecture abroad. Many of them also write literature for children. Some of them explicitly declare their *ta'ahud-i adabi* or literary involvement: Shafirnush Parsipur speaks of her writing as a *historical commitment*;[19] Muniru Ravanipur, who is often questioned about her peculiar writing style, justifies the choice of a literary language only if this is comprehensible to the majority of the readers.[20] Others animate the protagonists – not only the female ones – of their pages with their own commitment: the little Abud who happened to see closely the Iran–Iraq conflict, teaches his friends that war is not worthy of being simulated, not even as a game;[21] the old retired colonel Ariyanifar, anti-clerical and laic, steps into the street to defend a religious man accused of being a provocateur and therefore maltreated by the police;[22] another child, this time a girl, weaves a singular friendship with a prostitute, Kanizu, and defends the friendship against all hostilities, first of all that of her mother. It is not Kanizu who is corrupt, says the girl, but the society which drove her to behave like that.[23]

For other writers, commitment means defending traditions and values belonging to their culture by affirming, at the same time, women's rights not to be socially constrained by the values themselves. In this perspective, the stories in the collection *Suridan-i Minakari* (The Enamelled Collyrium Box)[24] by Mansura Sharifzada are significant. The tales are populated by female figures who act within settings strongly connoted by local colours: more than a protest against the customs and habits of a culture, Sharifzada asserts women's right to play a role inside that culture.

Another way to retrieve one's own culture is shown in *Laila dar Nisf-i Jihan* (Laila in Half of the World), a collection of two long short-stories by Pari Sabiri[25] who turns to indigenous literary elements such as: (a) the title *Laila* ... which paraphrases that of a diary written by Sadiq Hidayat and then used by Jamalzada as a title for the autobiography of his childhood; (b) the elaboration of a text with a combination of poetry and prose, according to the best classic Persian tradition; and (c) the use of the word *qissah* (story, tale) to qualify her narrative, as a homage to the Persian fabulist archetypes. Pari Sabiri stresses her choice in the introductory note to the collection entitled *Qissah Chist?* (What is a story?) in which she affirms that, in order to write her tales, she went back:

> to the roots of my country, of my story, of my existence. I woke up in the historical memories full of glory of Iranian people, in the splendour and in the misery of Isfahan.[26]

Other writers prefer to affirm the secret, hidden needs of the human beings whose psyche they explore by using literary, instead of scientific, language: the stories by Tahirah Riyasati's in *Shat-i Khiyal* (The Flux of Fantasy)[27] are almost a collection of clinical cases whose protagonists are on the borderline between normality and transgression and in which political conflicts are represented through personal conflicts that occur in a person's intimate sphere.

The utmost expression of this trend is represented by Sharhnush Parsipur: the stories in *Aviziha-yi Balur* (The Crystal Pendants)[28] are all pervaded by the sense of their protagonists' loneliness. Parsipur identifies some of the evils which afflict human beings (both women and men) such as a lack of communicability and a loss of identity, in the harsh life of the big city. About ten years later, Parsipur returned to these issues in her novel *Zanan-i bidun-i Mardan* (Women without Men) and gave them a female perspective. The novel is an allegory populated by many metaphors animated almost exclusively by women: the metaphor of lack of communicability even among members of the same family; that of transgression, above all in the sphere of female sexuality; the metaphor of the construction of personal growth and independence. Every woman develops her own consciousness independently from the others, but there is a common denominator which evolves in each protagonist and brings them all to escape from the urban contest (Tehran) to lead them to the natural environment (Karaj). But it is not only this 'ecological' issue that places Parsipur's narrative in the midst of the international literary stream: the Iranian women who give life to the novel share problems and aspirations with women spread all over the world. While local connotations (historical, political, social issues which appear between the lines of the story) should not be disregarded, they are not crucial to the narrative itself.

In other words, we may say that Parsipur's narrative affirms universal values. According to this perspective, we can also examine the production of one of the emerging female fiction writers, namely Farkhonda Aqay: in her *Sada-yi Dariya* (The Voice of the Sea)[29] a woman on holiday, while lying on the beach, is covered with shells and pebbles by her little daughter. When she gets up, she cannot get rid of them, in spite of her efforts. As the years pass by, the pebbles sink under the woman's skin, which remains smooth, while she continues to bear the weight of the little stones. The story ends with the woman's plea to those who have come to take her away: she is not a leper, she maintains, she is like the shore from which the sea takes away its pebbles.

The message, I believe, is clear: a woman can bear everything, she is used to swallowing any problem during her existence, but she has to do it silently. She is not even allowed to show her forbearance, because this means that she has the courage to perceive her capability to manage difficulties and serious problems by herself. Moreover, the protagonist of the tale is also a 'woman without man' as there is no mention of a husband in the whole story. She, as well as some of Shahrnush Parsipur's heroines, pays a price for her consciousness: the 'others' think that she is sick, or, rather, mad. And, as we know 'modern literary movements have appropriated the schizophrenic woman as the symbol of linguistic, religious and sexual breakdown and rebellion'.[30]

Mad or not, many heroines, but also heroes, of Persian contemporary female fiction live in between two contradictory levels of reality, the natural and the supernatural. This mode of writing is also called 'magic realism', and, in the Persian literary world, the unquestionable queen of this genre is Muniru Ravanipur.[31] This is not the place to enter into the polemic about the dependency of Muniru Ravanipur on the South American authors' models for her literary choice. We will just recall that Ravanipur's frescos of people's lives in southern Iran have indigenous precursors such as Sadiq Chubak and Mahmud Daulatabadi. Rather, it is to stress how the resort to the presence of natural and supernatural elements is very common in the literary production we are examining. In addition, the authors frequently intertwine the oneiric dimension with the real one, with no solution of continuity. In *Biqarar* (Anxiety) by Azardukht Bahrami, it is difficult to discern when Mahnaz, the restless protagonist who inexplicably rejects her lover and ruins her life with her own hands, is talking about her present life or about her past remembrances.[32] And we cannot find out if the shy and not pretty Shahla in the story *Hasti*, by Makama Rahimzada, has a real love story with her taxi-driver Hasti (which is not a male proper name, but means 'existence'); or, as her beautiful and merciless sister says among the laughs, she

> invented another story: as when you pretended you had a suitor who sent letters, and instead it was you who wrote them![33]

In some case the symbolism or the surrealism is so obscure that it interferes with the comprehension of the text itself.

One might wonder whether this is a literary trend which has been expanding among Iranian writers, or if it is an expedient behind which the authors hide their ideas, concepts and sympathies from censors' eyes. Whatever is the explanation, female fiction writers in Iran are also exploring different styles inside their own individual production and it often happens that various styles mix and blend together even in the same story.

Conclusion

The examples discussed in this chapter show that there are several Iranian women authors who are able to criticize moral and religious values which support Iranian social and domestic structures, to advocate unwarranted rights and to denounce abuses by inserting these issues into a general contest which transcends the historic and political moment. Their literature is not only the sociological mirror of the society in which the authors live, nor a mere reflection of the problems these women face in their everyday life *because* they are women. Most of this literary production is to be positively valued as a literary event, as a qualitative step in the history of Persian literature. These authors produce literature while remaining within the realm of their own culture, of their language, of their experiences.[34] Indeed, we may describe this literature using the words with which Hamid Dabashi defined the best expression of contemporary Persian literature:

> a literature conscious of aesthetic measures and principles, yet deeply rooted in the tumultuous soil of its social and cultural reality.[35]

Notes

1 Published in 1970 in Tehran and edited by Javad Nurbakhsh.
2 Shireen Mahdavi, 'Women and Ideas in Qajar Iran', *Asian and African Studies*, 19 (1985), pp. 187–197, p. 188.
3 *Ma'ayib al-Rijal: Vices of Men*, edited with an introduction by Afsaneh Najmabadi, Chicago, 1992.
4 There are several publications on Iranian women's activities at the turn of the century. See for example Eliz Sanasarian (1982) *The Women's Rights Movement in Iran*, New York and Parvin Paider (1995) *Women and the Political Process in Twentieth Century Iran*, Cambridge.
5 See *Crowning Anguish, Memoirs of a Persian Princess from the harem to Modernity, 1884–1914*, edited with introduction and notes by Abbas Amanat, translation by A. Vanzan and A. Neshati, Washington, DC, 1993.
6 *Savushun* has two translations into English: *Savushun, a Novel about Modern Iran*, by M.R. Ghanoonparvar, Washington, DC, 1990; *A Persian Requiem* by Roxane Zand, London, 1991.
7 Heshmat Moayyad in his preface to the volume he edited (1991), *Stories from Iran. A Chicago Anthology 1921–1991*, Washington, DC, p. 9.
8 This fact has been also recognized by Iranian male authors: see for example Jamal Mirsadiqi in his preface to the anthology of short stories *Dastanha-yi Panjshambah, Adabiyat-i Mu'asir-i Iran*, Tehran, 1375/1996, p. 8. By stressing the fact that seven out of ten authors of the anthology are women, Mirsadiqi forecasts a female future for Iranian fiction.
9 *A Room of One's Own*, London, 1945, p. 67.
10 Here I give to 'feminist' a restrictive connotation, meaning the approach, matured in the USA and in Europe, which depicts women as merely passive victims of patriarchy.
11 From the collection *Hayvan*, Tehran, 1985, pp. 103–35.
12 Shiva 1990.
13 From the collection *Bih Ki Salam Kunam*, Tehran, 1980, pp. 227–238.
14 First published in *Kitab-i Kum'ah* 1,5 1979, pp. 35–80.
15 In *Stories by Iranian Women since the Revolution*, translated by Soraya Paknazar Sullivan, Austin, 1991; A. Rahmani, 'A Short Hike', pp. 127–37; F. Kuhi, 'Mrs Ahmadi's Husband', pp. 162–72.
16 'Sheherazade Unveiled: Post-Revolutionary Iranian Women Writers', in *Stories by Iranian Women*, p. 8. Farzaneh Milani is also the author of the pioneering and brilliant work on Iranian women writers (1992) *Veils and Words, the Emerging Voices of Iranian Women Writers*, London and New York. Since then, a number of articles have been published in English on Iranian women writers, among which see Kamran Talattof, 'Iranian Women's Literature: from Pre-Revolutionary Social discourse to Post-Revolutionary Feminism', *International Journal of Middle East Studies*, 29, 4 (1997), pp. 531–58; see also (2000) *The Politics of Writing in Iran. A History of Modern Persian Literature*, Syracuse, by the same author.

17 'Veiled Voices: Women Autobiographies in Iran', in A. Najmabadi (ed.) (1990), *Women's Autobiographies in Contemporary Iran*, Cambridge, p. 5.

18 See W. Hanaway (1990), 'Half Voices: Persian Women's Lives and Letters', in *Women's Autobiographies*, p. 61.

19 Interview in *Dunya-yi Sukhan*, 17, 1988, p. 9.

20 Interview in *Dunya-yi Sukhan*, 35, 1991, p. 45.

21 Qudsi Quzinur, 'Aboud's Drawings', *Bidaran* 1981, in *Stories*, 1991, pp. 88–9.

22 *Kiyd al Kha'inin* (Traitors' deceives) by Simin Danishvar, in *Bih Ki Salam Kunam?* (Whom shall I greet?), pp. 242–66.

23 'Kanizu', from the homonymous collection by Muniru Ravanipur, Tehran, 1991, 3rd ed, pp. 7–29.

24 Tehran, 1995.

25 Tehran, 1991.

26 P. Sabiri, *Leila*, no page.

27 Shiraz, 1991.

28 Tehran, 1977.

29 From the collection *Raz-i Kuchik* (*The Little Secret*), Tehran, 1993, pp. 67–72.

30 Elaine Showalter (1985), *The Female Malady: Women, Madness and English Culture, 1830–1980*, New York, 1985, p. 204.

31 On this topic see N. Rahimieh, 'Magical realism in Moniru Ravanipur's *Ahl-e gharq*', *Iranian Studies*, 23, 1990, pp. 61–75.

32 Unpublished MS, by courtesy of the author. I want to thank here the Iranian women writers whom I met in Tehran in the summer of 1996 and who entrusted me with their short stories (some of which were unpublished) when I decided to make the Italian public aware of the phenomenon of women's literary activity in post-revolutionary Iran. I published some of these short stories in an anthology, *Parole svelate, racconti di donne persiane* (*Unveiled Words, Stories by Persian Women*) Padova, 1998. I want also to remember the late Hushang Golshiri, who patronized this meeting hosted by Parisima Mayel Afshar, my friend and supporter, who deserves heartfelt thanks: without her help, my anthology and the present chapter could not have been written.

33 Unpublished MS, by courtesy of the author.

34 There is also a flourishing literature produced by the Iranians in the Diaspora: on it (and also on literature in Iran) see 'Selections from the Literature of Iran 1977–1997', special issue of *Iranian Studies*, Col. 3, pp. 3–4, Summer–Fall 1997.

35 'The Poetics of Politics: Commitment in Modern Persian Literature', *Iranian Studies*, 18, 2–4 (1985), pp. 147–88, p. 172.

seven

Gender and the Army of Knowledge in Pahlavi Iran, 1968–1979

Farian Sabahi

Introduction

This article will discuss the Women's Literacy Corps programme (*sipah-i danish-i dukhtaran*), its implementation, achievements and difficulties.[1] Established in Iran in 1968, it aimed to increase women's participation in the country's modernization and in the White Revolution (*inqilab-i sifid*) which took place in Iran in the period 1963 to 1979 during the reign of the late Muhammad Reza Pahlavi (1941–1979).

The Women's Literacy Corps extended the Literacy Corps programme (*sipah-i danish*) to women. An educational programme started in 1963 as point six of the White Revolution, the Literacy Corps gave young men above 21 and holding the diploma of secondary education (mainly urban low and middle-class youth) the option of spending their two-year military service in rural areas, teaching those children between the ages of six and twelve years who had not yet attended school up to the second grade.

The programme was mainly implemented in villages near the main town and thus had a limited impact on the literacy rate of rural women. In this chapter I will focus on the consequences for those who served in the programme and look at the impact of the experience on the young, urban, middle-class and educated women who joined. In contrast with their male colleagues, my female interviewees declared that, while serving in the Literacy Corps, they were not interested in politics at all. However, the movement against the Shah saw the active participation of some of the illiterate female population and the educated urban women.[2] Due to their background, it is reasonable to assume that some of the urban middle-class women who joined the Literacy Corps were later involved in revolutionary activities, especially amongst the leftist opposition. However, the deaths in the aftermath of the Revolution of 1979, the exile of the opposition, and the secrecy that often envelopes a revolutionary past, have been overwhelming obstacles to the discovery of interviewees with specifically this kind of political background.

The Women's Literacy Corps programme formed part of the relationship between the state and women in Iran. This article will attempt to evaluate the effect of the programme on the lives and education of women, and will seek to give facts and data to that purpose. It will also provide some indicators of the contribution of the Women's Literacy Corps to state control of Iranian feminism, but that topic as a whole must await a more specific future study.

This research is based on documents collected in archives (National Archives at College Park Maryland, Foundation of Iranian Studies at Bethesda Maryland, UNESCO archives in Paris and International Bureau of Education in Geneva) between 1996 and 1999. I have supported written sources with oral history[3] by holding informal interviews in Iran and in the United States. Though I had a list of questions, I gave my six interviewees – obviously a narrow sample compared to the 37,508 young women involved – space to talk about what they wished.[4] Apart from personal data, and that on the cohort in which they were drafted, as well as the barrack and village in which they lived, I asked questions such as:

- Why did you join the Literacy Corps?
- Had you had any previous rural experience?
- What sort of problems did you have to cope with? Did you speak the same language as the villagers?
- Did you teach both children and adults?
- Which subjects did you teach?
- For how many days a week did you used to work?
- Did you take any holidays without asking the permission of your supervisor?
- What was the supervision like?
- Where did you live?
- Did you pay for food and accommodation?
- What was your salary?
- Did you bring any books with you?
- Which sort?
- How did people react to your presence?
- Did you or any of your colleagues get married to villagers?
- From which background did you come?
- Did you have any political ideas at that time?
- Did you keep a diary?
- Do you have photographs?
- Did you keep your uniform?
- Anything else you remember?

Interviews have been particularly important in understanding women's personal development after being members of the Literacy Corps. But, to what extent does memory change after 20 or 30 years? Though reliability is an evident problem, oral history permits a shift of focus from the institutional level to an informal one, and therefore provides witnesses from every social class and a more realistic account of the past.[5] Given the documents found in the archives and the information obtained through interview, the following issues will be examined: female education, the Women's Social Service Law, the aims of the Women's Literacy Corps, and its implementation, achievements and difficulties with specific reference to the women drafted into the corps. With regard to achievements, I will focus mainly on the literacy rate. Since my research has not been conducted in Iranian villages, I shall not examine the impact of this programme on other aspects of village life. The effect of state intervention on rural communities has been examined elsewhere. Goodell, for instance, has given a negative reading of it.[6] I have not come to the same conclusion because of the difference in focus – mine on women drafted into the Corps, and hers on women taught in the villages.

Female education

According to Afary, modern Iranian feminism is rooted in the first stages of Iranian nationalism and in the Constitutional Revolution of 1905, when women belonging to different religions and sects actively took part in protests, and physically defended the constitutionalists, providing them with financial and moral support. As in the case of Indian women during the swadeshi boycott (1905–1908) against the British, some Iranian women boycotted imported European textiles to free the nation from dependence on western goods. Moreover:

> activist women, many from the upper classes of society, began to organize themselves in anjumans and opened new girls' schools, adult education classes, health clinics, and a variety of other institutions. They received no financial support from the newly formed government, which expressly barred women from the political process; yet, despite their small numbers they managed to bring about important changes in the lives of many urban women.

Female education was given particular attention. Instead of spending on dowries, some women suggested saving that amount for girls' education. Though Sheikh Fazlullah Nuri had issued a *fatwa* against women's education, arguing that it would change the role of women in Islam, women kept on creating *anjumans* and educational institutions. Faced with strong clerical opposition, women argued that female emancipation would strengthen family ties and advance the nation and would not be, as denounced by some mullahs, a dismantling of the gendered order and the demise of the Muslim Shi'ite culture.[7]

Following the Constitutional Revolution of 1905, Iran experienced two main periods of state-building, the first in the 1930s under Reza Shah and the second in the 1960s and 1970s with Muhammad Reza Shah. In the first stage, women's status was seen as a symbol of the modernity of the new nation and the new state, while afterwards it became the symbol of the modernity of the monarch and his progressive benevolence towards them.[8] In Iran female education and feminism thus followed a path different from nearby Turkey, mainly because the Ottoman state was much more powerful than the Iranian one and this influenced the way nationalism developed. In fact, modern Turkey rose from the ruins of the Ottoman Empire and Atatürk created a new secular state where no space was left for the clerical forces who:

> had compromised themselves by backing occupying powers, while the whole period of the Young Turks had created wide acceptance of a new concept of Turkish nationhood, based partially on non-Islamic definitions and affiliations.

By contrast, in Iran:

> a significant part of the Shiʿite clergy had supported the Constitutional Movement, and despite periods of alienation from the secular constitu-tionalists, it continued to keep its traditional legitimacy as the voice of the people.[9]

Interwoven with the objectives of nation-building, national identity, strategy of socio-economic development, and modernization, the 'women question' (*masa'il-yi zan*) in Iran should be analysed together with: the influence and different views of the ulama, bearing in mind that they were responsive to different sections of society; the appropriation of the issue by the Pahlavi regime; its relationship to the changes the state was going through; and its consequent reinterpretation.[10]

During Reza Shah's reign, women's participation in the workforce, particularly in the bureaucracy, in teaching and in factories, was supposed to help build the Iranian state.[11] In 1918 a Teachers' Training College for women was opened in Tehran; *Danish* (Knowledge), an eight-page weekly newspaper and the first women's journal was published in 1911; and in 1936 women were admitted to the university.[12] However, by the mid-1930s Reza Shah had closed all independent women's societies and magazines, and started to take over the 'women question'.[13] With the help of the Ladies Clubs, adult classes were opened in private secondary girls' schools in Tehran, Tabriz and Rasht. Women's interest in education was reportedly so high that more than one thousand illiterates registered. In addition, in Tehran the Ladies Club organized classes to teach foreign languages.[14]

With Muhammad Reza Shah, the state appropriation of the 'women question' continued in the sense that all initiative – even of a charitable nature – was centralized and came either from the government, from the Shah himself or from his twin sister Princess Ashraf. Women's rights were to be 'royal grants'. Also the people involved changed: on the one hand, under Reza Shah women activists came from an elite background, were mostly involved in charitable work and, consequently, enjoyed a position of personal prestige; on the other hand, the new generation operating under Muhammad Reza Shah was composed of almost anonymous figures serving within the Women's Organization of Iran, which centralized all activities.[15]

In the early 1960s the literacy rate among Iranian women was still very low, mainly because of the lack of facilities, different priorities and marriage at a very young age. Since by law no government school was supposed to be co-educational apart from the first four years of primary school and in the universities, separation of female and male students also represented a major problem. Though not compulsory, segregation continued as a natural behaviour at college level. In the main cities particular consideration was usually given by the Ministry of Education to girls' secondary schools, such as the Reza Shah School in Tehran. Education was indeed considered the best way towards women's rights, amongst which female suffrage had a pre-eminent position.

According to a US Foreign Service despatch of 1960, the campaign for women's rights during the reign of Muhammad Reza Shah started with a demand for the right for women to vote and of election to public office. However, rather than being very well-organized, Iranian feminist leaders were divided, apathetic or too interested in being socially prominent. The impression was thus that the more socially prominent among these women were not so much interested in female suffrage as in getting themselves elected as the first woman Deputy or Senator in Iran. At the same time, some people thought that female suffrage should not have been a real concern since there was no point in having the vote in a country where elections are not free.[16]

However, the observations of the above American source are contradicted by Paidar. According to her research, during the period of nationalist struggle in the decade after Reza Shah, Iranian women were intensely politically active in both public political protest and the women's rights campaign, but the results are not obvious because on the women issue Mussadiq's nationalist movement had the same programme as the state.[17] In the aftermath of the Mussadiq period, women's enthusiasm and political participation were focused on the campaign for suffrage. In 1959 this issue was brought up in the Majles. However, the clergy strongly opposed female suffrage and Ayatullah Borujerdi vetoed the government's plan to hold a women's day parade in Tehran requested by the Federation of Women's Organizations. As a consequence of such strong objection by the clergy, the Majles dropped the issue of female suffrage, but Iranian women kept on fighting for their own rights.[18]

In November 1962 a decree for the election of provincial councils implicitly granted to women the right to vote and to be elected. But, at the same time, religious opposition made the government withdraw the decree. As a consequence, on the occasion of the referendum of 26 January 1963 women were invited to put their votes into separate ballot boxes which were not counted. Only on the occasion of the elections to the National Consultative Assembly on 17 September 1963 were Iranian women eventually given the right to vote.[19]

In February 1964, on the occasion of 8 Esfand, Tabriz celebrated the first anniversary of the Shah's order that women be given the right to vote, but speeches were mainly focused on the past and scarcely mentioned the future. In fact, Mrs Azmudeh, married to the commander of the Tabriz-based Second Division, and Mrs Bazargan, whose husband was the Rector of Tabriz University, vaguely spoke in 'flattering generalities about both the rights of women and the general tenor of the Iranian White Revolution'. Mention of female suffrage was made only in connection with the celebration itself. Though women did not seem extremely committed to struggling for more rights, they set up a large dinner-dance and were thus able to collect some $2000 in order to organize night classes for illiterate women in Tabriz.[20]

The following month, with the advent of Mansur's government and the first election after women's suffrage, six women won seats in the Parliament and two became senators. The number of women elected gradually increased. The reform of the electoral law granted women voting rights and it was thus identified with the emancipation of women, rather than with a revision of the parliamentary system in order to bring it in line with the needs of the time.[21] Indeed, the official propaganda defined the new steps as the emancipation of women with which Iran turned full circle to the times of the first Persian Empire, when:

> under the Achaemenians, women occupied a very privileged position. They could hold high offices in state administration and in religious orders and received equal pay for equal work. Details of labour conditions recorded on 180 tablets found at Persepolis show that the wage for a highly skilled woman was three or four times that of an unskilled man.[22]

The official propaganda juxtaposed women's position in pre-Islamic times with the twentieth century reality in which, according to Islamic rules:

> women had very few rights at all. A man could divorce his wife any time he felt like it. He could refuse her permission to travel, to go out to work or to spend even one night away from home.[23]

Women's participation resulted in the enactment of the Family Protection Law and in changes in the procedures regarding divorce, marriage and child custody.[24] However, the process leading to reform was slow, as women were not of sufficient significance to expect government consideration of their views or demands. Yet, minority groups were particularly active and enjoyed international contacts which became useful in terms of advice and financial assistance.[25] An American diplomat observed that upper class women belonging to religious and ethnic minorities were the first to be educated formally, but amongst the lower classes illiteracy was widespread.[26]

Foreigners also helped in many ways. Since 'Iranian feminist leaders believe (whether justly or not) that their recent successes have been the result of their own abilities and hard work' and 'they are consequently little disposed to listen to the suggestions of outsiders, and are concerned that they may be identified too closely with Americans', the U.S. Embassy in Tehran suggested that 'any attempt to help Iranian women must be in a low key and should in general be based on individual contacts'. For instance, Iranian and American women were brought together by the international conference on 'the role of women in the community' held in Tehran in April 1963 and sponsored by the Committee of Correspondence, a private organization devoted to the promotion of women's rights. Furthermore, besides its leader and specialist grants, USIS (United States Information Service) increased its emphasis on women organizing teas, concerts and lectures in order to bring together Iranian women and Americans living in Tehran, and through an adviser on Women's Affairs employed in the cultural branch, frequently in touch with local women's organizations and in charge of setting up seminars, assisting in establishing Iranian branches of international women's clubs, translating publications of American groups and helping American ladies visiting Iran.[27] Films such as *A Small Triumph* and *A Gift of Time* and publications such as *U.S. Women Today* were available to individuals, associations and magazines devoted to women, such as *Ittila'at-i Banuvan*, and to newspapers having sections for female readers. USAID material was also made available at its Technical Reference Library in the form of books, pamphlets, voter education, family courts, juvenile delinquency, property and divorce laws, women's education, social service and welfare activities. American help to the reform process also involved grants and exchange programmes. However, those sent to the United States for further education were members of the upper class only: Mrs Ozra Ziai was a prominent women's leader and, when she went to the United States on a Leader Grant, Secretary of the High Council of the Iranian Women's Associations and Under Secretary in the Ministry of Housing and Development; Mrs Mehri Alai-Ramzi, who received a Specialist Grant, was already Programme Director of Television of Iran: Mrs Mehranghiz Dowlatshahi received a full Leader Grant, and then became Majles deputy; two partial Leader Grants were awarded to Dr Mehri Ahi and to Dr Zafar-Dokht Ardalan, associate professors of Tehran University; Specialist Grants were also given to Mrs Sharafat Akbar, working in social welfare, and to Mrs Ghodsi Rahbari, speaker for Radio Iran.

As witnessed by foreigners, the Iranian stage was 'littered with the debris of government-sponsored groups and parties and organizations that have been launched, then forgotten or scuttled'.[28] Feminist activities were dominated by 'strong rivalries and a general failure to cooperate'.[29] Ms Firuz and Ms Dowlatshahi were, for example, presidents of the Council of Women and Rah-i Nau, two different associations sharing the same aims. Besides, in Tehran, there were two rival associations of Armenian women and a few organizations dealing with female charities such as the Federation of Women's Organizations of Iran, the 17th Dai Society and the High Council of Women.

Apart from these groups in Tehran, the Azerbaijan Council of Women in Tabriz played a role in establishing eleven literacy centres for adult women and family advice centres. The Council set up branches in Marand, Maragheh, Saran and Azarshahr. Its members were so committed as to be able to overcome a crisis of leadership caused by the transfer of the husband of one of the founders. In fact, the key figures of the Council were the wife of the Central Governor, the wife of the Chancellor of the University of Tabriz and the wife of a senior army officer. Since they belonged to upper class families, they shared little with the traditional Azerbaijani lady wrapped in the chador. The Azerbaijan Council of Women was able to teach 500 women literacy, hygiene and family care; to establish welfare committees to solve personal problems; to pay their fines and set free some women in prison and advise them on how to become useful citizens.[30]

The first reason for such slowness in the reform process was the contemporary characteristic of Iranian feminism as groups supervised by the regime, composed of a few hundred aristocratic ladies, revolving around Princess Ashraf and aiming at opening up a few positions for women in the government and related agencies. In other words, such Iranian feminism never really had to struggle. Benefits were generally bestowed from above. Secondly, Iranian feminism lacked the large national aspirations and idealism of the most successful Asian feminist movements. Thirdly, the government's fear of angering the clergy and other conservative forces, with which the regime already had difficulties, was clearly stated by Mehranghiz Manuchehrian, senator and veteran feminist who was asked by a young modern Iranian woman why the feminists did not struggle for a constitutional amendment banning discrimination on sexual grounds. Furthermore, Mehranghiz Dowlatshahi, the Kermanshah deputy, told an officer of the American Embassy that non-controversial questions of family law would have shortly been dealt with in a bill. Accordingly, since it was sensitive in religious terms, inheritance was not included in the draft submitted by the women parliamentarians to Princess Ashraf for clearance by the Shah on 9 January 1965.

The above features inevitably went against the transformation of Iranian feminism into grass-roots organizations recruiting among lower and middle class women. According to a report on Iranian feminism prepared in January 1965 by the American Embassy in Tehran, in comparison with Turkey, Iranian feminism did not have the 'zeal for social reconstruction, never rallied around a truly charismatic leader like Kemal Atatürk and did not massively reject the inhibiting traditional past'. And, in comparison with Palestinian women after 1918, the Iranians 'never participated as equals in the reconstruction of a nation on a socio-religious basis'. The Iranian government introduced women's rights mainly because 'some movement towards feminist goals was necessary to preserve and enhance the image of reform so essential for the support and aid they hoped to get from the outside world'. However, 'in a country in which men have few rights of voluntary group activity for the advancement of their interests, there are severe limits to what the women can do for the promotion of their particular concerns'.[31] From when the Majles convened in September 1963, the Iranian government made no movement on the legal front: women still needed their husbands' permission to obtain a passport; they received a different inheritance quota, unless specified in their marriage contract; they could not start a divorce action; and they were allowed custody of a child only up to the second year of age for boys, and to the seventh for girls. Moreover, before employing women, many government agencies and commercial firms still required letters of approval from fathers and husbands.[32]

In 1964 the Department of Women's Activities had been created, aimed at educating girls and women. One of the first six women to be elected as member of Parliament, Farrokhrou Parsa was appointed Minister of Education in 1968 and fought for women's education until she retired in 1975.[33] However, according to anti-regime propaganda she paid a high price for her devotion to women's rights. In fact, in December 1979, charged with 'expansion of prostitution, corruption on earth, and warring against God', she was not permitted a defence attorney, was declared guilty even before the beginning of the proceedings, wrapped in a sack and machine-gunned.

Amongst the many women's associations present in Iran, the Council of Iranian Women was founded in 1943 by Safieh Firuz. At the outset called the Women's Party of Iran, it later had to change its name because of numerous objections, as up to then no political party had claimed to be a woman's political party.

According to a document of 1960, the last Majles elections saw the establishment of women's committees within the two leading parties, but participants soon realized the hopelessness of the situation and gave up.[34] From 30 October to 5 November 1965 a congress of the High Council of Women's Associations of Iran took place in Tehran and, for the first time, brought together 60 delegates from women's local organizations. After an inaugural address by Princess Ashraf, a panel addressed the issue of the role of women in contemporary Iran, the participants visited the Tehran School of Social Work, a Baluchi woman from Zahedan presented crafts and talked about the organization of cottage industries in her area, and also participated in the birthday celebrations of the crown prince. The congress was useful in terms of meeting people, discussing issues, learning about leadership training and receiving material. Yet, according to *Kayhan International* and to the American Embassy in Tehran, both the Congress and the associations shared the same difficulty. Indeed, the dominant theme in Iranian feminism was said to be:

> the individual's push for the limelight and desire to enhance her own prestige, even at the expense of project coordination and overall benefit to Iran.[35]

Though this is only one view and it is unfair to reduce Iranian feminism to such individualism, an example of this lack of co-ordination was given by the literacy

classes established by the High Council of Women's Associations of Iran in order
to teach several thousand illiterate girls. While a process of reorganization was
taking place, confusion played a major role and funds from the sale of books
published by Franklin Publishers moved from the Council to the Committee for
the Eradication of Illiteracy.[36]

The Women's Social Service Law

Following the implementation of the Literacy Corps in 1963, a few Iranian
women leaders asked for educational programmes for rural girls.[37] At the same
time Parviz Natel Khanlari, Minister of Education, made public the statistics on
the 500 to 1 ratio of illiterate men to women in Iran.[38] Later, he insisted on a
volunteer programme for educating urban women, but did not mention any
plan for rural girls.[39]

Within this context on the evening of 3 January 1965 – on the occasion of
the 29th anniversary of Reza Shah's removal of the veil in 1936 – Princess Ashraf
addressed a gathering of 4000 women at the Muhammad Reza Shah stadium,
and ostensibly answered a request from Farrokhrou Parsa – at that time a Majles
deputy from Tehran – by announcing that Iranian women would be allowed to
form a Literacy Corps and thus 'march shoulder with our brothers in this holy
campaign'. On 5 January Muhammad Reza Shah approved the formation of the
Women's Literacy Corps under Ashraf's official patronage, and headed by Turan
Ahi.[40] Funds were allocated from the Ministry of Education, the High Council of
Women's Organizations which already sponsored a similar project and was
chaired by Parsa, and the National Committee for the World Campaign Against
Illiteracy formed in early November 1964, chaired by the Shah himself, with his
sister Ashraf as vice-chairman and Shoja-ed-din Shafa of the Ministry of Court
as general secretary.[41]

However, the programme merely seemed to continue a project begun two
years before under the Women's High Council which aimed at training, for four
months, women volunteers with high school or junior high school education in
order to send them to large and medium towns to teach girls aged from 7 to 20. In
two years, this programme had trained 500 volunteers teaching in 525 classes
attended by a total of 14000 women. Funds for the project were provided by the
Imperial Welfare Organization – of which Princess Ashraf was vice-President –
through the High Council. At the start books were given free, but since children
were not taking care of them, five rials were charged in order to make pupils feel
that their texts were valuable.[42] In other words, by the end of 1965 the plan mainly
involved the continuation and expansion of the High Council's programme for
teaching girls in cities and towns, without sending teachers to villages. Yet, external
observers were hoping for the extension of the programme to the villages, though
'deep-rooted Iranian mores', and the low number of women actually available to
move to rural areas, were already foreseen as major obstacles.[43]

The Women's Literacy Corps eventually went beyond the newspaper headline stage. On 15 July 1968, according to the provisions of the Women's Social Services Law, women and girls with high school diplomas would be called to military service. According to this law, unmarried women with high school and higher degrees and without dependants could serve in rural or backward urban areas near their home for a period of eighteen months. More precisely:

> All girls who had received their high school diploma and are between eighteen and twenty-five and all those who had received higher degrees and are under thirty will be invited to carry out these services.[44]

This law was advertised in the Iranian press, which called for women willing to enter the teaching profession.[45] Actually, the Women's Social Service Law was not very clear. Though women were supposed to enter the corps on a volunteer basis, article ten introduced a mandatory element for female college graduates, apparently in contradiction with the letter of the law:

> The services mentioned in this law are obligatory for women whose degrees are higher than high school, provided they meet the age requirements.[46]

Therefore, although the Women's Literacy Corps called for volunteers, the government considered itself empowered to call them up. According to article three, exemption was granted to (1) married women and women with children, (2) women who were the only wage-earners in their families, and (3) women who were either physically or mentally disabled. According to article thirteen, exemption was also granted to women who, at the date of the ratification of the law, were employed by the government or government related agencies, and to those women who, while serving, had obtained higher degrees. Though formally exempted, women in groups (1) and (2) could volunteer.[47]

Aims of the Women's Literacy Corps

In an interview broadcast by the BBC and reported by *Kayhan International*, Princess Ashraf promoted the establishment of a women's literacy corps which could target a particular niche: rural women.[48] The possibility of forming a corps of women to be rural teachers on the same lines as the Literacy Corps was announced by Muhammad Reza Shah in an official speech.[49] Creating awareness among the masses and obtaining support from the government and from women was a twofold aim. According to Mahnaz Afkhami:

> Special programs to combat illiteracy among rural women were not demanded solely on the basis of women's right to education, but as a necessary means of modernization. Special vocational training for women was sought not only on the grounds of their rightful access to better-

paying jobs, but for the sake of eliminating sociocultural problems inherent in large-scale importation of foreign labour.[50]

The Women's Literacy Corps was thus not only a weapon against illiteracy. As declared by a corps-woman, human rights sounded irrelevant to:

> a pregnant, illiterate village woman who was doing her chores as she breast-fed one baby, tried to extricate her skirts from the clutches of another child, and kept a worried eye on her two other children fighting and screaming nearby.[51]

As in the case of corps-men, women serving in the Literacy Corps had educational, hygienic and social goals. Among their educational aims were teaching rural women and children, preparing and using educational facilities, trying to establish libraries in schools, instructing Girl Scouts and Girls for the Red Lion and Sun (the Iranian Red Cross), participating in training courses and seminars set up by the Ministry of Education in order to improve teaching styles, and guiding rural girls and women in house-keeping. Hygienic duties were the development of personal hygiene, achieving and maintaining community hygiene, keeping schools clean and tidy, and co-operating with health and hygiene agents in case of emergency. Social duties were arousing an interest in learning, encouraging participation and cooperation in social and group activities, familiarizing peasants with their social rights and responsibilities, and informing rural girls and women of the country's important events and news.[52]

According to the first article of the law which established the Women's Literacy Corps, these cultural, educational, hygienic, health and social services were 'the holy responsibility of the women of this country'. According to the same article, the Women's Literacy Corps aimed at increasing 'the participation of women in the social transformation of the country and in the implementation of the Revolution'.[53] Furthermore, the creation of this corps contributed to the solution to the chronic shortage of teachers willing to move to rural areas, the high unemployment rate among graduates and the difficulties in entering university.

Implementation

On 23 September 1968 the first cohort of 1895 corps-women started their six-month training in 16 centres: Tehran, Rasht, Sari, Tabriz, Rezaeeh, Kermanshah, Ahvaz, Shiraz, Kerman, Mashhad, Isfahan, Qazvin, Sanandaj, Khorramabad, Hamadan and Zahedan.[54] The total number of hours during the training period was 936, of which 792 were in education and 144 were spent on military training. The topics included education and child psychology, Literacy Corps management, administrative and educational duties and responsibilities, teaching methods, sociology, co-operation, personal and community hygiene, family planning, principles of house-keeping, artistic handicrafts, and military education (self-defence).[55]

On 21 March 1969 the first cohort set off for the villages. Corps-women were usually assigned to one of the nearest villages to their home town.[56] As stated by the six women I interviewed, they could either commute every day or rent an apartment with other corps-women and return home for the week-end. In contrast to the corps-men, who mostly received free accommodation from the *kadkhoda* (village head-man) and whose meals were usually cooked by their pupils' mothers, the corps-women I interviewed clearly stated they payed for accommodation and cooked their own meals. However, they were frequently given eggs, fruit, vegetables and yogurt.[57]

According to an issue of the magazine *The Education Corps*, the Women's Literacy Corps was not only involved in teaching rural women, but rather exercised a broad range of activities:

> During the years 1969 and 1970 they have built or repaired tens of thousands of kilometers of roads, hundreds of bridges, funeral homes, slaughtering houses, public bathrooms and schools. They have collected vital statistics of the people and livestocks in their districts, numbered the houses and helped women in their housekeeping work.[58]

However, during my interviews I did not come across women who built roads, bridges and so forth, whilst Azizeh Ashoori and Nushir Saiai stated they taught knitting, sewing and cooking.[59] Corps-women were dispatched to villages close to towns, where villagers were usually already familiar with basic hygienic principles. An interviewee mentioned birth control meetings, but birth control was actually under the provisions of the Health Corps, as indicated by a photograph published in an issue of the magazine *National Geographic* in which a woman serving in the Health Corps was distributing birth control pills and disease-prevention information near Shiraz.[60]

Upon finishing their service in the Literacy Corps, all women were employed as permanent teachers by the Ministry of Education.[61] According to article seven of the Women's Social Service Law, women who had completed their service had priority in employment within government institutions and organizations linked to the government, and also in applying for study and research scholarships. For women who came from a lower and lower-middle class background, the teaching profession was the only way to become independent and the only possible alternative to being a housewife. The corps-men's situation was different. Only 50 per cent of them applied for a permanent position as teachers, mainly because men could choose among several jobs. In the case of women unable to attend university, entering the Literacy Corps was the best way to receive the training and the experience needed.

Furthermore, when the Women's Literacy Corps were established, the Teachers' Training College had been closed and the same programme was carried on within the training course for the Literacy Corps. A further reason for the different choices made by men and women after serving in the Literacy Corps was their working conditions: while women were teaching in villages near their towns, men could be sent to distant rural areas with neither basic facilities nor good communication to urban centres. Therefore, for a man being a rural teacher was not the most attractive scenario. Table 7.1 shows the number of women trained in the Literacy Corps between 1969 and 1977.

Table 7.1 Number of trained Women's Literacy Corps, 1969–1977

Year	Cohort	Number of women	Total for the year
1969	first	1891	
1969	second	820	2711
1970	third	967	
1970	fourth	1030	1997
1971	fifth	1023	
1971	sixth	953	1976
1972	seventh	1910	
1972	eighth	1730	3640
1973	ninth	1692	
1973	tenth	1946	3638
1974	eleventh	1963	
1974	twelfth	2374	4337
1975	thirteenth	2577	
1975	fourteenth	3036	5613
1976	fifteenth	2838	
1976	sixteenth	3636	6474
1977	seventeenth	3053	
1977	eighteenth	4069	7122

Source: M.A. Farjad (Ministry of Education, Undersecretariat for Research and Educational Reconstruction, Centre for Educational Research and International Cooperation), *System of Education in Iran*, No. 1, Tehran, February 1978, p. 22.

Achievements and difficulties

Before the implementation of the Women's Literacy Corps there were 438 girls attending urban schools for every thousand boys, while in rural areas the proportion of girls fell to 225 to every thousand boys; in 1976 the rural ratio of girls for every thousand boys was 295 and this increase was directly attributed to the Literacy Corps.[62]

Many articles were published in the Iranian press. In 1971, for instance, the newspaper *Kayhan* wrote about a five-day gathering of 258 corps-women in

Manzarieh. Divided into 43 groups of six fellows wearing the military uniform and sleeping in tents, these corps-women were taught how to mix in the villages and how important the Women's Literacy Corps experience was.[63]

In 1973 the magazine *Zan-i Ruz* dedicated four pages to this topic under the title 'Women are looking for freedom and happiness'. According to this issue, on the tenth anniversary of the White Revolution, the Iranian family was described as a happy one in which both husband and wife had to be responsible, female students outnumbered men in the university, peasants praised the land reform, workers were grateful for the privatization of state-owned factories, the villager's son prayed and waited for the arrival of a literacy corps-man who taught him how to read and write, and the Iranian woman could share the same rights as her male counterparts. According to *Zan-i Ruz*, by allowing women to vote, to be elected and to choose any job, and granting them more rights by means of a new Family Code, the Shah had eliminated the last social shame and stripped away a chain of slavery.

As a direct consequences of the new provisions, the Iranian woman had to manage her house, but she was not allowed to shut herself up at home. By contrast with her ignorant, subdued, weak and neglected grandmother, she had woken up after a millennial sleep. In a seminar held at Tehran University and quoted by the press, Dr Zafar Ardalan defined the White Revolution not only as a means of empowerment for Iranian women, but also as a way to further develop their personalities in terms of personal sacrifice and the opening of different careers. At the same time, sociological studies showed how recent developments had contributed towards a different male perception of their wives, mothers and daughters, so that they were now favourably inclined to the education of the younger generation. As a consequence of this attitude, while in 1963 only 31 per cent of girls attended primary school, ten years after the beginning of the White Revolution this percentage had increased to 46 per cent. In the case of secondary schools, female attendance increased four times and male attendance only three times. According to a study mentioned by Ardalan, in 1963 only 4183 girls were able to enroll at the university, that was 17 per cent of the total national number. Three years later this figure moved from 17 per cent to 20 per cent and then increased again. Moved by a new spirit of responsibility, by the tenth anniversary of the White Revolution the number of women attending university had risen seven times and reached 28869. Achievements at school paved the way for success on the work front: 27 women entered the political team of the Minister of Foreign Affairs, 23 were judges in the Ministry of Justice which employed a total of 243 female workers, among whom two were medical examiners, 10 helpers and one an accountant. Moreover, in 1973 42 women worked in village courts of justice. In conclusion, the whole article in *Zan-i Ruz* praised financial independence as a *conditio sine qua non* for Iranian women to be free and equal to men.[64]

In connection with the role played by literacy corps-women, it has already been mentioned elsewhere that many parents did not want their daughters to sit in a class with boys and with a male teacher. Khomeini had rejected co-educational schools as destroying 'the chastity of girls and the masculine powers of boys'.[65] And also the Fada'iyan-i Islam had attacked the idea of co-educational schools and suggested that women should receive the sort of education appropriate for their duties within the family.[66] An official document refers to this problem in the following terms:

> Our rural people, as a result of some religious taboos, did not send their girls to school'.[67]

And rural people in the village of Sarbandan near Tehran were recorded by the social worker Najafi as saying: 'A boy to teach our girls! Never. For a girls' school we must have a woman teacher.'

As a consequence, the villagers wrote a petition asking the Minister of Education for a female teacher.[68] After the arrival of the female teacher, in a village whose inhabitants had declared they 'had no girls', 35 women and girls showed up.[69] Yet none of my interviewees mentioned that girls did not attend or that their fathers were worried about them sitting in a class with boys and a male teacher. This was only the case, according to my interviewees, with young women (about 15 years old) who were attending the first grade because no school had existed before the arrival of the Literacy Corps. However, this difference in the sources may be explained by the location of the women I interviewed, mainly in rural areas near the capital.

The creation of the Women's Literacy Corps contributed to the solution of the low attendance of girls. According to an official publication, the percentage of girls attending classes in the villages increased from 22.5 per cent to 43.8 per cent.[70] However, official Iranian statistics are hard to believe, and since corps-women were not employed in distant rural areas, their impact on girls' education was, at any rate, limited. Corps-women shared some of the corps-men's difficulties, such as the high drop-out rate whilst children helped their families in the fields and pastures. The main difficulty was to make illiterate village women aware of their rights and persuade them to exercise them. Many examples of this obstacle are shown by a UNESCO officer for the Adult Literacy Pilot Project in Khuzestan: 'The first step was to create motivation for literacy, particularly among the womenfolk'.[71]

Linguistic problems did not seem to affect women because they were assigned to villages near their home town where people spoke their same language. None of my interviewees recalled a mullah's opposition to the programme. Azizeh Ashoori even showed me a picture, possibly taken for propaganda purposes, in which she was wearing the mini-skirt provided as uniform while she was talking to the village mullah.[72]

In the case of other women teachers not belonging to the Literacy Corps, due to their job schedule, they rarely joined the afternoon female gatherings in the courtyards, a time when 'ideas and attitudes were assessed'.[73] Therefore, though loosely wrapped in their chadors whilst walking in the village street heading towards the school, their ideas and behaviour were in some ways considered 'foreign'. The use of a uniform contributed to a different social position of corps-women, who were seen more as government agents, and did not fit exactly into the category of 'women' to the extent that in some cases they were selected as *kadkhoda* of the village were they served.[74]

Conclusions

Corps-women were generally urban, low and middle class, educated, but without any previous rural experience. During my interviews I encountered a great enthusiasm. Most corps-women recalled that time as the best in their life, underlined by how they learned to tackle problems and how much they grew up in terms of personal experience. Zahra Rezai praised her experience in the corps in her accounts, '*The last hour of my service* and *I don't want to leave the heaven I have built*', published in an issue of the magazine *Literacy Corps*.[75] It was an official publication, and therefore she expressed a good opinion of the programme. But even those who were against the regime had to admit that this experience had a great impact both on the rural female population and on the well-educated women who served in it, mainly in terms of human and working experience. In fact, this programme gave young women the chance to develop a more independent way of thinking and style of living, plus the experience needed in order to become a teacher. From a social perspective, the Women's Literacy Corps helped bridge the gap between townsfolk and countryfolk.

As already mentioned, corps-women taught in villages near their own towns and their impact on the literacy rate of rural areas was thus limited. By comparison, this programme also had less political impact on the corps-women's personalities than on the corps-men's. All the women I interviewed had, at the time of their service, no interest in politics. They were much more involved and committed to teaching than to anything else. Furthermore, compared with their male colleagues, women served near their home towns, often commuted and thus did not need to escape during the week or term-time in order to go back to their families.

Though my focus has been mainly on corps-women themselves, regarding the people's reaction to the presence of corps-women in rural areas, their suspicion could be interpreted as arising from fear of extension of state control, of possible western influence and of a perceived threat to Islam, rather than as an objection to the education of women *per se*.

Indeed, female education is perfectly in line with what is recorded about the Prophet's beliefs. In fact, according to al-Baladhuri's *Futuh al-buldan* ('The conquests of countries'), in the pre-Islamic era Hafsa, one of Muhammad's wives, was taught how to write and read by al-Shaffa al-Adawiyya, a woman belonging to the Bani Adi tribe to which 'Umar ibn al-Hattab also belonged.

After the Prophet's marriage to Hafsa, she was asked to continue studying under al-Shaffa and to learn the art of calligraphy.[76]

Last but not least, a few corps-women met their husbands while serving in the Literacy Corps. Rohanghiz Lashgari remembered that the *kadkhuda*'s grandson had asked for her hand, but she had no feelings for him and thus refused.[77] Zahra Rezai had two female colleagues who married while serving in the villages and judged these marriages as successful and, since divorced, she regretted to some extent the fact that she had not done the same.[78] Azizeh Ashoori married a corpsman who insisted that she join the Literacy Corps; at the time of her training in the barracks in Tehran she was pregnant and, after having given birth she served in Tavalesh near Rasht, in the province of Gilan where her in-laws lived and could thus look after her newborn child.[79] Nushir Saiai also married a colleague in the Literacy Corps; after having taught in a village for six years, she married a young man whose family lived in the village where she had been dispatched; at that time she was 29 and he was 24, he was serving as literacy corpsman in Tabriz and, when he returned for a holiday they met and married within a week. They are still happily together.[80] However, not all marriages were successful. Zahra Tanhai, for instance, married a villager but divorced.[81] According to Ma'sume Moghaddam, marriages between corps-men and corps-women had the highest probability of lasting due to the common understanding deriving from sharing the same working experience.[82]

Appendix: Sketches of interviewees

Corps-women

Ashoori, Azizeh: Fourth cohort of the Women's Literacy Corps, after 6 months training in Tehran in the barracks of Heshmati she served for 18 months in Tavalesh, a village with 400 inhabitants near Rasht in Gilan. Born in Astara in Gilan (1950), diploma in Tehran (1969), married to ex-corps-man Gholamreza Sadrai (1967), a teacher in primary school. She retired in 1996.

Lashgari, Rohanghiz: Third cohort of the Women's Literacy Corps, after 6 months training in Tehran she served for 18 months in Aderan-e Shariar, a large village in the province of Tehran on the road to Saveh. Born in Tehran (1951), diploma in Tehran (1967), unmarried, BA in Education Management at Tehran University (1977), MA in Consultance and Educational Guidance, now owner and principal of a nursery, Shi'a Muslim.

Moghaddam, Ma'sume: Third cohort of the Women's Literacy Corps, after 6 months training in a school in Orumie in Azerbaijan, she served for 9 months in the village of Dereshk and then for a further 9 months in Sadeghian, respectively 5 and 3 km from Salmas. Born in Maku in Azerbaijan (1950), diploma in Salmas in Azerbaijan (1969), married to ex-corps-man Hassan Irandoost (1974), BA in from Teachers Training College for Literacy Corps, now a teacher in the last year of high school (in the year which prepares students for the university), Shi'a Muslim.

Rezai, Zahra: First cohort of the Women's Literacy Corps, after 6 months training in Tehran in the barracks of Heshmati she served for 18 months in Aderan-e Shariar, a large village in the province of Tehran on the road to Saveh. Born in Tehran (1948), diploma in Tehran (1967), married to a bank employee (1976) and divorced (1979), now a teacher in a primary school, Shi'a Muslim.

Saiai, Nushir: First cohort of the Women's Literacy Corps, after 6 months training in Tehran in the barracks of Heshmati she served for 18 months in Aderan and Robatkarim, in the Shariar area in the province of Tehran, respectively 30 and 65 km from the capital. Born in Tehran (1946), diploma in Tehran (1967), married to a bank employee (1975), primary school teacher, Shi'a Muslim.

Tanhai, Zahra: First cohort of the Women's Literacy Corps, after 6 months training in Tehran in the barracks of Heshmati she served for 18 months in the Shariar area in the province of Tehran. Born in Tehran (1947), diploma in Tehran (1967), married to an employee of the Ministry of Education (1974), teacher in a guidance school (the level after primary school), Shi'a Muslim.

Other interviewees

Afkhami, Gholamreza: Served as Chief of the Literacy Movement. He now manages the *Foundation for Iranian Studies* in Bethesda, Maryland.

Afkhami, Mahnaz: Served as secretary-general of the Women's Organization of Iran (1970–79) and Minister of State for Women's Affairs (1976–78). She is now Executive Director of *Sisterhood is Global Institute* in Bethesda, Maryland, www.sigi.org

Dowlatshahi, Mehranghiz: Served for three terms in the Majles and then became Ambassador in Denmark. Now she lives in Paris.

Golshiri, Hushang: Novelist and literary critic. In 1999 he won the Osnabrueck prize with the book *Der Mann mit der roten Krawatte* (Verlag C.H. Beck, München, 1998) and is among those who are trying to refound the Writers Association. Born in 1937, he is normally based in Tehran. However, the recent (1998) killings of Iranian intellectuals obliged him to go into hiding for a few months.

Goudarznia, Azam: Served in the Ministry of Education for 37 years and in the last 4 years of her service she worked with the Women's Literacy Corps as deputy Dean of their school. She was also Dean of Reza Shah Senior Secondary School in Tehran. She lives in Washington DC.

Honar, Ali Muhammad: Born in Shiraz (1941), diploma in Shiraz (1959), graduated in Persian literature (1964), MA (1965), married (1967), university professor before the revolution of 1979 and now high-school professor of Persian literature. Served in the Reconstruction and Development Corps.

Khoi, Esmail: Poet. Born in Mashhad in 1938, he was educated in Iran and in England. After having obtained his degree in philosophy at the University of London (1966), he returned to Tehran where he became a lecturer in philosophy. He lives in London. According to Ali Rezavi, Khoi's revolutionary poetry was widely read amongst literacy corps-men.

Lahiji, Shahla Intellectual and publisher (Roshangaran & Women Studies Publishing, Tehran).

Naraghi, Ehsan: Born in Kashan in 1926, professor of sociology at Tehran University (1957–79), director of the Institute for Social Studies and Research (1958–79), scholar and advisor to the secretary-general of UNESCO in Paris (1983–present).

Peyvandi, Saeed; Following his older brother Bijan, he enrolled in the Literacy Corps and found himself in Behdesht (on the road between Tehran and Mashhad). This village was mainly inhabited by Bahais and, in fact, this was the place were the Bahai prophetess Tahereh chose not to wear the veil. He teaches at Paris University.

Rassekh, Shahpour: Born in Tehran in 1924, professor of sociology at Tehran University (1958–79), civil servant in the Plan Organization and Chief of the Central Planning Office of the Plan Organization, consultant to UNESCO in Geneva.

Ryan, John: Having completed his Ph.D. on Iran at Stanford University, he was hired by UNESCO and thus went to Iran from September 1973 to February 1979 as Director of IIALM, an organization mainly focused on adult education and partly financed by Tehran.

Tunis, Eric: Served in the Peace Corps in Iran, 1967–69, in Sistan and Baluchistan. After many years in the American Embassy in Islamabad, he is now (1998) employed at the American Embassy in New Delhi.

Tussi, Muhammad: General Director of the Ministry of Education (1961–76), Chancellor of Isfahan University (1966–78), Deputy Minister of Science and Higher Education (1963–76) and last director of the Literacy Corps programme before the Islamic Revolution.

Notes

1 This chapter is part of my Ph.D. dissertation from the School of Oriental and African Studies, London. I made extensive interviews in London, Iran, Geneva, Paris, Pakistan, Venice and the United States during 1997 and 1998. I am indebted for funding to the University of Bari, the University of Bologna and the Consiglio Nazionale delle Richerche in Rome. My thanks go to all those mentioned in the footnotes for answering my questions. See Farian Sabahi (2001) *The Literary Corps in Pahlavi Iran (1963-1979): political, social and literary implications*, Lugano.

2 E. Sansarian (1982) *The Women's Rights Movement in Iran: Mutiny, Appeasement and Repression from 1900 to Khomeini*, p. 107.

3 According to J. Vansina (1985) *Oral Tradition as History,* London, p. 196: 'Oral traditions are not just a source about the past, but a historiology of the past, an account of how people have interpreted it. It is a hypothesis, similar to the historian's own interpretation of the past. To consider them first means not to accept them literally, uncritically'. Oral tradition implies 'communication that presents 'news' and communication which represents an 'interpretation' of existing situations' (p. 3). Furthermore, 'Selectivity and interpretation weight more heavily on oral tradition than on written sources. This is because, once a written source exists it becomes permanent, it is subtracted from time' (p. 191). In defence of oral history R. Finnegan (1992) *Oral Traditions and the Verbal Arts. A Guide to Research Practices,* London, p. 48: 'Oral historians rebut traditional historians' scepticism about oral sources by the positive point that oral recordings can be *more* rather than less 'objective' than written documents. A face-to-face situation allows for direct questioning and probing in a way not open with documentary sources'.

4 M.A. Farjad (Ministry of Education, Undersecretariat for Research and Educational Reconstruction, Centre for Educational Research and International Cooperation), *System of Education in Iran,* n. 1, Tehran, February 1978, p. 22.

5 P. Thompson (1978) *The Voice of the Past,* Oxford, pp. 5–6.

6 G.E. Goodell (1986) *The Elementary Structures of Political Life. Rural Development in Pahlavi Iran,* New York and Oxford.

7 J. Afary (1996) *The Iranian Constitutional Revolution, 1906–1911,* New York, pp. 177–208.

8 A. Najmabadi (1991) 'Hazards of modernity and morality: women, state and ideology in contemporary Iran', in D. Kandiyoti, (ed.) *Women, Islam & the State,* London, pp. 55, 63.

9 Najmabadi, 'Hazards', p. 56.

10 N. Tohidi (1994) 'Modernity, Islamization and Womein in Iran', in V.M. Moghadam, (ed.) *Gender and National Identity: Women and Politics in Muslim Societies,* London, p. 111; Najmabadi, 'Hazards', p. 51.

11 *Ibid.,* pp. 53–4.

12 *Ibid.,* p. 55.

13 *Ibid.,* p. 56.

14 Imperial Government of Iran, Ministry of Education (Division of Adult Education), *Adult Education in Iran 1938–1939,* Tehran, 1938 IBE, p. 18. On p. 44 there is a photograph taken in Tehran in summer 1937 showing a summer class for women teachers of elementary schools. The women are unveiled.

15 Najmabadi, 'Hazards', pp. 60–1.

16 Foreign Service Despatch from Harry H. Schwartz (Counselor of Embassy for Political Affairs signing for the Chargé d'Affaires as interim) at the American Embassy in Tehran to the Department of State in Washington and for information to all consulates in Iran, official use only, 9 November 1960, n. 248, *Activities and Progress of Iranian Women and Feminists Groups,* RG 59 General Records of the Department of State, Central Decimal File 1960–1963, 888.46/11–960 HBS, NARA (National Archives in Maryland).

17 P. Paidar (1995) *Women and the Political Process in Twentieth-century Iran,* Cambridge, p. 134.

18 *Ibid.,* pp. 140–1.

19 A.K.S. Lambton (1969) *The Persian Land Reform 1962–1969,* Oxford, pp. 108–9.

20 Airgram from Carleton S. Coon Jr. (American Consul) at the American Consulate in Tabriz to the Department of State and for information to Tehran, Khorramshahr, Mashhad and Isfahan, limited official use, 4 March 1964, n. A-31, *Women's Day in Tabriz,* NARA EDU 12–4 Iran, RG 59 General Records of the Department of State,

Central Foreign Policy Files. According to the Iranian Ministry of Education *Report on Educational Development in 1966–1967 Presented to the Session of the 30th International Conference on Public Education*, IBE, Geneva-Tehran, July 1967, p. 17, on 8 Esfand 1341 (27 February 1962) women were given equal political and civic rights as men.

21 'Electoral law', in *Kayhan International*, 26 October 1967.

22 *Iran Almanac and Book of Facts 1973*, Tehran, 1973, pp. 376–7.

23 *Ibid.*, p. 376.

24 'For the first time', in *Kayhan International*, 26 October 1967.

25 9 November 1960, n. 248, *Activities and Progress of Iranian Women and Feminists Groups*, NARA.

26 Paidar, *Women*, p. 32.

27 Airgram from Martin F. Herz (Counsellor for Political Affairs, signing on behalf of the Ambassador) at the American Embassy in Tehran to the Department of State, 13 April 1964, n. A-552, *Women's Activities*, limited official use, NARA SOC14–2 Iran, General Records of the Department of State, Central Foreign Policy Files 1964–1966, Social, Human Rights and Race Relations.

28 Airgram from Carleton S. Coon Jr. (American Consul) at the American Consulate in Tabriz to the Department of State and for information to the American Embassy in Tehran and to the American Consulates in Isfahan, Khorramshahr and Mashhad, limited official use, 13 January 1965, n. A-19, *Women's Activities in Tabriz*, NARA SOC 14–2 Iran, RG 59 General Records of the Department of State, Central Foreign Policy Files 1964–1966, Social, Human Rights and Race Relations. And attachment written by the Steering Committee of the High Council of the Women in Eastern Azerbaijan, *A Brief Report of Activities*.

29 9 November 1960, n. 248, *Activities and Progress of Iranian Women and Feminists Groups*, NARA.

30 13 January 1965, n. A-19, *Women's Activities in Tabriz*, NARA.

31 Confidential airgram from Martin F. Herz (Counsellor for Political Affairs, signing on behalf of the Ambassador) at the American Embassy in Tehran to the Department of State and for information to Ankara, New Dehli and Tel Aviv, 20 January 1965, n. A-388, *Iranian Feminism as a Social Force*, NARA SOC14–2 Iran, General Records of the Department of State, Central Foreign Policy Files 1964–1966, Social, Human Rights and Race Relations. The sense of superiority to the common Iranian women was also emphasized in an interview held on 8 October 1998 with Azam Gudarnzia in Bethesda Maryland, once Dean of Reza Shah Senior Secondary School in Tehran.

32 20 January 1965, n. A-388, *Iranian Feminism as a Social Force*, NARA.

33 M. Afkhami (1984) 'Iran: a future in the past – the "prerevolutionary" women's movement', in R. Morgan (ed.) *Sisterhood is Global. The International Womens' Movement Anthology*, New York, p. 330; 'Evolutionary politics and revolutionary change: 1965–1978. Activities and achievements of the Women's Organization of Iran', in *Iran Nama*, special issue on Iranian women, 1997, pp. 389–412; and interview, Washington DC, 8 October 1998.

34 9 November 1960, n. 248, *Activities and Progress of Iranian Women and Feminists Groups*, NARA.

35 Airgram from William A. Helseth (First Secretary who signed for the Ambassador) at the American Embassy in Tehran to the Department of State and for information to the American Embassy in London, limited official use, 29 November 1965, n. A-368, *First Congress of the High Council of Women's Associations of Iran*, NARA SOC 15 Iran, General Records of the Department of State, Central Foreign Policy Files 1964–1966 Social, Human Rights, Race Relations.

36 29 November 1965, n. A-368, *First Congress of the High Council of Women's Associations of Iran*, NARA.

37 *Kayhan International*, 8 and 29 January 1963.
38 *Kayhan International*, 2 February 1963.
39 *Kayhan International*, 31 January 1963.
40 *Iran Almanac and Book of Facts 1969*, Tehran, 1969, p. 532.
41 Confidential airgram from Martin F. Herz (Counsellor of Embassy for Political Affairs signing for the Ambassador) at the American Embassy in Tehran to the Department of State, 13 January 1965, n. A-370, *Women's Literacy Corps*, NARA EDU 9–1 Iran, RG 59 General Records of the Department of State, Central Foreign Policy Files.
42 13 January 1965, n. A-370, *Women's Literacy Corps*, NARA.
43 29 November 1965, n. A-368, *First Congress of the High Council of Women's Associations of Iran*, NARA.
44 Article 2 of the Women's Social Service Law, in *Education Corps*: 1970, p. 33.
45 'Sipah-i danish-i dukhtaran' in *Kayhan*, 7 Aban 1346 (29 October 1967).
46 Ministry of Education, *The Education Corps Magazine*, summer 1970, p. 34.
47 Ministry of Education, *The Education Corps Magazine*, summer 1971, p. 14.
48 'Princess' new plans to help women', in *Kayhan International*, 12 November 1967.
49 'Literacy corps', in *Kayhan International*, 26 October 1967.
50 Afkhami, *Iran*, p. 332.
51 *Ibid.*, p. 332.
52 Ministry of Education, *The Literacy Corps Magazine*, summer 1971, pp. 26–8.
53 *Ibid.*, p. 14.
54 *Ibid.*, p. 26.
55 *Ibid.*, pp. 26, 28.
56 *Ibid.*, p. 14.
57 Interviews in Tehran with Rohanghiz Lashgari, 15 May 1997; Zahra Rezai, 15 May 1997; Azizeh Ashoori, 20 May 1997; Nushir Saiai, 27 May 1997; Zahra Tanhai, 22 May 1997.
58 Ministry of Education: 1971, p. 13.
59 Interviews, Tehran, 20 and 27 May 1997.
60 W. Graves, 'Iran: desert miracle' in *National Geographic*, January 1975, picture p. 3.
61 Ministry of Education: 1970, p. 34.
62 Institute for Research and Planning in Science and Education, *Report of the Iranian delegation to the UNESCO International Conference on Education, XXXIII Session, Geneva, 15–23 September 1971, on Main Lines and Trends of Educational Development in Iran 1970–1971*, Tehran, September 1971, p. 3; The Imperial Government of Iran, *Report on Educational Development in 1971–1973 Presented to the XXXIV Session of the International Conference on Education, Geneva, September 1973*, Tehran, March 1973, p. 2; Farjad, *Education*, pp. 19–20.
63 'Paikha-yi danish dar rustaha', in *Kayhan*, 26 Khurdad 1349 (16 June 1970).
64 'Zan-i imruz, dar just va ju'i-yi azadi va kushbakhti', in *Zan-i Ruz*, 7 Bahman 1351 (27 January 1972).
65 R. Khomeini (1971) *Kashf al-Asrar* (*Revealing of Secrets*), Qum, pp. 313–14, quoted by Paidar, *Women*, p. 121.
66 Fada'iyan Islam (1939/1950) *Rahnama-yi Haqa'iq* (*The guide to the truth*), Qum, p. 56, in A.K. Ferdows, *Religion in Iranian Nationalism: The Study of the Fadaiyan-i Islam*, Ph.D. dissertation, Indiana University, quoted by Paidar, *Women*, p. 122.
67 Ministry of Education, 1971, p. 13.
68 H. Najafi and H. Hinckley (1960) *Reveille for a Persian village*, London, pp. 146–7.
69 *Ibid.*, p. 15.
70 M.R. Pahlavi (1967) *The White Revolution*, Tehran, p. 112.
71 R.J. Wiesinger (1973) *Light me a Candle. Two years of Literacy and Adult Education Work among the Women of Khuzistan*, Iran, Bombay, p. 159.

72 Interview with Aziaeh Ahoori, Tehran, 20 May 1997.
73 S.A. Wright, *Identities and Influence: Political Organisation in Dushman Ziari, Mamasari, Iran*, Ph.D. dissertation, Linacre College, Oxford 1985, p. 34.
74 Afkhami, *Iran*, pp. 336–7.
75 Interview with Zahra Tanhai Tehran, 22 May 1997, and her account (as Zahra Koohestani) in *The Literacy Corps Magazine*, 1971, p. 46.
76 A. Wafi (1998) 'I diritti umani e i cinque obiettivi della Shari'a', in A. Pacini (ed.) *L'islam e il dibattito sui diritti dell'uomo*, Turin, p. 58.
77 Interview, Tehran, 15 May 1997.
78 Interview, Tehran, 15 May 1997.
79 Interview, Tehran, 20 May 1997.
80 Interview, Tehran, 27 May 1997.
81 Interview, Tehran, 22 May 1997.
82 Interview, Tehran, 27 May 1997.

Bahartami primary school in Khosrowabad:

Literacy corpswomen Zahra Fazel, principal and teacher, decorating the school.

Literacy corpswomen

The Society for Rural Houses 10 October
1976 (800,000)

National Society of Parents and
Education 6 November 1969 (200,000)

Birth Centenary of Lord Baden Powell
22 February 1957

Iranian Girl Scouts
24 June 1968 (400,000)

20th Anniversary of Scouting in Iran
9 December 1972 (400,000)

Second National Iranian Girl Scouts'
Camp 16 July 1975 (1,2 million)

World Literacy Day
8 September 1973 (1 million)

Free Health and Education
11 September 1974 (500,00)

First Regional Seminar of Education and Welfare
7 November 1977 (2 million)

Teachers' Day
8 October 1977 (1 million)

Iranian Women's Organization
6 November 1966 (300,000)

International Literacy Symposium
8 September 1975
(1,5 million)

Stamps commemorating the Literacy Corps and the White Revolution

Formation of the
Literacy Army
15 October 1963 (300,00)

Six point reform law
26 January 1964
(300,000)

Six point reform law
26 January 1965
(300,000)

White
Revolution
26 January
1966
(300,000)

eight

From Islamization to the Individualization of Women in Post-revolutionary Iran

Azadeh Kian-Thiébaut

This chapter is largely based on personal interviews. It argues that the implementation of the shari'a in the aftermath of the 1979 revolution has paradoxically triggered the autonomization and individualization of women. Through their mobilization against the Islamization of laws and institutions, women have attempted to establish their authority in the family, as well as in political, religious, judiciary and other institutions. To this end, religious and secular female social activists have initiated the reinterpretation of Islamic laws and traditions. Women's social struggle against gender segregation has also led to a radical change in their self-perception. They no longer allow themselves to be considered only as mothers and wives. Women's new demographic, social and economic behaviour has consolidated their autonomization and individualization: they are increasingly better-educated and active in the job market; their average age of marriage is higher than before; and their fertility rate has sharply declined.

A minority of educated upper and upper-middle class women participated in the Constitutional Revolution (1906–11), and the Movement for the Nationalization of Oil under Mussadiq (1951–53). However, the 'Islamic revolution' was the first Iranian social movement to draw the massive and active participation of various social categories of women with distinct cultural and ideological aspirations (from modern to traditional, and from religious to secular). Through their collective political involvement, women powerfully attested to the failure of authoritarian modernization and the Western acculturation of the Pahlavis (1925–79), and stressed their own importance as social and political activists for the first time in Iran's history.

These women erroneously came to be considered as fervent advocates of traditionalist values of gender inequality. The reasons for this were two-fold:

127

Western observers wrongly analysed the 'Islamic' revolution as anti-modern and traditionalist, because the majority of women demonstrators were veiled; and in Western eyes, veiling and subordination correlate. The result was an ongoing irrational hostility against a stereotyped image to which Iranian women do not correspond. Sweeping generalizations that followed were thus the logical outcome of such perception, when in fact, Iranian women are actually heterogeneous in terms of their social and family backgrounds, aspirations, mode of life and demands.

In the course of the revolution, various categories of women adopted the Islamic veil for different reasons: while secular women used the veil as a symbol of national unity against the Shah's regime, the traditionalists' thick black chador symbolized their Shiʿite ideology and culture, and their aspirations to an exclusive society ruled by Islamic laws. For the Islamist youth who were influenced by the teachings of the radical religious intellectual, ʿAli Shariʿati, veiling symbolized their distinct identity and their struggle for a just and inclusive society. Shariʿati was a French-educated Third-Worldist who had a modern and militant interpretation of Shiʿism. He attempted to transform religion into the ideology of liberation in order to change society. Shariʿati also denounced the westernization policies of the Shah, and, following Frantz Fanon, proposed cultural introspection, a return to original values.[1] The following statement by an Islamist militant who is from a traditional religious middle-class background, and like many young Islamist activists was a Shariʿati follower prior to the unfolding of the revolution, demonstrates that the veiling of these women was by no means a symbol of their subordination to traditional religious views:

> Shariʿati attempted to revise religious traditions. Following his teachings, we denigrated traditions. For example, we were against pilgrimage which we considered as worshipping an idol. We considered supplication as superstitious. We regarded prayer as a means of struggle. … When I was a high-school student, I used to wear a small scarf and a short dress over my pants. Then when I started participating in the protest movement, I wore the chador. Yet, by wearing it I did not intend to cover my head or body. Like many other women what I meant to do was to mark my identity. We wore the chador as the symbol of our struggle for a just society'.[2]

The stereotyping of women in post-revolutionary Iran has also led to the undermining of their efforts to re-appropriate modernity and to provide new interpretations of religious laws and traditions in order to promote women's status. Paradoxically, the implementation of the shariʿa has made women major protagonists of social, cultural and political change, regardless of their social status and political stands. Autonomization and individualization are also outcomes of the struggle of these major protagonists who challenge institutionalized gender inequality.

During the first years of the revolution, Islamist women who considered themselves the heirs of the revolution collaborated with the Islamist state to oppress secular women. Some even achieved upward social mobility by obtaining the administrative posts of the dismissed secularists. Yet, the excessive privileges granted to men by the shari'a and the personal status law in matters of marriage, divorce, child custody after divorce, led to the dissatisfaction of the female population. Furthermore, the thrusting aside of women from the public sphere gradually led to the disillusionment of some Islamists who realized that the implemented segregational policies concerned all women regardless of their convictions. This disillusionment in turn led to the emergence of gender sensitivity among them and ultimately to their mobilization against sex discrimination. An Islamist activist who prefers to remain anonymous, maintains:

> The authorities only needed us to demonstrate in the streets, but when the revolution triumphed they wanted to send us back to domestic work. I then realized that revolutionary social activity was meaningless when women were losing their rights, and started to defend women's rights.[3]

The outbreak of the Iraq–Iran war (1980–88) mobilized the country's resources, and was a major impediment to the flourishing of debates on the condition of women. Although Islamist women contributed to war efforts, and some were recruited by the Pasdaran (revolutionary guards) and the Basij (volunteers), women's social role was not recognized by the power elite, who considered women primarily as biological reproducers and houseworkers. In addition to traditional instruments of propaganda such as mosques and Friday prayers, the state ideology on women was perpetuated by modern communication networks, especially television and cinema. As well as the media, schoolbooks were used to propagate the image of women as asocial beings who prefer to stay at home. The plight of gender-sensitive women was also overshadowed by the predominant values of self-abnegation, devotion and sacrifice, rooted in the Shi'a culture and internalized by the young volunteers (*basijis*), hundreds of thousands of whom served at the front. Moreover, the clerical and the political elite, who attributed all shortcomings and problems to the force of circumstances, used the war as a pretext to dismiss women's social problems:

> Like many others, I actively participated in war efforts. We established emotional ties with Imam Khomeini and thought that through martyrdom we would achieve communion with God. Many of us lost our loved ones in the war. ... Yet, I also realized that women's condition was alarming. Not only were they losing their rights but were also faced with immense social problems caused by the war. Female prostitution and delinquency was increasing among widows and orphans who had lost their heads of households. But each time we wanted to emphasize these social problems, the power elite restrained us under the pretext that the country was at war.[4]

During the revolutionary period (1980–86) and the war, women's attempts to highlight their sufferings did not find much echo in the state-controlled media. Back then only three women's magazines, namely *Payam-i Hajar* (edited by Azam Taliqani), *Nida* (edited by Zahra Mustafavi, Ayatullah Khomeini's daughter) and *Zan-i Ruz* were published. The first two were the organs of specific women's associations and had their own editors and staff.

Zan-i Ruz, published by the traditionalist/conservative *Kayhan* press company, was the only available forum for other Islamist women activists. Shahla Sherkat, who later founded *Zanan*, Mahbubeh Ummi, the editor of *Farzana*, Tayyibeh Iskandari, the current editor of *Zan-i Ruz*, and several others composed the editorial board and staff of this magazine in the 1980s. In the early 1990s these women finally obtained the right to publish their own magazines and to present their own ideas. Shahla Sherkat, the editor in chief of *Zanan*, one of the leading women's magazines, argues:

> I was the editor in chief of *Zan-i Ruz* for ten years. It was an invaluable experience and I think that it is thanks to this experience that *Zanan* can now serve women. But I faced limitations and had disagreements with directors of Keyhan press company. I ultimately felt that I did not have enough space for my activity. As a result, I decided to publish a different magazine and obtained the authorization to publish *Zanan* before I was dismissed from *Zan-i Ruz*. ... Now I have much more freedom and much wider contacts with women. In *Zan-i Ruz*, we were in contact only with a specific group of women, whereas now I have come to know many women intellectuals and specialists. They work with us and provide us with their knowledge of women and their problems. We also have established wider international relations. As a result of all of this I realized that despite historical, cultural, legal, or social differences, women throughout the world shared a number of problems and that in order to solve them we should use each other's experiences.[5]

With the end of the war new policies were implemented to reconstruct the devastated infrastructures and to reorganize the economy. Specialization and know-how thus gained importance. None the less, the country was faced with a great shortage of specialists, many of whom had migrated to foreign lands. Educated, secular women, who had earlier been purged from the public sphere and had now become indispensable to the implementation of 'reconstruction policies', seized the opportunity to reappear gradually in the workplace. Active secular women created their own informal groups and started to organize debates on issues relevant to the condition of women. Women's role in Iran's modern history, motherhood, employment, feminism, and strategies to adopt with regard to Muslim women activists, were among the topics discussed. Under the pressure of the emerging civil society, the government authorized relative freedom for the press, and several hundred new journals and magazines, including women's, started publication.[6] In the absence of political parties, the press plays a crucial role in presenting different cultural and political tendencies within society. Through their journals and magazines, modernist religious and secular intellectuals demand freedom of thought and expression, and the philosophical, cultural and political opening to the Western world.[7] Likewise, women started to organize, and to publish books and magazines protesting against the institutionalization of gender inequality. The scope of debates on the condition of women expanded, and conferences started to be organized on various aspects of women's and family issues. University professors, researchers, and liberal professionals who were members of secular informal groups, all participated in the running of public conferences. The first conference of this kind, entitled 'Social Participation of Women', was arranged in 1993 by Tehran's Women's Commission and a study group in the department of social sciences and humanities at Shahid Beheshti University. Several secular economists, sociologists, political scientists, artists, psychologists, lawyers, and jurists debated the economic role of women, women's rights, women's political participation, the effects of industrialization on women's status, and women's cultural and artistic activities. They also presented a critical reading of Islamic texts. Concomitant with these changes, a new generation of female Islamist social and political activists offering modern discourses and programmes has emerged. They are graduates of domestic or foreign universities and are often English speaking. Contrary to traditionalists, they are open to the outside world and share a modern reading of Islam. They argue that Islam is a dynamic religion and should be adapted to the realities of a society at which women's economic, social and political activities have become an integral part. The editors and the staff of some newly published women's journals and magazines are among them.

Zan (edited by Faizeh Hashemi-Rafsanjani) started publication in summer 1998, but was closed down in April 1999 by the Islamic revolutionary court for publishing a message from Iran's former empress, Farah Diba, and printing a cartoon that made fun of the law of blood money, which permits one who has caused loss of life to avoid retribution by compensating monetarily the family of the victim. Another publication is *Huquq-i Zanan*, which is edited by Ashraf Girami-Zadigan, the former editor of *Zan-i Ruz*. Also represented in this new generation are some deputies of the Fifth Majles (convened in 1996) including Suheila Jiludarzadeh, Fatimeh Ramizanzadeh, Marzieh Siddiqi, and Ma'sumeh Ibtikar, the vice-president in charge of the protection of environment. The increasing involvement of women in public life and their airing of their demands has gradually led to a change in the dominant ideological discourse on women. The authorities now acknowledge women's social role and are more attentive to women's specific problems.

Ayatullah Khomeini's death (in June 1989), and the revision of the constitutional law, provoked a crisis of consensus both at the societal level and among the religious and political elite regarding the leadership of a jurisconsult (*vali-yi faqih*). According to the new version of the constitution, being a source of imitation (*marja'-i taqlid*) is no longer a prerequisite for the spiritual and religious leader of the Islamic Republic (*vali-yi faqih*). Ayatullah Khamene'i, the new leader, is not a source of imitation, and has not succeeded in asserting his claim to such authority. This lack of consensus has allowed the emergence or the enforcement of modernist interpretations of Islam by some religious intellectuals and clerics, including Abdulkarim Surush, Grand Ayatullah Yusif Sani'i, and Hujjat ul-Islams Muhammad Mujtahid-Shabistari, Muhsin Kadivar, Seyyed Muhsin Saidzadeh. These intellectuals and clerics, who also publish in the widely-read magazines and journals, including *Kiyan, Rah-i Naw, Khurdad, Subh-i Imruz, Jahan-i Islam,* and *Nishat,* attempt to reconcile Islam with democracy, and to separate religion from the state. They admit that concepts of western political thought have entered Iran and have made significant changes in the political culture of the post-revolutionary Iranians who now aspire to economic, social, political and cultural progress. They also maintain that political power should acquire its legitimacy exclusively through founding its authority on the public will. In view of achieving this progress, they propose a synthesis of Islamic traditions and western modernity.[8]

These endeavours have found tremendous support among educated Islamists, especially women. Shahla Sherkat argues:

> Radical legal changes are needed to solve women's problems. Because many articles of the civil code are based on the shari'a, its reinterpretation proves necessary and women should be involved in this undertaking. Our understanding of religion varies in each historical period, and religious interpretations should account for factors of time and space.[9]

The newly published magazine *Huquq-i Zanan* prints articles to reject men's unilateral right to divorce and challenge the established views on the subject:

> To make their point, the proponents of men's right to divorce refer to the Quran, whereas no such evidence is found in the relevant Quranic verses. ... Moreover, the Quran authorizes the Prophet's wives. ... to get their divorce.[10]

Nahid Shid, an Islamic lawyer who has both a religious and a university education and has initiated several amendments to the divorce law, especially *ujrat-ul misl* (the principle that says when a man files for divorce, his wife can ask to be compensated by her husband in return for the housework she has carried out during the marriage) maintains:

> The bulk of the enforced laws can and should be changed because they are not divine orders. They are based on secondary orders. Blood money is one of them. It was determined when men were valued as warriors who contributed to the expansion of Islam, while women were devoid of such social values. Times have changed and the law should reflect this change ... This law cannot be functional in a society in which women are medical

doctors, university professors, engineers, and the like. Blood money should be the same for men and women.[11]

Religious women are also challenging men's right to polygamy. For example, *Payam-i Hâjar*, edited by Azam Taliqani, the daughter of the late radical cleric Ayatullah Mahmud Taliqani, was the first to publish an article (in 1992) refuting the legalization of polygamy and proposing a new interpretation of the *al-Nisa* verse:

> The analysis of the Quranic verse on polygamy shows that this right is recommended in some specific cases and exclusively in order to meet a social need in view of expanding social justice. ... Contrary to the state in ancient times, the modern state and its social institutions were conceived to assist needy families. Therefore, polygamy has no social function to fulfil. ... It has been shown that in reality it is pleasure rather than charity that motivates men to become polygamous.[12]

Common grievances have led to the emergence of an unprecedented gender solidarity between secular and modernist-Islamist women.[13] The editors of some women's magazines, especially those of *Zanan, Farzana,* and *Huquq-i Zanan,* demand the contribution of secular women specialists. This call for co-operation has provided both a challenge and an opportunity for secular social activists. Some secular lawyers, jurists, economists, sociologists, artists, historians, novelists and film directors have taken up the challenge and seized the opportunity to present their opinions and works through writings and interviews with these magazines. Indeed, these secular intellectuals, who were forced into isolation for several years, have adopted a new strategy of asserting their social identity through writing. These specialists discuss various aspects of gender inequality, analyse its causes and consequences, and propose solutions. They have thus contributed tremendously to the awakening of the female population. Mehrangiz Kar, a renowned lawyer who regularly contributes to the magazine *Zanan,* and has published several books on social, economic and legal issues, argues:

> When the war ended, we [secular intellectuals] felt that the social and political circumstances were less hostile to the publicizing of our opinions than during the war. We thus started publishing our writings on the condition of women and gradually entered the cultural and social realms. None the less, as secularists, we are still faced with restrictions which every now and then force us to temporary silence. Thus, before publishing our works, we first appraise the situation and only if it seems appropriate do we publicly express our ideas. We all have the impression that writing strengthens us. We feel that a force is born inside us that is stronger than the power of the proponents of gender segregation.[14]

Likewise, Shirin Ebadi a renowned jurist who was Iran's first woman to become a judge (in 1969), decided to assert her identity through writing. When the revolution unfolded, she was a court president. Following the application of the shari'a, she, like other women judges, lost her post on the grounds that women are too sensitive by nature and subject to manipulation. She was relegated to administrative work in the ministry of justice but decided to resign and work as private legal consultant:

> I was a court president until 1979. Although I had not been a political activist prior to the unfolding of the revolution, I had religious leanings and was quite optimistic about religion. Therefore, I joined the general trend and became a revolutionary. When Ayatullah Khomeini, who was in France, demanded that public sector employees oust cabinet ministers from their offices, I, along with a group of revolutionaries at the Ministry of Justice, went to the Minister's office and asked him to leave at once. Because I was the only woman of the group and was quite well-known at my work (some even said that I had a chance to become the minister of justice) the minister looked at me and said 'do you know that if the mullahs get to power the first thing they will do is dismiss you?' I said that I preferred to be a free human being rather than a judge in captivity! But after the revolution I was dismissed from my post. Back then, the clerics had not become predominant. I was not dismissed by the clerics but by my own colleagues who had a university education. ... They gave me an administrative position ... I could not bear the humiliation and after a while applied for early retirement and started working as a legal consultant. Although I earned much more than when I was a judge, I was not satisfied because my new job was not as prestigious as my previous post. ... I came to the conclusion that I should do something else to prove my social identity. ... As a woman jurist, I have always been sensitive to the issue of gender ... I thus started to write books and articles ... to show the shortcomings of the legal system.[15]

The very act of writing has strengthened the position of these women specialists and has made them role models for other women, especially the younger generation.

While women propose legal changes and present their own readings of the Qura'nic verses and Islamic laws, the actual implementation of change in the existing laws under the Islamic Republic requires recourse to *ijtihad* (interpretation of religious laws and traditions). Following the death of Mrs Amin-Isfahani, a woman *mujtahid* (doctor in jurisprudence) in the early 1980s, Iran is, for the time being, devoid of women religious authorities. The shortage of women *mujtahids* has led some religious women to create women's religious seminaries. Fatemeh Amini founded the first religious school for girls (called Maktab-i Tauhid) in Qum in 1972 with the support of the late Grand Ayatullah Kazim Shari'atmadari. She is now in charge of an independent religious seminary in Tehran called Fatima-i Zahra. She maintains:

Society needs women doctors and engineers as well as women *mujtahids*. But there is an important resistance against women attaining the degree of *ijtihad* (interpretation). Without these obstacles, which seriously hinder their training, we could have had at least fifty women *mujtahids* since the revolution. We believe that according to the Quran, men and women are equal. ... Our aim here is to educate women *mujtahids* as well as women capable of finding solutions to women's problems, including their social problems. We are independent and have over 250 students, many of whom are also university students. Like at other religious seminaries, they study for four years. In addition to ordinary curricula, which are common to other religious seminaries, we also offer courses on public health, ecology, and the like. These are taught by university professors. Our goal is to contribute to women's development by giving impetus to their creativity, thereby also increasing their self-esteem.[16]

Young women, including university or high-school students, increasingly seek religious training and enrol in religious seminaries. In 1996, of 62731 students in religious seminaries, 9995 or 16 per cent were women.[17] During the training of women *mujtahids*, the issuing of religious edicts (*fatva*) is limited to qualified men. Thus, the support of high-ranking clerics, the only authorities who can bring about change in the existing laws through new interpretations, proves necessary. In order to obtain their support, both the editors of women's magazines, and secular women jurists and lawyers are increasingly interacting and discussing with clerics and religious intellectuals in an attempt to persuade them of the justice of their cause. Women's efforts have shown results for some specialists of Islamic law and jurisprudence, including Ayatullahs Yusif Sani'i and Bujnurdi, Hujjat al-Islams Muhsin Sa'id-Zadeh and Muhaqiq-Damad; and Husayn Mihrpur and Ahmad Akuchakian now contribute to these debates through their writings or interviews with women's magazines. They often endorse women's proposals to adapt Islamic laws to the realities of Iranian society in which women are active in social, cultural, economic, religious and political fields. Some go even farther and encourage women to mobilize and to defend their rights. For example, Hujjat al-Islam Muhaqiq-Damad publicly criticized women for their lack of mobilization when special civil courts which exclusively dealt with family cases were closed down:

I blame women, including journalists, Majlis deputies, and specialists who did not rise up against the closing down of these courts which defended women's rights. You women did not even write an article or organize a meeting to protest and defend your rights. Today, if a woman takes her case to the court, her problems will be dealt with in the same courts that criminals are being judged, i.e. in courts where there is no specialist in women's rights. In these courts, the same judges who deal with the case of a criminal also deal with the case of a woman who has family problems.[18]

He then criticized his fellow country men for their misinterpretation of the Quran:

> Islam is the religion of justice, compassion, righteousness, and women's rights. A man who lies or betrays, a man who is authoritarian or a murderer is spiteful. When did the Prophet say that such a man can take four wives? Unfortunately, all they [men] have understood from Islam is that they are entitled to polygamy.[19]

Likewise, following the late Ayatullah Muqaddas-Ardibili, Grand Ayatullah Yusuf Sani'i argued that Islam does not forbid women from becoming judges or *mujtahids*, and that they can deliver religious edicts and become political leaders.[20] Ayatullah Mar'ashi, the head of the penal laws revision committee declared that according to the existing laws women could become judges.[21] As a response to women's social struggle, Ayatullah Khamene'i stipulated that 'Islamic principles on such issues as employing women as judges or in other posts should be studied and discussed'. There has been a lot of debate on women's issues, but only small steps have been taken, and there is much work to be done.[22] It was also on the issue of women that the Leader and other senior clerics, including fervent traditionalists like Ayatullah Jannati, Tehran's temporary Imam of Friday Prayers and the head of the Council of Guardians, criticized the Afghani Taleban as 'un-Islamic', and said they gave Islam a bad name by stopping women from working out of the home and girls from attending schools.[23]

Among women's demands, those which do not contradict the Qur'an are met more easily than those which are incompatible with the Qur'anic verses. If women's aspirations to social, political, economic and cultural activities are about to be met, it is because the Qur'an does not prohibit such activities for women. This is clearly not the case with the Islamic veil which will remain compulsory, even though it is now clear that 20 years after the revolution, and despite severe punishments, including imprisonment, compulsory veiling has not obtained the intended results. Women, especially the younger generation who are born or raised under the Islamic Republic, increasingly utter their discontent and oppose compulsory veiling by leaving a lock of hair out, or putting on make-up, or modifying their long dark dress to give it a modern form. The refusal of these women to respect the Islamic dress code and the increasing number of 'badly veiled' women, which testifies to women's rejection of Islamist regulations, has in turn led the traditionalists to revive debates on 'Western cultural invasion and its promoters in Iran'. Faced with women's opposition against the main symbol of Islamist politics, and because veiling has become a political stake, the Organization of the Islamic Propaganda opted for a moderate stand by organizing a clothing exhibition in February 1993 at which colourful cloths and veils were substituted for thick black Islamic veils. This moderate stand was not approved by the traditionalists who severely criticized such colourful clothing, and argued that it would jeopardize the traditional chador (the most salient symbol of the revolution) which they unsuccessfully attempted to impose on women. Several women candidates for the Fifth Majlis reported that they were denied qualification by the Council of Guardians on the grounds that they did not wear the black chador. Shahla Habibi, then chair of the Office of Women's Affairs (created in 1992 as an offshoot of the presidential bureau), reacted to the traditionalists' attempts to impose the chador and maintained that it was not the only possible veil. *Zanan* took a stand against compulsory veiling by publishing on its cover page the picture of a 'badly-veiled' renowned woman movie director, who was also wearing Ray Ban type sun glasses. The heated debates on the issue of veiling as a political stake are far from reaching an end. Horse riding and outdoor cycling also became political issues when traditionalists announced that these sporting activities should be prohibited for women. As a reaction, many women, even those who had never touched a bicycle in their entire life, counteracted the traditionalist discourse through airing demands for outdoor cycling. Faizeh Rafsanjani, member of the Fifth Majlis, president of the Islamic Countries' Solidarity Sports Council, vice-president of the National Olympic Committee, and a member of the Islamic Republic's High Council for Women's Sport, endorsed their demand. She courageously spoke out against traditionalists and defended women's outdoor cycling:

> Women's outdoor cycling is neither illegal nor illicit. ... It has become a political issue because those who opposed it bestowed a political dimension on it. After all, their opposition was beneficial to outdoor cycling for now there is a significant demand for it.[24]

As a result of her courageous stand, she has gained tremendous popularity among women, especially the youth, but has simultaneously become the pet hate of fundamentalists. Advocates of traditionalism and fervent opponents of women's active presence in the public sphere, have published satirical articles and caricatures against her in their press.

The increasing social and political activities of Islamist women who reject traditionalist values and demand modern readings of Islam, has led many secular intellectuals, including Shirin Ebadi, Mehrangiz Kar, Nahid Musavi, a journalist, and Zhaleh Shaditalab, a sociologist and a university professor, unanimously to maintain that, despite regressions in women's rights, the revolution has radically changed the self-perception of women from traditionalist backgrounds and has ameliorated their status. Nahid Musavi argues:

> Islamist women are no longer confined to the private sphere of the home. They enrol in universities, actively participate in social, economic and political life and try to promote their status. The scope of change in their self-perception and status becomes clear when compared to traditionalist-religious norms and values according to which women are not allowed to leave the home without their father's or husband's authorization. Likewise, they are not supposed to talk with men who do not belong to

their family. The presence of several Islamist women in the Majlis, some of whom are outspoken, shows that despite the regressions these women have had important achievements.[25]

Mehrangiz Kar, whose secular and feminist stands have made her a renowned figure, summarizes the evolution of Islamist women:

> Compared to my generation in post-revolutionary Iran, girls, especially those who belong to religious-traditional families, are very ambitious. They have goals and do everything to achieve them. ... Influenced by economic and religious factors, traditional structures are undergoing change. Traditional families who, under the Shah, opposed statutory changes, saying that they corrupted women, now see religious authorities declaring that women's education or activity outside the family is compatible with religion. This new discourse is a consequence of Islamic women's participation in the revolution and war efforts and their rejection of their traditional roles. Their political involvement in the revolution and war efforts led to the strengthening of the Islamic regime. Yet, it simultaneously legitimized the demands of these women for the recognition of their social role, and they succeeded in forcing the power elite to officially recognize this. They continued airing additional demands to promote their status in both the private and the public spheres. As a result, traditionalist-religious families underwent change. Then, their daughters who were gradually involved in public life, went even farther, criticizing legal shortcomings and demanding equal rights with men. They keep telling the authorities that they supported the Islamic regime to acquire their rights, and that they are determined to make their voices heard. Because they refer to Islam, no religious or political authority can easily oppose or dismiss their legitimate demands. ... The economic crisis and inflation have led to the decline in the real income of households, the majority of which relied on a single source of income. As a consequence, the financial contribution of women has proved necessary. This has led fathers or husbands who were against their daughters' or wife's activity outside of the home to seek a job for them. The economic crisis has thus contributed to women's financial independence.[26]

In addition to the economic crisis, the privileges granted to men by the shari'a, especially their exclusive right to divorce and to polygamy, have caused anxiety among women, leading many to seek a job in order to become financially independent from their husbands. Several magazines have published stories of women who depended on their husbands for their survival and were abandoned after many years of marriage with no financial resources. The following is the story of a woman whose husband is polygamous. Although she is legally entitled to apply for a divorce, she refrains from doing so because she is financially dependent on her husband:

My husband and I were married eighteen years ago and have two children. He never authorized me to work outside of the home, and I accepted to be a housewife. Many years ago and without my consent he was married to a second wife and has a child with her. When I found out I protested and asked him what he planned to do. He replied that he wanted to keep both of us. I told him that I could not bear the humiliation. He said I could get my divorce and leave. Now I understand why he didn't want me to work. He wanted to keep me at home, he wanted to keep me isolated. He wanted to make sure that I would be forced to bear this life ... I have no job or revenues to take care of my children and myself. Therefore, I have no other choice but to remain his wife and live with him.[27]

In the words of Muhammad, a 55 year-old polygamous notary who pretends to have good relationships with both of his wives:

It is obvious that men want to dominate their wives. Women's economic dependence on men is the best way to guarantee men's superiority over women. Women's economic activity makes them independent and avoids their domination by men.

For many educated, working women, economic activity has become an integral part of their identity. These women who establish social relationships through their activity outside of the home, perceive work as a means to gaining autonomy and respect. Like many of her counterparts, Nahid, 32, who works for Isfahan's municipality, argues:

I have been working since the age of 18 and am used to work. I cannot stand staying at home. I think that housework is burdensome whereas activity outside of the home makes me feel that I am part of society. ... I absolutely need my financial independence. I cannot stand being paid by my husband ... I am also persuaded that my financial independence and my participation in breadwinning have earned me autonomy and decision-making authority. Besides, both my husband and my extended family respect me.

Women are also challenging traditional impediments through adopting modern demographic and social behaviour, thereby consolidating their autonomization and individualization. The increase in women's average age of marriage, the sharp decline in the fertility rate, better education and a general increase in women's activity, are among the unintended consequences of the modernization policies of the Islamic regime. Following the revolution, urban areas saw a rapid growth. The number of towns increased from 373 in 1976 to 614 in 1996; 47 of these have more than 100000 inhabitants, compared to 23 before the revolution. As a result, the majority of the population (61 per cent) now live in urban areas. To contain rural exodus, rural areas have been modernized. The majority of villages now have roads, electricity, drinking water, schools and dispensaries.

Although the Islamic regime did not succeed in curbing rural-to-urban migration, the gap between town and country has narrowed, as illustrated by literacy rates among the younger generation in both urban and rural areas: 93 per cent of the age group 6–24 are literate (97 per cent of males and 96 per cent of females in urban areas; 93 per cent of males and 83 per cent of females in rural areas).

With the readoption by the government of family planning and birth control in 1988, the birth rate has diminished sharply. The results of the first national census of the population under the Islamic Republic (in 1986) revealed a total increase of fifteen million in the population since 1976, the last national census of the population under the Shah. The annual population growth rate thus averaged 3.9 per cent, one of the highest in the world. The economic crisis, the lack of resources to respond to the needs of the young generation (in matters of education, health, employment, etc.) forced the government to adopt projects to diminish this birth rate, despite clerical opposition and the pro-birth traditions in Islam. The annual population growth rate is now 1.5 per cent, and the average number of children per family is now 3.2, as against 7.2 before the revolution,[28] 67 per cent of Iranian women now use contraceptive devices. Urbanization, a better education and the increasing participation of women in the job market (which was the result of the economic crisis, urban life, and women's drive to participate actively in the public sphere), have also led to an increase in the average age of marriage for women from 19.75 before the revolution to 22 in 1996. Women are also increasingly pursuing higher education. In 1996, of 966970 enrolled students, 393609 or 41 per cent were women. In 1998–99, for the first time since women had entered university in 1939 (five years after the creation of Tehran University), 52 per cent of the students admitted were women. This new social and demographic reality has contributed to the individualization of women, including the uneducated, who now tend to develop personal projects and think of strategies to achieve them. The following statement uttered by a 38 year-old illiterate rural migrant woman reveals the emergence of individual identities:

> Women should think of themselves and decide for what they want to do with their life. ... We should try to obtain what we want by mobilizing our own resources. We should not rely on other people's assistance, not even our families because if we do so we will be reduced to women in care, and will also allow others to intervene in our private life, making decisions for us ... I am very proud of myself because I work and earn my life. I cherish my independence even though being a janitor is not prestigious! I would have liked to work as a state employee in the administration. But I know I can't attain such a position or status because I'm illiterate and will never succeed in finding a job like this. Women who occupy these posts are all university graduates. For this very reason, I always tell my children that they should study well to become somebody. ... Despite financial problems, I

will never go back to my village. I like urban life. Here I feel I'm a part of the society. ... Educated active women who have authority, are financially independent, and provide their children with good education are my role models. I wanted to be like them, so I told my husband that I did not want more than two children, and that I wanted to work.

The rule of political Islam, which has proved incompatible with the realities of modern Iranian society, has led Islamic and secular women to join hands, re-appropriate modernity, and challenge institutionalized gender inequality. They emphasize their activity in the public realm and impose their own interpretations of Islamic laws and traditions to initiate legal reforms and modify traditional cultural perceptions of women. In doing so, they form an identity which is no longer founded on traditions. The result is that they now perceive themselves as women/individuals rather than exclusively as mothers and wives. A new self-consciousness and a desire to exist as an individual have emerged among them. By questioning traditional gender roles and identities these women are also constructing their own religious models, thereby acquiring autonomy *vis-à-vis* male religious authorities. In this undertaking, they both demonstrate the limits of political Islam and advocate the opening of religion to modernity.

Notes

1 For a discussion of Shari'ati's ideas see among others, Brad Hanson, 'The "Westoxication" of Iran: Depictions and Reactions of Behrangi, Al-e Ahmad and Shari'ati', *International Journal of Middle East Studies*, 15, 1 (January 1983).
2 Personal interview, Tehran, July 1994.
3 Personal interview, Tehran, July 1994.
4 Personal interview, Tehran, September 1994.
5 Personal interview, Tehran, September 1994.
6 Their number is now approximately 900. For a discussion see Zarir Merat, 'Les revues intellectuelles: l'embryon d'une agora', in Azadeh Kian-Thiébaut (ed.) *L'élection de Khatami: le printemps iranien?* Special issue of *Les Cahiers de l'Orient*, 1 (1998), pp. 87–102.
7 They include, *Kiyan, Zanan, Iran-i Farda, Adina* (prohibited from publishing in 1999) *Kilk, Guftugu, Jami'ih-i Salim* (prohibited from publishing in 1998), *Dunya-i Sukhan, Nigah-i Nau, Payam-i Imruz.*
8 See Azadeh Kian-Thiébaut, 'Les stratégies des intellectuels religieux et clercs iraniens face à la modernité occidentale', *Revue Française de Science Politique*, 6 (1997), pp. 776–97. And 'L'islam est-il incompatible avec la démocratie?', *Etudes,* September 1995, pp. 161–7.
9 Personal interview, Tehran, September 1994. See also the editorial of *Zanan,* I, 1 (February 1992) pp. 2–3.
10 Ali Andisheh, 'Farhang va talaq' (Culture and divorce), *Huquq-i Zanan,* 8. March 1999, pp. 16–17.
11 Interview, Tehran, February 1996.

12 Forouq Ebn-Eddin, 'Luzum-Islah-i Qavanin-i Talaq, T'addud-i Zujat va Hizanat' (The necessity for the reform of laws concerning divorce, polygamy, and child custody), *Payam-i Hajar*, 19 Shahrivar 1371/10 September 1992, pp. 28–9.

13 For the alliance between secular and Islamist women, see among others, Ziba Mir-Hosseini (1996) 'Stretching the Limits: A Feminist Reading of the Shari'a in Post-Khomeini Iran', in Mai Yamani (ed.), *Feminism and Islam: Legal and Literary Perspectives*, London, pp. 285–319. And Azadeh Kian, 'Des femmes iraniennes contre le clergé: islamistes et laïques pour la première fois unies', *Le Monde Diplomatique*, November 1996.

14 Personal interview, Tehran, July 1994.

15 Personal interview, Paris, March 1995.

16 Personal interview, Tehran, October 1994.

17 The 1996 National Census of the Population and Housing, p. 77–81.

18 See his speech in a seminar at the Tehran University, published in *Zan-i Ruz*, 1559, 19 Khurdad 1357/9 June 1996, pp. 4–5.

19 Mohaqeq Damad's speech in a seminar at Tehran University, pubished in *Zan-i Ruz*, 1559, 19 Khurdad 1357/9 June 1996, pp. 4–5.

20 See Ayatullah Yusuf Sani'i's interview with the magazine *Payam-i Zan*, published by the Qum religious seminary, n.63, Khurdad 1376/May 1997, pp. 6–9.

21 Zanan, 5, 32 (January–February 1997), p. 62.

22 Quoted by the state-run Tehran radio, Reuter, Tehran, 18 November 1997.

23 Ibid.

24 Personal interview, Tehran, July 1996.

25 Personal interview, Tehran, July 1996.

26 Personal interview, Tehran, September 1994.

27 Fatemeh Qasimzadeh, 'Zanan dar Dadgah, Mardan dar Dadgah' (Women in the court, men in the court), *Jami'ih-i Salim*, 24 January 1996, pp. 45–6.

28 Marie-Ladier Fouladi, 'Aperçu démographique', in Azadeh Kian-Thiébaut (ed.), *L'élection de Khatami, le printemps iranien?*, special issue of *Les Cahiers de l'Orient*, 1 (1998) p. 11.

nine

The Politicization of Women's Religious Circles in Post-revolutionary Iran

Azam Torab

Based on anthropological fieldwork conducted in 1993 in post-revolutionary Iran, this article describes the organization and politicization of women's religious circles which increased rapidly in the years leading up to the revolution of 1978-9. The focus is on the activities of rival female preachers, around whom the circles were formed, and who became increasingly popular, gaining large numbers of adherents among women.[1]

I argue that the upsurge in women's religious activities must be seen as part of an increasingly politicized religious environment rather than any essential 'Islamic' world-view or so-called fundamentalism. In the context of the debates about the relationship of religion and state, religious gatherings have become forums for demonstrating political affiliations as well as prayer and worship, resulting in fragmentation among women's religious circles. This interplay of religious practice and 'politics' is part of women's bid for political participation in a field which cannot be challenged so easily by a male-centred regime that defines itself on the same grounds. I use 'politics' in the sense of a bargaining process among several forces or contending groups over rules and discourses.[2] Despite the state's attempts at religious monopoly, women's religious meetings often work as counter discourses to state ideology, rather than being a channel for it, even if there are some overlaps. I argue, therefore, for a view of religious gatherings as of gatherings in any other social and cultural arena, where individuals struggle over social accomplishment and legitimate a definition of their social reality.

Neighbourhoods of piety

My introduction to women's religious gatherings called *jalasa* was through an established and respected preacher in south Tehran and whom I will call Mrs Umid. When I first asked her permission to attend a *jalasa* led by her, she asked me about the type of *jalasa* I was interested in for my research and proceeded to give me an account of the motives and different levels of competence of female preachers who preside over *jalasa*. She first talked about those whom she called 'revolutionary' (*inqilabi*) and who she said had become 'official spokespersons' (*sukhangu-yi daulat, hukumati,* 'governmental') and 'part of the establishment' (*qati-yi urganha shudand,* 'mixed in' with the establishment). Some others, she said, resembled the majority of uneducated dirge cantors (*rauza-khan*). Finally there were those who, she said, were educated, not materialistic and who taught 'the language of the Qur'an' rather than 'merely the Arabic language' taught in schools. Their sole aim was, she said, to be a guide (*rahnama*), and to fight against superstition (*khurafat*) and innovation (*bid'at*).

Mrs Umid's idioms of distinction made me aware of how people defined themselves politically and that *jalasa* were contested forums. She herself came across as an orthodox preacher, though interestingly one with independent views. After giving me the address of her next meeting, Mrs Umid cautioned me to appear with the proper *hijab*: the black chador and opaque black stockings. Correctly assuming that I did not normally dress that way, she alluded to our different social circumstances and the city's north–south divide. Mrs Umid drew variously on this divide as a way of locating her standpoint. I therefore begin with the city's division, not as a 'setting' or 'background', but as an integral part of the social interactions in my subsequent account.

The city divided

Tehran's marked social, economic and political divisions are both striking and well-documented.[3] The more affluent high level bureaucrats and professionals live by choice in the western-style residential northern parts of the city. The more traditional southern areas, where Mrs Umid lived, are inhabited by small traders and retailers, skilled workers, artisans and lower income salaried employees. Even further south live the working class and migrant populations of semi- and unskilled labourers. And coming from the north, I could not help noticing women covered in the black chador, instead of the post-revolutionary headscarf and overgarment (*mantu-rusari*) common in the north.

After the revolution of 1978–79 there were plans to desegregate the city. Revolutionary rhetoric radically challenged the prevailing social differences which were one of the key issues that had led to the revolution.[4] Ayatullah Khomeini's quest for 'social justice' (*'idalat-i ijtima'i*) became the maxim of the revolution. The more radical political factions of the Republic, whom Mrs Umid referred to as 'revolutionary' (*inqilabi*), called themselves *maktabi* (doctrinaire, ideologically committed, from *maktab*, school of thought), a label that disguised many hues within.[5] Their ardent supporters championed the cause of the masses with a language of class-warfare and oppositional slogans such as 'down-towner'/'up-towner' (*pa'in-i shahri/bala-yi shahri*), the 'oppressed masses'/the 'powerful elite' (*mustaz'afin/mustakbarin*) and 'party of God'/'idol worshippers' (*hizbullahi/taghuti*).[6] In compliance with the ideals of social justice, a series of populist measures were introduced,[7] but despite a certain amount of mobility, the north–south divide continues to exist.[8]

The enforcement of the dress-code or *hijab* (modesty) after the revolution was in part an attempt to replace markers of difference by dress, although it was widely propagated as a preserver of public morality and modesty. During the Shah's era, the chador was a highly conspicuous marker of social distinction along class lines. Those who wore a chador were derided by the 'west-toxicated' (*gharb-zada*) middle classes as '*ummul* (pejoratively 'traditional').[9] None the less, the enforcement of *hijab* by the Islamic Republic encountered widespread resistance, including by many pious women who themselves insisted on *hijab*. Their reproach was directed at the ideological manipulation of a practice which they perceived to be the most visible marker of social distinction and respect between themselves and the secular or impious. The chador was in effect a 'gatekeeper' to Mrs Umid's circles, without which they would never admit anyone into their midst. In persisting in their mode of dress, they wished to assert the moral superiority and exclusivity of their style of life. They did not want the state to redefine this for them.[10]

The claim to moral superiority operated as a powerful form of self-validation in the context of persisting social and economic inequalities. Conversations and discussions during the *jalasa* revealed a sharp contrast between the perceived reality of their daily lives and the hopes and illusions that they had harboured under the revolutionary maxim of 'social justice'. The feeling of malaise was wide-ranging: black market prices and endless queues for mundane daily necessities (bread, milk, washing powder, medicine and many more) due to shortages caused by the war; galloping inflation and the poor state of the economy; problems of health care and housing; the creation of a new privileged class of elites; a continued lack of freedom of expression. There was also sadness and embitterment for the loss of loved ones in the war. The distress felt by the relatives was aggravated by the limit set to public expressions of grief by the discourse of 'martyrdom in the name of Islam' as a highly prized ideal. Mothers of martyrs had to be celebrated for raising sons who were prepared to die for their faith. The majority of 'martyrs' had been recruited from down-town, as is evident from the numerous street names in the neighbourhoods, each of which had been renamed in memory of a martyr who had lived in that street.

The failure of the revolution to use its potential to shift social boundaries effectively has been a cause of tension, even hostility, between north and south, and in certain contexts, made it all the more important to insist on difference.

Mrs Umid was proud to identify herself and her followers as 'down-towners'. Her language of contest was replete with sardonic comments, which she used playfully during the gatherings – 'We the third class' (*tabaqa-yi-sih*), 'We the 'traditionally backward' who wear the chador' (*'ummul-i chaduri*) – conjured up images of the 'westernized up-towners' who, before the revolution, had used these negative phrases to describe women like herself.

A north-south division along social and economic lines is too simple. As Mrs Umid's telephone statement indicated, there were many internal political divisions within her neighbourhoods, as within the entire city space. As I shall show, the political behaviour of women's *jalasa* circles cannot be understood simply in terms of 'class' (an abstract category). Nor can it be said that the 'religious' character of the *jalasa* arises from any single religious 'world-view'. Rather, I argue that the politicization of the *jalasa* relates more to the quasi-institutional networks of the circles formed around preachers like Mrs Umid, and arises from a complex intersection of variables such as gender, age, education, political interests and strategies of individuals, as well as 'class' positions, at a particular historical juncture.[11]

The formation and the organization of the *jalasa* circles

It is not easy to map the beginnings, frequency and configuration of women's religious circles. By contrast to men's *hay'at*, which are named associations with formal membership and are well-documented,[12] there is a dearth of research and information on women's religious circles and activities. With the so-called religious revival in the years leading up to the revolution of 1979,[13] there was a rapid increase in women's religious activities alongside the astonishing growth from the 1960s of men's religious associations, which were crucial in instigating the revolution.[14] Significantly, they tended to be based in the less-privileged down-town quarters, which have been centres of protest and rebellion in the modern political history of Iran. At a time of political uncertainty, religious leaders gained adherents, *jalasa* gained momentum alongside an astounding boom in female preachers and other religious 'professionals' such as Qur'an teachers and reciters, and cantors of dirges and eulogies for Shi'i saints. There was also a substantial increase in publications and sale of religious books, such as books of supplications and the Qur'an.[15]

With the proliferation of religious activities in the 1960s, women began to form distinct religious circles around the *jalasa*. I use the term 'circle' to avoid any conception of a neatly bounded solidarity 'group'. The women's *jalasa* circles were comparable to men's *hay'at*, but they were characterized by relative flexibility without formal membership. They were also structurally and economically independent from men's religious groups. The meetings I attended in Mrs Umid's neighbourhoods were generally sponsored on a monthly basis by a few individual women in each circle who had sufficient space and the material means to do so. Some had been sponsoring *jalasa* on a specific day of the month for over 20 years. The gatherings were usually held on an open-house basis (*'umumi*), often rotated from house to house on an itinerant basis (*jalasa-yi sayyar*), making a daily circuit from house to house of the *jalasa* circle concerned throughout the year. Others were held on a fixed basis (*jalasa-yi sabit*), usually in a mosque or in religious institutes called *Husainiyya,* which some women had created in their homes (see below).

People generally heard about home-based gatherings by word of mouth, or, on important religious anniversaries, also by a suspended flag (green or black) outside the front door. Although *jalasa* were open-house and designated as 'public' (*'umumi*), this ethos of openness stood in tension with the desire of some circles, such as Mrs Umid's, for exclusivity and a certain amount of closure *vis-à-vis* outsiders. Unfamiliar newcomers, such as myself, were welcomed with a degree of caution and were subjected to indirect scrutiny. A *jalasa* circle's separateness from other circles was marked by both choice of a preacher and terminology. Each *jalasa* circle centred on a powerful freelance female preacher like Mrs Umid. They were the focal axes of the *jalasa* circles and acted as a moral and religious guide. The women of each circle who regularly attended each other's meetings referred to each other by the term '*jalasa*-fellow' ('same', '*ham-jalasa*'). The prefix 'same' (*ham*) assumes a certain closeness and moral unity in each circle, marking its separateness from other circles. Arguably the treatment of everybody as if they were equal is a subtle reproduction of inequality. Indeed, the social prestige of preachers and sponsors *(bani)* was considerable. A preacher's popularity was reflected in the number of followers and high attendance at her gatherings. Home-based meetings could easily attract over 100 women, as with those led by Mrs Umid, while mosque or institute-based meetings would attract several hundred women. Popular preachers had engagements every day of the year. On major religious anniversaries they were invited to preside over several gatherings a day, so that they had to decline some invitations.

When the women held their meetings, men were absent or kept out of sight. The meetings usually took place in the early afternoons, a time when their husbands or other male members of their households were least likely to be at home. This radical spatial segregation with unrelated men was less rigidly maintained in the homes in the north of the city. Men's religious associations also held their meetings by rotation in the homes of their members throughout the year, but mosques and the preacher's pulpit (*mimbar*) are the centre of men's religious activities.

Even though mosques are considered to be the central institutions for all worshippers, they are primarily masculinized spaces. Women must enter by a side entrance, are assigned a peripheral space, may not occupy the pulpit to preach, and may listen to prayers and sermons of male preachers only over a loudspeaker. Religious rules forbid women entry during menstruation, which is commonly conceived of as being the source of female pollution. The denial of equal access to communal centres of worship is an example of the radical

home teachers, Qur'an reciters and cantors of eulogy or dirges. Despite the recent measure of recognition gained by some female preachers, only male clergy may interpret religious laws and perform important daily functions, such as leading prayer and performance of the rites of life course ceremonies (marriage, divorce, funeral). The designation for female preacher is 'speaker' (*guyanda*, from *guftan*, to speak, to talk) or simply 'madam' (*khanum*, also woman, Mrs) Their male counterparts are designated *va'iz* (from *v-'-z*, to interpret). Moreover, prestigious religious titles are reserved for men who act as spiritual and moral leaders. These include honorific titles like *marja'-i taqlid* ('source of emulation'), *hujjat al-islam* ('proof of Islam'), *ayatullah* ('Sign of God') and *mujtahid* ('authority' in jurisprudence and theology), men who define the religious laws which shape everyday life. A woman can in theory become a *mujtahid*, but only one woman in recent times, Mrs Amin from Isfahan (d. 1977) is known to have been allowed this title. Thus, despite the encouragement of institutionalized women's religious education, there is still a great deal of ambivalence towards their religious professionalization.

The state's interest in women's religious education is complex. It can only be understood in the context of the secularism of the Shah's regime, which the clergy perceived as a threat to their social and moral order, in particular regarding their understandings of gender roles and values.[20] Secularized women of the Shah's era had to be 'civilized', not only by proper 'dress' (i.e. veiling), but through discipline and control of their thought and conduct. In this sense, women's access to religious education is related to the official character of that education, as a channel for state ideology. This ideology is grounded in the gender bias inherent in dominant Islamist discourses on *'aql/nafs*. *'Aql* is usually translated as reason and rationality, which, as Nancy Tapper argues,[21] has wider implications of social responsibility; *nafs* is the animal part of human nature and includes passion, lust, desire. Many religious scholars often use the attributes of 'reason' and 'emotion' in a highly gendered way. They argue that women's reasoning capacity is overrruled by emotion, which justifies laws that treat women as legal and economic dependents, while associating men with authority, control of resources and social prestige ('honour'). They argue that men and women may be equal before God, but they have different physical, emotional and mental capacities, and that as a result, men and women have different potentials, rights and responsiblities. In effect, the dominant legal discourse denies women control over many aspects of their own lives.

Any authoritative discourse creates, even if inadvertently, the seeds for resistance and contestation. Eickelman offers insights into the interplay between advanced education and religious activism.[22] He argues that, despite claims to reinstating some 'authentic' traditions, religious activists or 'fundamentalists' inadvertently create new forms of religious understanding and action through a process which tends to 'objectify' religion. There is now an increasing volume of literature which discerns a tendency to 'pragmatism' and 'rationalization' of religion among 'Islamist' women who advocate their own gender interests and the emergence of a self-ascribed 'Islamic/ist feminism' in Iran.[23] The encouragement of religious education has in practice not led to the desired enforcement of official ideals which institutionalize gendered inequalities. Despite its ideological nature, the opportunities created for advanced religious education have strengthened a 'feminist' view among younger women who advocate their own interests. As an independent preacher with views of her own, Mrs Umid was highly critical of the ideological nature of this mass religious training. She had indicated this in our first conversation. For her, faith was not something to be questioned or reasoned with. We shall see, however, that this view did not preclude intellectual activity and novel interpretations of texts by her.

The varying levels of education and training of preachers constituted one of the main underlying sources of tension among them. They ranged from the older, theologically untutored women to the many younger, theologically-trained women. They had not gained their authority equally. Some had done so on the basis of openings provided by the state. Mrs Umid, like others of her generation, had sought training in the traditional way at home, in turn selecting and training younger women by example in her style of leadership, during the gatherings which she led. These older women resented the sudden flood of younger, theologically-trained preachers. Mrs Umid denounced the younger generation as ideological 'newcomers' (*taza majlisi shudaha*, 'those who have become newly part of *jalasa*'). In her view, they were not sufficiently grounded in the religious source books to be able to offer informed commentaries and explain the precepts, thus misleading people who did not generally study the books themselves. This resentment may have been partly connected to a perceived threat. Younger women were eroding the monopoly which older local preachers had hitherto maintained over textual interpretation. In addition, they were moving up the religious hierarchy by virtue of their formal training and official recognition, rather than through judgement, selection and the protection of the older generation, thereby diminishing the latter's sphere of influence. The competitive climate was aggravated by the possibility of shifts in allegiance by followers, and by the flood of a range of other women who have gained popular followings as intermediaries for vows and supplications.

Mrs Umid had to contend with six other 'established' female preachers, and several less prominent ones, in her neighbourhoods. Rivalries among them were not always explicit, for such behaviour was theoretically reprimanded in the religious sphere where humility and modesty were supposed to prevail. The effectiveness of a preacher depended on observing these rules. It was evident in such unassuming statements about their own qualifications as, 'I am only a guide', as Mrs Umid said, adhering to the rules she herself helped to construct. But modesty was only part of a more complex pattern. Indeed, the conduct of the female preachers was not unlike that of the male preachers in the local mosques who competed with each other for attendance. In both instances, fame rested on the invited preacher and prayer leader in charge. In this sense, *jalasa* circles were more like networks of political alliances centred on a single woman, and thus is similar to men's religious associations, contradicting the categorical images of competitive males and passive women presented in summary accounts of Muslim social and political relations.[24]

The politicization of *jalasa*

The upsurge of the *jalasa* and the increasing numbers of women who attended must be seen as part of an increasingly politicized religious environment in the years leading up to the revolution of 1979. Piety and political opinions were no longer an individual's own affair. *Jalasa* contrast sharply with previous accounts of a range of women's collective rituals in Iran, which have mostly been dismissed by the commentators or the religious establishment as marginal, domestic and of little significance except to women themselves: they were perceived as places where women pursued goals as 'women'.[25] *Jalasa* were important forums for demonstrating not only one's piety, but significantly also for rallying support for the revolution, enabling female preachers to wield a degree of political influence. This was a novel opportunity for women of a certain social background to participate in politics. Many of the *jalasa* circles, including Mrs Umid's, had supported the clergy against the Shah's regime. After the revolution, however, tensions had surfaced during the *jalasa* following disillusionment with expectations of social justice raised by the revolution. Differences also surfaced between rival preachers over their understanding of the revolution and the nature of a religious revival based on diverse political theories of just leadership.

One of the key issues of the revolution was the relationship between religious and temporal authority. The fall of the Shah and the collapse of the Pahlavi regime gave rise to the integration of religion into the state and a conflation of religious and political leadership. Crucial in bringing about the 1979 revolution was the millennial doctrine of the Hidden Imam (*Imam-i Ghaib*), the Twelfth Imam of the Shi'a (b. 255 AH/868 AD), who, according to Shi'i doctrine, did not die but disappeared from the sight of ordinary people in the 'Great Occultation' (*Ghaibat-i Kubra*), in order to reappear at the end of time (*Ruz-i Ma'ad*, 'the Promised Day'). Until such time, he is 'the Lord of the Ages' (*Sahib-i Zaman*). Belief in his imminent reappearance to bring justice, when oppression and corruption reach a high level, is a fundamental tenet of Twelver Shi'ism. This belief theoretically denies legitimacy to any form of political power or government by temporal rulers, on the grounds that this would be a usurpation of the prerogatives of the Hidden Imam.[26]

Although the doctrine of the Mahdi is a fundamental tenet of Twelver Shi'ism, it has undergone re-evaluation in modern Iranian history according to context and in line with political rivalries.[27] It provided the clergy with the rationale for protest and rebellion against unjust rule by the Shah and was crucial in bringing about the revolution of 1979. However, for the masses, as Momen notes,[28] the clergy cast the revolution in terms of the Karbala tragedy and a perceived injustice, emphasizing Imam Hussain's protest, revolt and martyrdom in the cause of justice. By contrast, after the Revolution, that same doctrine which the clergymen had employed to depose the Shah, was now employed by them to legitimize their own rule, based on the controversial concept of 'the mandate of the jurist' (*vilayat-i faqih*).[29] None the less, as we shall see, the doctrine of the Mahdi continues to provide ordinary believers with hope for the justice they had been promised but denied.

The background to the concept of *vilayat-i faqih* is complex. It is popularly attributed to Khomeini (1902–89), who argued in a series of lectures given in Najaf in 1969–70, that all the executive powers of Imams, including government, devolved upon the jurists (*fuqaha*), whose authority had hitherto been generally considered limited to the implementation of the shari'a. This argument has become known as *vilayat-i faqih*, the guardianship or government of the jurist. According to some interpretations, the concept implies a claim to absolute authority as the representative of the Hidden Imam during the occultation (cf n. 29). The idea was disputed by some influential Ayatullahs who acted as *marja'*. They tended in practice to support the separation of powers and adopted a quietist stance, as a way, allegedly, of indicating disapproval of the new concept. Since each *marja'* commands large followings of 'imitators' (*muqallid*), their pronouncements have obvious extensive social and political consequences, even after death, because people can remain followers of a deceased *marja'*, a practice called 'remaining with the dead' (*baqa-yi bar miyyit*). All these differences among the *marja'* filtered down to the *jalasa* and constituted one of the vital underlying tensions between the preachers and the *jalasa* circles that had formed around them.[30]

Preachers had a crucial influence on *jalasa* participants as to whom they should choose as a *marja'*. The self-designated *maktabi* preachers generally followed Khomeini's teachings. Among these were many younger, university-trained committed women. In their continued loyalty to the revolutionary ideals, the *maktabi* preachers had linked themselves with the more radical factions of the establishment. Mrs Umid, by contrast, was a follower of those *marja'* who reportedly pursued a quietist, 'anti-political' stance, such as the Najaf-based Khu'i (1899–1992), Gulpayigani (1899–1993) and Tabataba'i Qumi (1911–95). During the *jalasa*, Mrs Umid propagated the millennarian ideology of the Hidden Imam, but her concern was not with continuity of existing structures of political authority. For her, as an independent preacher with her own views, the promise of salvation and justice lay in the early reappearance of the Mahdi, which she emphasized particularly in fervent supplications at the end of each *jalasa*.

The political motives of preachers was generally explicit in their commentaries, in the way in which they concluded the *jalasa* they led, and more generally through their support or rejection of state sponsored rituals, such as *dah-yi fajr* ('dawning of a new age', literally ten days of dawn) celebrating the anniversary of Khomeini's return and the success of the Revolution. The differences among preachers affected the choices of those who attended rituals. Indeed, the very choice of attending or sponsoring a particular ritual, and the way it was held, were political statements and affected the emotional texture of the rituals.

Mrs Umid, who saw politics as outside her understanding of religion, presented her own meetings as religious and spiritual in content, but represented those led by others as politicized. 'True religion', she said, should not be polluted with 'politics' (*siyasat*). None the less, her desire to separate 'religion' and 'politics', though seemingly innocuous and pietistic, was fraught with political sensitivities. Definitions of the boundaries of these notions are highly variable. Her choices and interpretations of the Qur'an during the gatherings did not preclude a subtle engagement with wider social and political concerns. It soon became evident that freedom of speech, which had been one of the rallying points of the revolution, did not include freedom to criticize the new regime and its doctrines. Her denial of political engagement was a veiled criticism of the situation. This is a good example of piety as a politically charged, contested 'process', rather than as an apolitical consensual 'state'.

As sites of contestation, the importance of women's *jalasa* far exceeded their modest domestic appearance. A measure of their perceived importance was suggested by official plans to bring *jalasa* under state control. One of the ways in which these plans were realized was indirect surveillance through tacit support for some women preachers in exchange for political loyalty, as indicated by Mrs Umid in her first conversation with me. Another way was stated explicitly by an official of the local branch of the 'Organisation for the Propagation of Islam'.[31] She told me that, in order to prevent the dissemination of 'superstitious' and 'subversive' ideas, a major objective of their plans was to provide training with obligatory certification for so-called 'propagators of Islam' (*muballighin-i islam*), the official designation for 'preachers', who would then ideally act as channels for state ideology.

The diversity among rival preachers gave rise to a variety of different interpretations for the same texts and threatened to undermine the more universalist pretensions of the prevailing religious interpretations of the state. Plans for intervention in the *jalasa* by the state must be seen in the context of these women's active, and pluralist, religious engagement. What emerges is an opposition between the doctrine of the state and that of the general 'superstitious' masses, who, as perceived by the clergymen leaders, could distort 'the true religion' at this crucial historical post-revolutionary juncture, when the desire for homogeneity and coherence is of particular significance for the more conservative elements in the theocratic state.

Outline of the *jalasa* and techniques of the preachers

Jalasa[32] were generally similar, at least on the surface. All the meetings included Qur'an recitals and exegeses of the Qur'an (*tafsir*) by the preachers. Most meetings included lessons on ethics (*dars-i akhlaq*), combining preaching, teaching and moralizing, often with *hadith* examples. All women's gatherings were generally convivial and included some form of refreshment. While the preachers' talks were primarily intended to be didactic and moralistic, they often digressed to current affairs and sometimes generated discussions. Sponsors generally dedicated their rituals to (*bi niyyat-i*) a preferred Shi'i saint, often as a votive pledge (*nazr*). According to Shi'a doctrine, the saints are thought to be alive and present. Their physical death is of no concern, as attested by visits to their distant shrines. The common belief in the presence of the saints sanctified rituals dedicated to them and imbued all refreshments and food served with grace (*barakat, tabarruk shudan*), in which ritual participants could partake. The women conceived of grace as emanating from God and God's Words, the Qur'an being its most tangible manifestation.

The outline description given here is based on the daily *jalasa* rounds conducted by Mrs Umid. These generally followed the same pattern. They lasted two to three hours and were held routinely in the early afternoon between the mid-day and afternoon devotions. The atmosphere was generally one of a friendly formality, fairly open and flexible. Mrs Umid's place, as with all other preachers, was always well-defined at the top end of the room. Her seat was marked by a blanket covered with white linen, a back cushion and a low table covered by a tablecloth, with a large Qur'an, a *Mafatih* (a comprehensive book of supplications) and one or more copies of books of the precepts or religious rulings of the *marja'.* Seating was otherwise egalitarian. The other women sat on the carpet shoulder to shoulder facing Mrs Umid with their headscarves on but their chadors draped around their shoulders.

Typical of each meeting was a first session of about fifteen minutes of intoned recitations in Arabic prescribed in the *Mafatih*. Mrs Umid usually appointed one or two participants for these recitals which they performed competently while the others followed quietly moving their lips accordingly. A second session of about thirty minutes was devoted to discussions of the religious precepts or rulings (*ahkam, vajibat*).[33] Mrs Umid introduced a particular theme from the precepts, offered her explanation, then waited for questions from the women concerning the problems encountered in trying to adhere to the rules in specific situations.

The most common stated objective of the meetings was to give ordinary people the opportunity to pose questions to preachers regarding these precepts, so as to ensure their correct application in daily life. Most of the women with whom I spoke considered it their religious duty to attend *jalasa* in order to learn these precepts properly. Indeed, the main bulk of the questions revealed their preoccupation with the details of correct application of the precepts, rather than with wider theological issues. Although Mrs Umid disapproved of excessive preoccupation with detail (*vasvas*) and emphasized a focus on the intent and purpose of an act, she understood and empathised with the women's needs and problems. Their questions acted as a spur for her to find ways of reinterpretating the religious rules to which they were committed to adhere. Her talk on the precepts created its own dynamic and sparked off further questions from the participants, who were inspired to look at the complexities of their daily lives afresh. She encouraged women's attendance at the *jalasa*, saying that even if the husband of any woman forbade her to attend the meetings, her religious obligations overrode her religious duty to obey (*tamkin*) her husband.

The purpose of this and the next session was to instruct and Mrs Umid's talk was didactic and moralistic, but never tedious. She would often change register, breaking off in the middle of sentence or phrase to tell a joke or an anecdote. At the end of the session dealing with the precepts, the participants often showed their appreciation of the way Mrs Umid conducted her performance with loud rounds of *salavat*, formulaic praises and greetings to the Prophet and his successors in Arabic.[34] *Salavat* could be initiated spontaneously when someone was moved by a preacher's talk and its loudness and frequency was a reliable indicator of the response of participants. *Salavat* was sometimes used strategically, for instance when attention began to falter, or when a dispute arose, thus reminding everyone of their common Shiʿi identity.

A third session of about sixty minutes, almost half the time of the entire meeting, consisted of free exegesis of the Qur'an by Mrs Umid. She began by reciting one or more verses herself in a speaking tone, followed by a row of *salavat* initiated by her, usually 'To all our martyrs from the beginning of Islam to the present "Leader" (*rahbar*)', by which all present knew she meant the Mahdi. Following this, she either translated the verses verbatim, or, more often, gave a summary, then, depending on the available time, asked a few of the participants to recite some more verses, correcting their mistakes. Only then did she proceed to deliver her commentaries, during which participants generally posed no questions, except occasionally when they asked for elucidation of a point made.

A final session of about fifteen minutes of the meeting was devoted again to intoned recitations of set Arabic prayers from the *Mafatih*. For instance, on Thursdays, the eve of the Mahdi's expected day of reappearance, they recited special supplications, such as *duʿa-yi ghaibat*, to hasten his reappearance. Mrs Umid's love for the Mahdi and her millennial fervour was obvious. He was an important figure in Mrs Umid's prayers in all the meetings. Sometimes, the mere mention of the 'Mahdi' gave rise to sobs, and each time his name was mentioned, everyone stood up, ensuring that their veils were properly in place.

Depending on whether it was a calendrical occasion of joy or sorrow (*jashn* or *ʿazadari*) relating to events in Shiʿi history, the meeting would be extended with either joyful eulogistic *mauludi* poems accompanied by a steady, rhythmic hand-clapping, or with dirges (*zikr-i musibat*) and ritualized weeping. Mrs Umid ended the meetings formally by petitioning God with a series of spontaneous supplications (*duʿa*) in Persian, requesting for instance, 'Guide us in the right path, forgive our sins, grant health and happiness for everyone and the dead spirits, help the unfortunate, the ill, bring justice'. These concluding supplications often showed the special concern of the preacher or a participant known to her. Some preachers included petitions requesting, for instance, 'The release of prisoners of war/political prisoners', or, 'The rightful return of Jerusalem to Muslims', or, 'Destroy the enemies of Islam'. Mrs Umid's petitions always included a plea for the Mahdi's reappearance, 'God strengthen our faith so that we do not doubt His return', 'Lord of the Ages appear soon, next Friday'. Mrs Umid's final words were a row of *salavat* dedicated to 'our Leader', inviting all those present to join in a loud chorus. All those present knew who she meant. By contrast to Mrs Umid's hidden discourse, so-called *maktabi* preachers generally concluded the *jalasa* with popular revolutionary slogans like 'Neither East nor West, until the revolution of the Mahdi, keep Khomeini'.[35] They hailed named political leaders with loud choruses of triple *salavat*, which were followed by designating Khomeini as 'Our leader, the representative of the Lord of the Ages' (*rahbar-i ma Khomeini naʾib-i Imam-i Zaman*). The *jalasa* were clearly forums demonstrating political affiliations as well as prayer and worship.

During the final session, the sponsoring hostess served tea again, and depending on the occasion, also sweet pastries and fruit or some form of votive food, which the participants eagerly took for its grace. Most participants left promptly after the refreshments, but some went to Mrs Umid before she left to hand over their religious taxes, ask for personal advice or the interpretation of a dream.

Few preachers commanded the same degree of attention as Mrs Umid. A language that commands attention is an 'authorized language', invested with authority and legitimacy by those for whom the speech is performed.[36] Her rhetorical skill and wit reinforced her command of the situation. She knew how to control the focus of everyone's attention by being finely attuned to their responses, skilfully changing pace, tone and volume in her talks. When attention began to falter, she drew on a repertoire of apposite jokes or anecdotes, sometimes two or three in a row. Her sense of humour was remarkable, as was her skill in maintaining the right mood (*hal*) by changing register. Her simple style of talk was inclusive, so that her talks were not restricted to the literate and learned. In familiar speech, constraints and conventions fall, so that there is always the possibility of taking an unofficial approach. Her frankness was sometimes combined with cautious remarks such as 'All that is discussed or heard during a meeting should not be repeated outside'. No matter how monological her talks may have been, the *jalasa* led by her had an interactive quality. The active response of Mrs Umid's 'listeners' was clear from their laughter, smiles, and spontaneous loud choruses of *salavat* when they chose to convey their appreciation for what she said.

Despite a general similarity, the *jalasa* varied crucially according to the preachers, their style of leadership, and in procedure, and in the time spent by preachers on each topic (exegesis, precepts, recitals and supplications). A further crucial difference was the degree of attention, discussion and participation by attendants. All of these depended on a preacher's authority, style of leadership, verbal savvy and rhetorical skills. Commentaries made by preachers varied in style, content and emphasis according to a preacher's age, education, training, personal interests and her political orientation. These were not secret, but openly discussed. The age range of their followers varied accordingly. With time I learned of some recurring descriptive tropes that the women used to categorize the preachers according to their personal preferences: 'good at *hadith*' meant variously: 'entertaining', not 'political enough', or not particularly 'learned'. 'Accurate at exegesis' (*tafsir-i daqiq*) stood for formal theological learning. 'Free exegesis' (*tafsir-i azad*) stood for the capacity to relate the text to current social and political concerns. *Imruzi* (of the day; moves with the times) could refer to the politicized religious activism of *maktabi* trained preachers, or, to those who were regarded to have a more flexible attitude to the younger generation on matters such as *hijab*, employment, journals and books, TV, tapes and videos. Mrs Umid was admired by her followers particularly for her 'free exegesis'. Her exegetic narrative served as a telling commentary on wider social concerns. What mattered to her circle of followers, who were generally older and with little or no education beyond primary school, was not theological analysis, but a knowledge to which they could relate in comprehending their daily lives.

Learning, or perceived knowledge of religious texts, was a key attribute that legitimized a preacher's authority. Only recognized preachers were allowed to explain the precepts and perform Qur'anic exegesis. Judgements as to the extent and quality of 'learning' depended ultimately on popular appeal and on perceptions of learning, which involved attributions of grace (*barakat*), spirituality (*ma'naviyat*) and purity of intent (*niyyat-i pak*). Since Mrs Umid's circle of followers regarded her as informed and her intentions as anchored in faith, any novel textual interpretations she made were respected and seen as appropriate, rather than as un-Islamic novelties. Thus, *jalasa* were political arenas where authorities were made or denied.

Tropes for re-presenting knowledge: Qur'anic exegesis and 'Islamic jokes'

Exegesis (*tafsir*) is a learned discipline. It is the prerogative of the learned and constituted one of the competitive elements among preachers, who drew on this genre to establish their religious competence. It has often been said that Qur'anic passages and Hadith contain many apparently contradictory statements which can easily be used both for and against a point.[37] God's Words were oral and only written down at a later stage and it is generally known that an oral text is linked to the society out of which it is derived. Once the oral form is written down, it becomes fixed and decontextualized. Exegesis and interpretation are ways in which the text is re-aligned with modern realities. If the written text is hegemonic, the oral re-interpretation re-defines it. Interestingly, in Arabic dictionaries, the term 'Ayat, a Qur'anic verse, is translated as 'sign', which means that each verse 'stands for something else'; similarly, the term *vahy*, which is usually translated as 'revelation' of the Qur'an from God to the Prophet, is translated as 'a hint' in Arabic dictionaries, that is something that must be 'understood'. Both notions, which are central to the Qur'anic text, entail elements of interpretation.[38] That exegesis was an essential part of the meetings only shows that the 'authentic text' is only accessible through authoritative interpretation. In other words, utterances are not only signs to be understood, but to be evaluated, appreciated, obeyed and believed, all of which are signs of authority. In a sense, the recited verses of the Qur'an were not intended to provide information themselves, but to legitimize authoritative comments. In the end, 'exegesis' took on a new interpretative emphasis.

I present three versions of exegetical commentary on the famous Qur'anic passage concerning the dialogue between Moses and Khizr (S.18: 66–78) which has been subject to numerous interpretations. The three versions are by Mrs Umid and two other local preachers. One of them, whom I will call Mrs Imami, was the head of a local 'Institute for Religious Training' (*hauza-yi 'ilmiyya*) which she had set up in the early 1970s on the second floor of her own house. Mrs Imami was an established theologically-trained preacher known beyond her neighbourhoods. She was reputed as a radical *maktabi* supporter of the regime. Two enlarged black and white photographs of her two sons, both martyred in the war with Iraq, hung on the walls of the room where the gatherings took place. She had been proud of her sons and had never shed a tear for them, so I was told. The third preacher, the oldest in the neighbourhoods, was renowned for her fluent Qur'anic recitation and for being 'good at *hadith*', by which, as already said, the women meant variously 'entertaining', 'not political enough' or 'not particularly learned'. I heard the three exegeses performed by these three preachers by lucky coincidence during Ramadan, when I attended the meetings of various *jalasa* circles who were engaged in daily Qur'an recitals.

Three different commentaries on the same Qur'anic verses

I begin with the story in the Qur'anic text (S.18: 66–78) as narrated by Mrs Imami, the *maktabi* preacher. She was the only one who provided a summary. The other two preachers assumed that their listeners were familiar with the story.

Moses asks God for permission to follow the learned Khizr in order to learn from him. Permission is granted on the condition that he poses no questions and waits until told. During their journey, Khizr carries out three apparently irrational acts. First, he badly damages a ship by boring a hole in it. Then he kills an innocent youth. Finally, he rebuilds a crumbling wall without asking for renumeration, even though he and his companions are hungry and could obtain food for it. Each time Moses raises objections and queries the logic of the act, but is reminded that he is not allowed to pose questions until told. After the third objection, Khizr says they must separate since Moses has not abided by his promise. None the less, he provides Moses with the reasons for his actions before parting. He says that he damaged the ship because he knew that it would be confiscated by the king, thereby causing hardship to the ship-owners who are poor and make a living from the ship. He killed the youth because he knew that when of age, the boy will be an unbeliever, causing himself and his believing parents evil (*kufr*). He built the wall in order to safeguard a treasure buried underneath for two orphans, to whom the treasure belongs, until they can claim it themselves.

Commentary A

Mrs Imami commented on each of the three episodes of the Qur'anic text in turn. First she constructed a relationship between the incident of boring the hole in the ship, and recent objections by people in her neighbourhoods concerning state-sponsored fund-raising for Bosnian Muslims. I have paraphrased her speech as follows:

> I want to interpret these verses [concerning the boring of the hole in the ship] and relate it to our times and the objections (*i'tiraz*) raised to the leader of our revolution. People ask, why should we donate money for Bosnia? We ourselves have poor in our midst. The Qur'an says that if we ourselves do not know what is best for our times (*maslahat-i zaman*), like the boring of the hole in the ship, then we must take it as advisable (*maslahat*) for social and political reasons. Even a Prophet like Moses needed a higher source of reference for knowledge. If we look at the Qur'an and relate it to our times, we will see that the same issues that were relevant in those days are relevant now. Therefore, we must not criticize or object to policies. We can ask for the reasons, but must obey God's commands.

Her comments on the wall incident was posed as a series of questions:

> Why did Hazrat Khizr not ask for remuneration when he built the wall? Should we only do things to obtain divine reward? Is worship only for business (*tijarat*), or to go to Paradise and be free from pain (*'azab*)?

The commentary on the third incident was as follows:

> Now, how can we relate the killing of the youth by Khizr to our times. Nowadays America shouts 'Iran is terrorist'. Imam [Khomeini] says, whoever steals must have his hand cut off. At present, things are behind the curtain. Only when the 'Lord of the Ages' appears will all be clear. Those who are cancer to our society must have their necks and heads cut

off. *Insha'allah* God will waken us up. Our leader is the 'Deputy of the Lord of the Ages' (*Na'ib-i Imam Zaman*). His command is the command of Lord of the Ages. Obeying God, then his Prophet and Imams, and in His [the Twelfth Imam] absence, Imam Khomeini.

Mrs Imami's support of the concept of *vilayat-i faqih* as she interprets it is unambiguous. She emphasizes that in the absence of the Twelfth Imam, it is an unconditional duty to follow and obey the judgement and policies of the leader of the revolution, whom she refers to as 'Imam'. One could tease out a submerged hesitation in Mrs Imami's commentary. She said, for instance, that one may not object to those who hold supreme office, but one can still ask questions when their policy seems unjustified. Indeed Moses asked questions without being punished for doing so. Another submerged criticism appears to lie in the question she posed: 'Is worship only to be free from pain (*'azab*)?' Her use of the word 'pain' is unclear, but it conveys a sense of unease with present circumstances, as echoed in her phrase: 'At present, things are behind the curtain. Only when the "Lord of the Ages" appears will all be clear.'

Commentary B

Mrs Umid's comments were more summary than Mrs Imami's. Given the overall political climate of restraint, independent preachers had to be particularly careful when they touched on sensitive potentially political themes. After recitation of the verses and a very brief translation, Mrs Umid said that the text clearly showed that ultimate knowledge was reserved for God and those appointed by God, namely the Prophet and His twelve infallible (*ma'sum*) successors. She then stressed that even the Prophet's successors were not immune from fallibility, as was commonly believed, for they were mortals like everyone else; the difference between them and other humans was that they did not sin, even though they could have done so. She continued to argue that Khizr was also a mortal and not immune from sin and fallibility; thus Moses was justified in posing questions and to object when Khizr's actions seemed irrational and contrary to God's Will. After a short deliberately thoughtful pause, Mrs Umid then asked: 'Who could condone the wilful damaging of people's property and the murder of innocent persons?' She ended her talk by saying that after all, Moses was treated leniently by Khizr when he raised objections. He was not punished although his action led ultimately to their separation.

I understand this commentary as an oblique criticism of the regime and the lack of freedom of expression. Mrs Umid seems to be saying that, if such an elevated figure as Khizr accepts questioning, then it is permissible to question the actions of any leader. Thus, the current leadership should also accept questioning, and they should not necessarily punish those who do challenge them.

Commentary C

The third commentary is by the oldest preacher whose followers regarded her as being 'good at *hadith*'. In her gatherings, held twice weekly in her own house, the emphasis was generally on Qur'an recitation rather than commentaries on the verses. On this occasion, participants recited a whole section (*juz*) of the Qur'an twice over, covering several *sura*, including the story of Khizr and Moses. There was consequently little time for any extended commentary. None the less, the preacher did stop at the verses concerning Khizr and Moses to make a brief comment. After the verses were recited by a participant, she rephrased the text and said: 'Khizr said to Moses, don't be meddlesome (*fuzuli nakun*, being a busy-body), like we women are apt to be'.

The old preacher lived up to her reputation, confirming the women's judgement of her as being 'good at *hadith*'. With her simplistic comment, she inadvertently reproduced the gender bias inherent in dominant Islamist discourses on *'aql/nafs*, which has wider implications for social responsibility (see above). Bourdieu would call this a process of 'misrecognition' or 'symbolic violence'.[39] Accordingly, the gendered discourses are imposed upon women like this preacher in such ways that they are regarded as legitimate, obscuring the power relations which permit that imposition to be successful. Arguably, the old preacher could also have had her own interest in mind. Conformity has its rewards. As Henrietta Moore suggests,[40] taking up certain subject positions are bound up with issues of power, and with the material benefits which may be consequent on the exercise of that power.

By contrast with the old preacher, Mrs Umid and the *maktabi* preacher re-constructed the text skillfully and strategically to reflect their particular perspectives on wider social and political concerns of the day, and each seemed to have their own interpretation of the concept of *vilayat-i faqih*. None of the three preachers considered the possibility that their interpretation, or their perceived world, was only 'one' of many possible interpretations. The potency of the *jalasa* discourse lies in the 'language of authority'. Set within the framework of its divine origin, that language becomes the metaphor for truth and authenticity, which female preachers use to carve out a new public feminine discourse.

'Islamic jokes'

Jokes (*shukhi, latifa*) and jocular anecdotes (*hikayat*), like exegesis, were part of a process that gave an idea of how established norms are unsettled and social reality may change. Joking can be a covert expression of social and political commentary or criticism, but were explicitly said to be necessary as 'entertainment', to show that the *jalasa* were not solemn and dry (*khushk*) affairs. Mrs Umid's repertoire allowed her licence to be subversive, whether consciously intended or not. The prospect of official sanctions demanded that social and political critique be expressed obliquely, and by openly professing that one is apolitical. Tales of ill-informed mullahs who misled people were among Mrs Umid's favourite jocular anecdotes, especially those relating to Mullah Nasreddin (a folk figure), a popular vehicle for expressions of social criticism.

During a meeting, one of the participants asked Mrs Umid about the precepts concerning the distinction between 'pure' and 'impure' water (*ab-i mutlaq, ab-i muzaf*), and whether one is allowed to use sea water for ablutions. A clergyman had told the woman that sea-salt rendered the sea water 'impure'. Mrs Umid said that she had carefully searched the source-books but had found no reference to salt rendering water impure, so that the clergyman was either wrong, or else he must provide the reference to the source on which he had based his claim. And in the same breath, she went on:

> Mullah Nasreddin was on his way somewhere and he was wearing a turban. A man approached and asked him to read a letter because he was illiterate himself. The Mullah said he couldn't read it either. The man replied that he should be able to read it since he had a turban. Mullah Nasreddin took his turban off and put it on the man's head and said, 'Now you can read it for yourself'.

Humour and satire do not translate easily from one language to another. This is partly because they are elliptical and rely on taken-for-granted shared knowledge. But jokes are also often complex and can be interpreted differently by different people. One might consider jokes in the light of the notion of 'hidden transcripts',[41] which create spaces of autonomy and agency for the less powerful members of society in interactions with their rulers, apparently observing rules of deference and correctness, but simultaneously demonstrating resistance and contestation. Jokes do not merely 'express' or 'represent' an alternative reality or different interests, as Mary Douglas says,[42] but are themselves ways of constituting subjectivities in the context of relations of unequal power. It is in this sense that I agree with Douglas,[43] that jokes are an 'anti-rite', with elements of subversion, levelling of hierarchies, giving predominance to informality, unofficial values, paradoxes and dissonance, offering thereby alternative patterns with elegant economy. They reveal the arbitrary nature of established categories, lift pressure momentarily, and suggest other ways of structuring realities.

Conclusion

In the context of the Islamic Republic, it is worth reflecting on the importance of religious practice for providing women of a certain social background and age with unprecedented opportunities for political participation, social mobility and economic independence without losing face. Even if this opening is accompanied by hidden forms of control and discipline, it is enabling. By partaking of masculinized discourses and locally established idioms of gendered space, the women are able to appropriate and re-define the gendered boundaries of private and public, gaining self-accomplishment in defining their social reality. Some have done so by a creative reconstruction of domestic space into politically charged professional space of worship, which allows them the freedom to express alternative, even subversive, discourses. Others have exchanged a degree of political loyalty for mobility, positions of authority and economic independence. Thus, in the debates about the relationship of religion and state, *jalasa* gatherings suggest increasing fragmentation among women preachers and their followers, with a shifting tendency toward separation of religion and state. Women are not a homogeneous category and religious practice can reinforce relations of inequality. There were crucial differences and degrees of authority between different individuals in the women's circles of the same social background, based on control of material resources, local perceptions of 'learning' and purity, as well as political convictions and relationships to the state. In their *jalasa* meetings, the women not only did things for themselves as 'women', but also nurtured social, economic and political relationships, including those to do with men. As Marylin Strathern says, the excluded sex is always present by implication.[44] If activities are locally interpreted as the arena of one sex, the other sex is there as cause. *Jalasa* women's meetings partake of male defined religious discourses and practices, and even if their meetings are spacially feminized, these gendered domains often intersect.

Notes

1 Author's note: this chapter is based on my Ph.D. thesis (unpublished), 'Neighbourhoods of Piety. Gender and Ritual in South Tehran' University of London, 1998. I thank Vanessa Martin and Ziba Mir-Hosseini for their helpful comments on an earlier version of this paper. I gratefully acknowledge the support of Clare Hall, University of Cambridge, for a non-stipendiary Research Fellowship, and SOAS, University of London, for making me a research associate, and providing an academic context for writing and research.

2 See D.F. Eikelman and J. Piscatori (1996) *Muslim Politics*, Princeton, NJ, p. 7.

3 See C. Adle and B. Hourcade (eds) (1992) *Téhéran capitale bicentenaire*, Paris/Tehran; B. Hourcade (1987) 'L'homme vertical: un mythe, une ville, un divorce,' in *Teheran au dessous du volcan*, Hors Serie no. 27. Paris, pp. 60–8.

4 There is a vast literature on the wide-ranging and highly complex issues that led to the revolution of 1978–79. See, for instance, S. Akhavi (1980) *Religion and Politics in Contemporary Iran: Clergy–State Relations in the Pahlavi Period*, Albany; S.A. Arjomand (1988) *The Turban for the Crown*, New York, Oxford; S.A. Arjomand (1984) *The Shadow of God and the Hidden Imam*, Chicago; S.A. Arjomand (ed.) (1984) *From Nationalism to Revolutionary Islam*, Albany; S.K. Farsoun and M. Mashayekhi (eds) (1992) *Iran: Political Culture in the Islamic Republic*, London, New York; M.M.J. Fischer (1980) *Iran. From Religious Dispute to Revolution*, Cambridge; N.R. Keddie (1982) *Religion and Politics in Modern Iran*, New Haven: Yale University Press; N.R.

Keddie (1981) *Roots of Revolution: An Interpretative History of Modern Iran*, New Haven; N.R. Keddie and E. Hoogland (eds) (1986) *The Iranian Revolution and the Islamic Republic*, Syracuse; M. Momen (1985) *An Introduction to Shī'i Islam*, New Haven, London: Yale University Press, pp. 286–9; A. Najmabadi, 'Iran's Turn to Islam: from Modernism to Moral Order', *Middle East Journal*, 41, (1987), pp. 202–17; S. Zubaida (1993) *Islam the People and the State*, London, pp. 64–83.

5 For an extended discussion of the term *maktabi* and discourses adopted by them, see A. Gheissari 'Critique of Ideological Literature', *Iran Nameh*, Vol. 22, 2, (1994), pp. 233–58; A. Vali and S. Zubaida, 'Factionalism and political discourse in the Islamic Republic of Iran', *Economy and Society*, (1985), 14, 2, pp. 139–73.

6 See Arjomand, *Turban*, pp. 93–7, 103–5; Gheissari, 'Literature', pp. 239–47.

7 These included the establishment of the 'Reconstruction Crusade' (*jihad-i sazandigi*) and the 'Organisation for the Mobilisation of the Oppressed' (*basij-i mustaz'afin*), which functioned as urban and rural development agencies with the additional task of mobilizing support for the government (Vali and Zubaida, 'Factionalism', pp. 141–2, 170). Also, the south was allocated more green and recreational spaces. Confiscated houses and abandoned properties of the elite were handed to supporters of the revolution from the down-town areas, or were bought at a premium by a new class, enriched through the revolution, Hourcade, 'L'homme'.

8 Cf. Hourcade, 'L'homme'.

9 See J. Al-e Ahmad, (1981) *Plagued by the West*, trans. P. Sprachman, New York, (original publ. Persian *Gharbzadigi* 1962). The notion of 'westoxification' was central to Al-i Ahmad's (1981) influential pre-revolutionary social criticism of middle class Iranian 'women', 'spell-bound' by Western goods. It was not so much the 'west' that was the target of his criticism as the privileged middle classes who associated themselves with the west.

10 For a critical appraisal of the numerous studies on veiling, see N. Lindisfarne-Tapper (1997) 'Approaches to the Study of Dress in the Middle East', in N. Lindisfarne-Tapper and B. Ingham (eds), *Languages of Dress in the Middle East*, Richmond, Surrey, pp. 1–40, who rightly says that wearing a headcovering must be understood as a complex act which may generate a myriad of nuanced interpretations. See also J.W.Anderson, 'Social Structure and the Veil: Comportment and the Composition of Interaction in Afghanistan', *Anthropos*, 3, 4, (1982), pp. 397–420, for a rare earlier such study of veiling, and V.J. Hoffmann-Ladd, 'Polemics in the Modesty and Segregation of Women in Contemporary Egypt', *International Journal of Middle Eastern Studies* 19, (1987), pp. 23–50, for the politicized usage of the veil.

11 In his analysis of the political behaviour of the clergy during the Revolution of 1979, Zubaida argues that there is no straightforward correspondence between the abstract scheme of class (conventionally associated with Marxist analyses), economic divisions and political orientation and action; rather, in Iran, groups which can be distinguished as political actors are formed on the basis of cultural and institutional characteristics, *Islam*, ch.3, 72–76ff.

12 *Hay'at* may be local neighbourhood associations (*hay'at-e mahalla*), or based on a common professional interest (*hay'at-e sinfi*), with a designated title or distinct name, indicating the members' profession, geographical origin, their particular aspirations and type of religious sentiment and motivations in forming these associations, see Arjomand, *Turban*, pp. 91–3; F. Kazemi (1980) *Poverty and Revolution in Iran*, New York, pp. 63, 92–96; G.E. Thaiss 'Religious Symbolism and Social Change: the Drama of Husain', Ph.D. Dissertation, Washington University, St Louis, 1973, pp. 202 ff.

13 As Gilsenan notes, the so-called revival of Islam in the 1970s and after is not a revival at all, but a continuation of a tendency toward various significant religious movements

since the late eighteenth century as European influence became predominant. See M. Gilsenan (1990) *Recognizing Islam. Religion and Society in the Modern Middle East*, London, p. 18.

14 For accounts of men's religious associations see Arjomand, *Turban*, pp. 91–3; M. Borghei (1992) 'Iran's Religious Establishment in the Dialectics of Politicization' in Farsoun and Mashayekhi, *Iran*, pp. 57–81; G.W. Brasswell, 'A Mosaic of Mullahs and Mosques', Ph.D. University of North Carolina, 1975; P.J. Chelkowski, 'Iran: Mourning Becomes Revolution', *Asia*, 3, (1980), pp. 30–7, 44–5: Fischer, *Iran*; Kazemi, *Poverty*, pp. 63, 92–3; Thaiss, *Symbolism*, pp. 192 ff.

15 In 1973, the Qur'an was the perennial bestseller, with a sale of about 700000 copies, followed by the sale of 490000 copies of *Mafatih al-Jinan* (Keys to the Garden [of Heaven], simply called *Mafatih*), a comprehensive guide to daily supplication and worship; Arjomand, *Turban*, p. 91.

16 Women have sometimes been denied access to mosques, or permitted access if spacial gender segregation were maintained, and at times they were even allowed to give political speeches, as was the case with Aisha, the Prophet's youngest and rebellious wife, see L. Ahmed (1992) *Women and Gender in Islam*, New Haven, ch. 3, pp. 60–1, 75.

17 There is considerable dispute among the clergy as to whether communal Friday prayers and sermons are mandatory, and some forbade it at certain times because of its control by what they perceived to be an unjust government. See M.M.J. Fischer and M. Abedi (1990) *Debating Muslims*, Wisconsin, pp. 120–1, 293–4.

18 In 1974 there were 322 *Husainiyya* centres in Tehran; Arjomand, *Turban*, p. 92.

19 See P. Bourdieu (1992) *Outline of a Theory of Practice*, Cambridge, pp. 171–83. In his treatise on 'symbolic capital' Bourdieu includes qualitative social values such as prestige and renown as being perhaps 'the most valuable form of accumulation' in the community of his example.

20 See T. El-Or (1994) *Educated and Ignorant, Ultra-orthodox Jewish Women and Their World*, trans. H. Watzman, Boulder, ch. 2 describes the paradox of how Jewish women's religious education began as a result of a threat of secularism (the Jewish diaspora and later Zionism). Secularism meant the decline of women's traditional roles, and religious education was intended to reinforce orthodox ideals (that women should remain 'ignorant', confining themselves to their role as mothers and wives). Instead, literacy and acquisition of knowledge created circumstances for change, in that the orthodox women began to rethink the values they themselves had held.

21 See N. Tapper (1991) *Bartered Brides: Politics, Gender and Marriage in Afghan Tribal Society*, Cambridge, p. 15.

22 D.F. Eikelman, 'Mass Education and the Religious Imagination in Contemporary Arab Societies', *American Ethnologist*, 19, 4, (1992), pp. 643–55.

23 See F. Adelkhah (1991) *La revolution sous la voile, femmes Islamiques d'Iran*, Paris, pp. 108ff; Z. Mir-Hosseini (1996) 'Stretching the Limits: A feminist Reading of the Shari'a in post-Khomeini Iran', in M. Yamani (ed.) *Feminism and Islam. Legal and Literary Perspectives*, London; Z. Mir-Hosseini (1996) 'Women and Politics in Post-Khomeini Iran', in H. Afshar (ed.) *Women and Politics in the Third World*, London; A. Najmabadi (1998) 'Feminism in an Islamic Republic', in Y. Haddad and J. Esposito (eds) *Islam, Gender and Social Change*, Oxford, pp. 59–84.

24 Cf. N. Lindisfarne (1994) 'Variant Masculinities, Variant Virginities: Rethinking Honour and Shame', in *Dislocating Masculinity. Comparative Ehnographies*, London.

25 For an extensive discussion and overview of available literature on women's rituals in Iran, including accounts written in Persian by Iranian authors, see Torab, *Neighbourhoods*.

26 The Twelfth Imam has various titles: 'Lord of the Ages' *Sahib-i Zaman*, *Vali-yi 'Asr*, *Imam-i Zaman*, 'Messiah' or the *Mahdi* ('the rightly guided one', from the Arabic root

'*h-d-i*', from which derives the Persian word *hidayat*, 'to guide', often implying divine guidance). Another title is *hujjat*, from which derives the word *Hujjatiyya*, a reportedly clandestine society that began in the 1950s as an anti-Baha'i society and which is attributed with an extreme version of Messianic quietism, one that would readily acquiesce to oppression and corruption to hasten the return of the Mahdi, see Vali and Zubaida, *Factionalism*, p. 150; Momen, *Shi'i Islam*, p. 296; Fischer and Abedi, *Muslims*, pp. 48–9, 228.

27 For examples of how other Shi'i elements have been reconstructed in line with political realities see, Zubaida, *Islam*, p. 180.

28 Momen, *Shi'i Islam*, pp. 170–1.

29 On the concept of *vilayat-i faqih* and controversies over it among the clergy, see S. Akhavi (1986) 'Clerical Politics in Iran since 1979' in N.R. Keddie and E. Hoogland (eds) *The Iranian Revolution and the Islamic Republic*, Syracuse; Arjomand, *Turban*; M. Bayat (1985) 'Shi'a Islam as a Functioning Ideology in Iran', in B.M. Rosen (ed.) *Iran since the Revolution*, New York, pp. 21–9; W. Buchta, 'Die Islamische Republik Iran und die religos-politische Kontroverse un die marja'iyat', *Orient*, 3, (1995); Momen, *Shi'i Islam*; Vali and Zubaida, 'Factionalism'; S. Zubaida 'The Ideological Conditions for Khomeini's Doctrine of Government', *Economy and Society*, 11, 2, (1982).

30 Despite considerable difference among the leading scholars, their treatises give the impression of unity. Fischer distinguished five religious styles among the Qum clergy: popular, scholarly, mystical, privatized and revolutionary, *Iran*, p. 4. Similarly, the quietist stance of some leading *marja'*, such as Khu'i (1899–1992) and Tabataba'i Qumi (1911–95), made it difficult to judge their opinion, although others were more outspoken. See Akhavi, 'Politics' p. 62; Buchta, 'Republik'.

31 The umbrella organization in question was '*Sazman-i Tablighat-i Islami-i Kull-i Kishvar*' (the 'Nation-wide Organization for the Propagation of Islam'). These measures were under way at the time of my research. Further research would be required to see if, or how far, such plans have been implemented and their consequences.

32 For other descriptions of *jalasa* see, Adelkhah, *Revolution*, ch. 3; Z. Kamalkhani, 'Women's Islam. Religious Practice among Women in Today's Iran', Ph.D. Thesis. Bergen: University of Bergen; Torab, *Neighbourhoods*; A. Torab, 'Piety as Gendered Agency: a Study of *jalasa* Ritual Discourse in an Urban Neighbourhood in Iran', JRAI, N.S., 2, 2, (1996) pp. 235–52.

33 The religious precepts are published in the treatises of the *marja'*. The treatises are called 'explanatory text on problems [of religion]' (*risalat-i tauzih-al-masa'il*), or simply, 'book of precepts' (*kitab-i ahkam*). They are subdivided into a compendium of about three thousand 'problems' (*mas'ala*, from *su'al*, question), which set out to answer questions for lay people on their ritual duties. The precepts (*ahkam*) and ethics (*akhlaq*) together form the shari'a, which is derived from interpretations of the Qur'an and the Prophet's Traditions (*sunnat*).

34 The *salavat* formula is as follows: *Allah-u masallih 'ala Muhammad va 'ali Muhammad*, added often with *va 'ajjil farajahum*, which refers to a desire for the early reappearance of the Mahdi.

35 The slogan is: *Na sharqi, na gharbi, ta inqilab-i Mahdi, Khumaini ra nigah dar*.

36 Cf. Bourdieu, *Outline*, pp. 170–1.

37 In their interesting discussion of 'Qur'anic dialogics', Fischer and Abedi show the ideological, political and legal concerns in Qur'anic exegesis and in interpretations of Hadith. Of particular interest is their example of what they call 'Hadith game' surrounding questions of leadership in present day Iran, *Muslims*, ch. 2, pp. 112–43.

38 The importance of the notion of *vahy* for re-interpretations of the Qur'an was discussed by Dr Abdolkarim Sorush, a prominent religious intellectual, in a speech

delivered on the Prophet's birthday (8 December 1996) at a Shi'i religious Institute 'Mahfil-i 'Ali' in North Harrow.

39 P. Bourdieu (1997) *The Logic of Practice*, trans. R. Nice, Cambridge, ch. 8.

40 H.L. Moore (1994) *A Passion for Difference. Essays in Anthropology and Gender* Cambridge, p. 65.

41 See J.C. Scott (1990) *Domination and the Arts of Resistance. Hidden Transcripts*, New Haven; and J.C. Scott (1985) *Weapons of the Weak: Everyday Forms of Peasant Resistance*, New Haven.

42 M. Douglas (1991) *Implicit Meanings. Essays in Anthropology*, London, pp. 107–8.

43 *Ibid.*

44 M. Strathern (1988) *The Gender of the Gift*, Berkeley.

ten

Islam, Women and Civil Rights

The Religious Debate in the Iran of the 1990s

Ziba Mir-Hosseini

Introduction

A woman who enters a government building – a Ministry, or an Airport Terminal – anywhere in Iran will find herself undergoing a number of ritual procedures. Each such public space has a women's entrance, segregated from the men's. The ritual and the strictness of its observance vary with the nature of the space and the number of women present there. The closer to the seat of official power, and the more women there are – especially if they are from the secular-oriented middle classes – then the stricter are the rules of segregation and screening.

An example is the modern 20–storey block that houses the Ministry of Agriculture. Many current employees have worked there since before the 1979 Revolution, and a comparatively large number are women. As in other large government offices with many female staff, there is a single entrance, but once inside, a woman must first pass through a curtained enclosure, where she is received by female officials whose task it is to ensure that she is observing the correct dress code (overall chador is the ideal, but a long coat and scarf are also acceptable), and to tell her to remove her make-up.[1] Then she enters the elevator lobby, where she will discover four elevators, three for men, and one for women, though all are operated by men. These rituals are in force during office hours (8.00 am to 4.00 pm), after which there is no dress screening and no segregation of the elevators: as the elevator operator responded one evening with a grin, when I expressed surprise at finding a man in the women's elevator: 'after 4 o'clock we all become *mahram*' (i.e. close relatives, between whom mixing is allowed).

With public transport, one meets other extremes and paradoxes. In airport terminals there are separate doorways for 'brothers' and 'sisters', who meet up again immediately inside, while the more plebeian bus and railway terminals have no such separate entrances; yet city buses are divided by a metal bar: men travel in front, and women behind, and each have their own entrance; this segregation too is abandoned after about 8.00 pm in the evening, and it is not observed at all on private minibuses. And if you choose to take an ordinary shared taxi, you may find yourself sharing either the back seat or the front passenger seat with a strange man, in very close physical contact.

I begin with these observations, to convey a sense of the diverse and complex ways in which the Islamic Republic is trying to cope with the presence of women in the public domain. There are no definite rules, but a set of improvised rituals that people and organizations create, then modify when necessary. The existence of these rituals is due to the need to divide space according to what is understood to be an Islamic mandate; their modification is due to a practical need to stretch the limits set by that mandate.

Women's massive participation in the 1979 Revolution, and since then in political life, came as a real challenge to the clerics, the custodians of the shari'a. On the one hand, once they were in power, they had to recognize political expediencies and the realities of contemporary social life, including the fact that women are active in most fields of social and economic life, and that many of them are resisting the restrictions and discriminations to which they have been subjected in the name of shari'a. On the other hand, women's public presence and demands for equality subvert the notions of gender roles and relations constructed in traditional Islamic jurisprudence (*fiqh*).

This chapter explores some of the ways in which these dilemmas have been expressed in 1990's Iran, a country which has undergone a major shift in discourse and policies.[2] I contextualize and examine two texts representing opposed jurisprudential approaches to gender roles and boundaries. The first is a book by Ayatullah Ahmad Azari-Qumi, one of the most influential clerics of the first decade of the Islamic Republic, best known for founding *Risalat* in 1981, the daily newspaper which became the voice of conservative clerics, now referred to as the Traditional Right. Azari's book encapsulates the essence of the *fiqh* discourse on women which informed and shaped the gender policies of the Islamic Republic, remaining unchallenged until the early 1990s. The second text is a critique of Azari's views published in *Zanan* (Women), a women's magazine with an Islamic feminist agenda. Launched in 1992, *Zanan* is part of a reformist intellectual tendency that remained dormant during the years of war with Iraq (1980–88). This review, the first coherent major challenge to the official discourse on women, was written (under a pseudonym) by Sayyid Mohsen Sa'idzadeh, the most articulate clerical proponent of gender equality in Islam, and a regular contributor to *Zanan* until June 1998.[3]

Woman's image in the Islamic Order

Ayatullah Azari-Qumi's *Woman's Image in the Islamic Order* (Sima-yi Zan dar Nizam-i Islami, henceforth *Image*), is an extended version of an article published in *Risalat* in December/January 1991/92. In his Introduction, we find that he was prompted to write a book on women so as to counter the new 'conspiracies of world imperialism' which now present themselves in the form of a 'wholesale cultural invasion'. 'Cultural invasion' became an issue in Iranian politics soon after the end of the war with Iraq, and served a useful purpose in the faction-fighting following Khomeini's death. It is one of those vague ideological concepts which everyone is trying to find ways of confronting, and owes its power to its vagueness: it is the enemy within, which resists the ideological definition of Islam.[4]

Like others, Azari defines 'cultural invasion' by opposing it. He recommends a number of 'consolidation measures' and specifies three as the most important:

> First, expansion and clarification of the culture of *hijab* and the Islamic code of dress for women, through films, plays, publications or other means. Because, if the smallest breach is opened in this strong fortification, corruption and recklessness will expand to all other institutions and the way will be paved for the downfall of other Islamic values.
>
> Secondly, among the important actions that officials and ordinary people must pay attention to is the facilitation of marriage for youth …
>
> Thirdly, the role of the Islamic regime in containing cultural invasion in all its different dimensions is undeniable. The Islamic regime must exercise control over the press, public media, radio and television in order to ensure that they all encourage young girls, even children, to observe Islamic dress and chador (pp. 10–11).

These three points are the key to Azari's text and his gender discourse, which centres on women's appearance in public. Before the Revolution, when clerics like Azari were in opposition, the 'Image of Woman' and her place in their Islamic order were clear-cut. Women were not to be seen by strange men and their place was at home. But with the Revolution they came out, and since then they have continued to play an important role in consolidating the regime. Azari accepts these facts. Yet he cannot abandon or ignore the world-view and gender discourse of the traditionalists among whom he belongs. Women's participation in politics and society subverts traditionalist notions of the proper sphere of gender relations, and 'threatens society's moral fabric'. The solution he proposes is to regulate women's movements in public and in private, that is, to promote the 'culture of *hijab*.'

The main body of the book reveals other facets of this dilemma and Azari's way of dealing with them. The seven chapters are divided into sections, with titles accurately indicating their theme and content. Chapter One, 'The Image of Woman in Islam', contains the core of Azari's theological reasoning. It is about Fatima

Zahra, the Prophet's daughter and wife of 'Ali, the first Shi'i Imam; and must be read in the context of the official Iranian discourse, which portrays Fatima as embodying Islamic ideals of womanhood. This discourse dates to the mid-1970s, when 'Ali Shari'ati, the Islamic thinker and ideologue, in a lecture delivered in the *Husainiyya Irshad* (then the centre for Islamic intellectual opposition to the Pahlavi regime), addressed the crisis of identity faced by women in Iran, urging them – both Muslims who unquestioningly accepted traditional roles and those who aped the west and became mindless consumers – to follow Fatima's example as an ideal.[5] For Shari'ati, her life embodied the essence of Shi'i traditions and values of defiance, struggle and protest against tyranny and injustice.

Since the Revolution, 'Fatima as a role-model for women' has become (like 'cultural invasion') a shibboleth used as a source of legitimacy for gender discourses. Fatima and her image have undergone a transformation. Her birthday (in the Islamic lunar calendar) was officially proclaimed Mother's Day, and the week in which it falls is celebrated as Women's Week. She no longer stands for protest, defiance and justice, but for chastity, piety and submission. Iranian women are encouraged to follow her example.

This is implicit in two points Azari makes. First, 'if a woman wants to find her place in an Islamic society, in the eyes of God and the Prophet', she 'must adjust the programme of her life in accordance with *fiqh*'. Secondly, in order to do so, she must model her life on Fatima's. He draws a parallel between the pre-revolutionary era in Iran – which he refers to as 'the time of idols (*taghut*)' – and the pre-Islamic 'time of ignorance (*jahiliyya*)'. His thesis is that women entered a new era with the establishment of the Islamic Republic, more or less like the advent of Islam.

> In the time of idols – with few exceptions – [women] cared only for make-up and expensive clothes; and in their special dress, day and night they busied themselves with make-up and wasted their lives, and were happy that Western culture and its surrogate [Pahlavi] state had granted them this banal Western freedom. ... The deposed Shah regarded 'wearing the chador' as 'backward' and suitable for old women and the poor, who did not have beautiful clothes and comely bodies; he repeatedly said so ...
>
> Among the achievements of the Islamic Revolution which are the cause of pride and honour ... is the evolution that has occurred in this class [women], which has amazed the entire world.
>
> A world that has imposed all kinds of corruption on women, especially sexual corruption, now witnesses that a *creature named Iranian Muslim woman* has reached such a degree of self-sacrifice, dignity and honour that her role in fighting world oppression, if not greater than man's, is certainly no less. Perhaps one can say that the secret of the victory of the Revolution was the active participation of Muslim women.
>
> They sent their children to the war fronts to welcome the burning bullets of the merciless enemy, and with an open face and a heart full of

patience and gratitude sacrificed [their sons] for Islam. With all this, they see themselves as indebted to God, religion and the Leader (pp. 31–4).

Chapter Two, 'The Personality of Woman in Comparison to Man', contains what can be considered the ideological centre of Azari's text. Here we see Azari's version of the theory of sex and gender complementarity, which, as articulated by Mutahhari in pre-revolutionary Iran, became the official discourse of the Islamic Republic.[6]

> The Creator has created men and women to complement each other. Both are independent and move towards a defined goal, but one cannot fulfil his/her duties without the other. Men and women are both human and humans are superior to other creatures. Both have the same positive and negative qualities; both can be either just or corrupt, both can be believers or non-believers ...
>
> On the first day of creation, God addressed Adam and Eve in the same way; both were summoned to obey God, given the mission to come to earth and accept divine guidance, and threatened with a dire fate if they strayed ...
>
> Woman has appropriated the privilege of carrying the child and rearing it for a long period. Men and women have shared specific duties and roles in the conception and rearing of children, they also have shared specific duties in making themselves pure and continuing human life. Both are blessed with the same divine gifts. Heavy jobs are assigned to men and light and delicate jobs to women; but they are the same in human value and greatness. The advantage of divine religions, in particular the sacred religion of Islam, over other schools is that men's and women's duties and responsibilities stem from their creation and nature; so all responsibilities are given to men (pp. 37–40).

Azari then counters objections by traditionalist clerics who still consider women's presence in public as a violation of the sacred laws of Islam. He makes a case for women's full participation under the following headings: (1) [women's] participation in politics and total submission to the Islamic ruler; (2) women's personal wealth; (3) women's [right] to inherit; (4) reward for women's pious deeds; (5) acquiring knowledge; (6) enjoining the good and forbidding evil.

Azari invokes seven Qur'anic verses and one *hadith* of the Prophet. All seven verses imply gender equality. The first (Mumtahanah, 12) invites women to declare their allegiance to the Prophet; the second (Nisa, 32) tells men and women that whatever each earns is theirs and neither husbands nor wives should interfere with each other's wealth; the third (Nisa, 7) indicates that women, like men, inherit wealth from parents and relatives, however much there is; the fourth (Nahl, 97), the fifth (al-Imran, 195,) and the sixth (Ahzab, 35) all confirm that God rewards and punishes believers, both men and women, according to their deeds; the seventh (Tuba, 71) enjoins both men and women to help each other to keep to the correct path. The *hadith* also implies equality: 'acquiring knowledge is obligatory for Muslim men and women'.

Without referring to the arguments of those who invoke the same verses to argue for gender equality in Islamic law, Azari signals his consent by saying that they are proofs of the 'permission that Islam has given women to participate in politics, provided it has the sanction of the Islamic ruler.' The only commentary he provides is under the last heading, enjoining the good and forbidding evil.

> Men and women believers are components of an Islamic collectivity and responsible to others. If ladies always stay at home, the important duty of 'enjoining good and forbidding evil' – which heads all duties – will be left unperformed. It is true that, regarding the question of jihad and armed defence, [women] have no duty, but even this Ruling is confined to a time when there are enough men. Women's presence in armed conflict is not obligatory, but this, and their participation in medical work, nursing and other behind-the-lines tasks, are among their most important duties. Likewise, in early Islam women took part in treating the wounded (p. 46).

In the final part of the chapter, Azari offers a rejoinder to those who argue for gender equality. It encapsulates how traditionalist clerics perceive women's employment outside home, whether in the West or in Muslim societies, as cruelty and exploitation, and how they consider any form of dress that is not chador as tantamount to nakedness.

> In capitalist countries, where their greedy men's only objective is to acquire more capital and to exploit the rest, including women, in the beautiful and magnificent name of 'equality for men and women', women suffer the greatest cruelty. With the pretence that women in Eastern and Muslim societies have been deprived of their human rights, and with the conspiracy that *hijab* is an obstacle to women's social activities, [men] have compelled Western women, in spite of their delicate nature, to do heavy work. Women are degraded; and through the expansion of the culture of nudity they are turned into pretty dolls for the satisfaction of [men's] lust. In order to cause the fall of Muslim women too, they have instilled doubts into their minds and have planted seeds of doubt in Muslim societies (pp. 49–50).

Chapter Three, 'Duties of Wives and Husbands towards Each Other', contains Azari's views on marital relations. It begins:

> One of woman's characteristics is her love of adornment. Women are raised in a variety of adornments. For her, adornment is among the necessities of life, and to display herself and to attract men's attention is important to her. At the same time, it is in woman's nature to be intimate with only one man, and this is a prized quality that compensates for her other weaknesses. ... Woman encapsulates a man's desire and yearning;

and in return man is created to be drawn to women and to manage human forces.

This mutual love and attraction is the basis for the creation of male and female, on which the division of labour in the family is based. The internal affairs of the home, which revolve around pure emotions and feelings, are entrusted to someone who has them [women], and affairs outside the home, which involve reason and wisdom, are entrusted to men. And because the general management of the family needs reason, wisdom and management skill, man is the ultimate decision maker and woman is the adviser in the internal affairs of the family and what relates to them (pp. 61–2).

To back this up, Azari cites Sura Nisa, 34, commonly invoked to argue that women should obey men since God has made men superior to women. In Azari's translation, interestingly, God made men superior because they are bread-winners; that is, he implicitly admits that the difference is social, not natural. But he leaves it there, and then elaborates on the notion of division of labour in the family, invoking a *hadith* in which the Prophet assigned matters concerning the inside of the house to Fatima and those concerning the outside to 'Ali. From this he concludes:

In all undertakings, the man is responsible and is the final decision maker. For example, the way a woman wears clothes and her appearance outside the home concern her husband, and in this matter a woman must obey her husband.

The first and most important quality in a good woman is to be obedient to her husband. She must in no way expose herself to the eyes of unrelated men and ruin her character under their lustful and poisonous gaze. In Fatima's words:

'The best thing for a woman is not to see and not to be seen by an unrelated man.'

It might be said that:

If it means that man and woman not only should not look at each other's faces and places of ornament but also should not converse except through a curtain or other barrier, such a command is impossible [to follow] in society.

In response it must be said: history records many occasions when Fatima talked with men, and they narrated her *hadith*. Therefore, the mentioned *hijab* and women's seclusion must be considered as 'ideal and desired *hijab*'; or the raising of such issues by Her Holiness must be considered a response to those who criticize the severity of [imposition] of *hijab* and see it as contrary to the values [of the Revolution] (pp. 62–4).

Azari devotes the rest of the chapter to reconciling this *hadith* of Fatima with his own position that Islam allows women to take part in political activities. On the one hand, he admits that it is impossible for men and women not to see each other in society and to avoid communication; on the other, he asserts that it is not lawful (*shar'i*) for a woman to look at an unrelated man; and he then makes a case for men's right to chastise their wives in order to keep them in line. He concludes:

> Women's obedience to men is obligatory in only two matters, which come to the same thing, that is the protection of the essence of the family, otherwise a man cannot give even the slightest command to his wife. A man must instruct his wife in what is permitted and forbidden, and cut the roots of corruption; he should not even house his wife in places where she can be seen by unrelated men. A man should not bring unrelated men to his house and let them be seen by his wife. A man must avoid buying and bringing [home] books and magazines and films whose teachings are harmful. When satisfying his own sexual urges, a man must consider the woman's right too, and avoid lechery and socialising with unrelated women and being alone with them in a room either at home or in his office (p. 69).

Azari's message becomes more explicit in the next three chapters, which contain his manifesto for proper gender relations and women's rights according to his version of the Islamic Order, his objections to the current situation and the way women appear in public, and suggestions how to rectify this. The solution he proposes is to regulate women's movements in public and in private, or in his words, to promote the 'culture of *hijab*.'

Chapter Four, 'The Role of Islamic *Hijab* in Keeping Society Pure', starts by defining *hijab*, both figuratively and literally.

> The protection of a woman's bounds and character is her modesty, and the importance of this issue is such that the Commander of the Faithful ['Ali] recommends to his son:
>
> > '[Ensure] if you can, that she does not recognize anybody but you.'
>
> Of course, observance of *hijab* in this way is impossible, because even Purest Fatima and her dear daughter Zainab and the wives of the Noblest Prophet could not abandon more important duties to reach the highest level of *hijab*.
>
> The Holy Verse on the particulars of *hijab* says:
>
> > 'Oh Prophet! say to your wives and your daughters and the women of the believers that they let down upon them their over-garments; this will be more proper, that they may be known, and thus they will not be given trouble' (Ahzab, 59) (p. 73).

Azari then engages in a kind of exegesis that makes little sense unless read in the context of post-revolutionary attempts to promote the chador as 'the supreme form of *hijab*'. His apparent goal is to establish that the Qu'ran's 'over-garment (*julbab*)' is the same as the Islamic Republic's chador. His main evidence is that the chador, like the *julbab*, is a piece of cloth placed over women's headgear, and is thus the best protection for their chastity. However, as soon as Azari has established this, he qualifies it by adding:

> It is better for [women] not to confine themselves to wearing only the chador, because, as narrated in a *hadith* by Umm Salma [one of the Prophet's wives]:
>
>> 'I was in the presence of God's Prophet; Maimuna [another wife] was there too. Blind Ibn Umm Maktum arrived. The Most Noble Prophet commanded: 'Go behind the curtain.' We said: 'O Prophet of God! Isn't it the case that a blind man cannot see us?' The Prophet responded: 'You are not blind. Do you not see him?'"
>
> From this order it clear that *hijab* must be such that men cannot see women and women cannot see men, whereas chador is not such, so in our country and other Muslim countries where it is customary for women to go out shopping and there is no barrier between men and women, [the situation] is contrary to this order (pp. 77–8).

In support, Azari produces three other Qur'anic verses on *hijab* (Ahzab, 32 and 33, and Nur, 31), and a *hadith* of Imam 'Ali: 'if possible do not give [women] permission to leave the house', relating them to contemporary issues:

> [We must therefore] restrict whatever can cause corruption or stimulate men's [sexual] desire, whether this corruption comes through looking at ears, hands and faces decorated with ornaments, or whether it comes through looking at body protrusions, even if the skin is covered.
>
> Therefore, tight trousers and stockings that reveal the shape of a leg, using perfume – which has stimulating properties – and the sound that comes either from the throat or from tapping decorated feet, or singing by men and women which stimulates sexual desire, all these cause corruption and are forbidden.
>
> Such corruption might afflict people by other means, some of which are as follows:
>
> 1. Reading stimulating novels;
> 2. Looking at pictures which can excite and corrupt men and women;
> 3. Watching bad films, even if the actors are unknown Muslim or even non-Muslim women;
> 4. Shaking hands with an unrelated women, even through a glove; touching a woman's body, even through clothing, if it is stimulating;
> 5. Joking and laughing with unrelated [people of other sex];

6. Even learning the Joseph Sura [the story of Potiphar's wife Zulaikha], if it
can have a bad effect.

This bizarre catalogue encapsulates Azari's sexual morality; directed at men as
well as women, both are expected to observe it. When it relates to women, he
calls it *hijab,* giving this concept a meaning far broader than the dress code.

Therefore a Muslim woman's character must be placed within such
confines that she will not be vulnerable to aggression by an unrelated
person, even in his imagination ... What has today become known as
Islamic *hijab,* which covers women's nakedness but displays the parts that
stimulate, is not Islamic *hijab.* Islamic *hijab* is what protects a woman's
character from man's aggression by any means (p. 81).

The chapter ends with a discussion of rules for looking at women. Three kinds of
look (*nigah*) should be avoided in all circumstances. The first is a look entailing
pleasure (*lizzat*), which he defines as:

a look and a touch that transforms a permitted action into a forbidden
one. Therefore, if a young man looks at his mother or sister or another
relative or touches their body with the intention of pleasure; or if a man
looks at another man, or even if a man or woman looks at or touches a
non-human entity; or even if they touch their own body in such a way –
this is forbidden. Only one's spouse is exempted here (p. 83).

Second is a look that entails *riba,* the fear that it might lead to a forbidden act,
even if pleasure or evil are unintended; for instance, looking at a woman's face
with the intention of describing it to someone else. Third is a look that leads to
chaos (*fitna*), resulting in a forbidden act, even if without the intention of
pleasure or evil: for instance, watching a film or listening to a story that might
have bad results.

Having said all this, Azari then raises a logical question:

If the rationale for *hijab* is to prevent men falling into corruption, then it
should suffice for men to guard their gaze; why such an emphasis on
women's observing *hijab*?

His answer occupies two pages: paraphrased, it reads:

It is for woman's human dignity that she must observe *hijab,* because one
difference between an animal female and a human female is that the
former will surrender to any male by instinct. If a woman does not cover
herself she may attract any man, and this is certainly not in her interest.
The human female has been created to be part of an order, and if she defies
the rules of this order she will be separated from it and might not be able
to rejoin a new order. This is what has happened to Western women. If a
woman understands properly why a man is attracted to her, she will feel
degraded, not respected, because he has seen her as a means of satisfying

his own sexual and animal urges; that is, he has considered her as a worthless animal. On this, Imam Sadiq says: 'looking at an infidel's pudenda is like looking at an animal's.' There is consensus among jurists that looking at an infidel woman's face and body is allowed. Some jurists object to looking at nomad or peasant women who because of their work and geographical conditions do not cover their heads or parts of their body ... because they consider it an insult to nomad and peasant women, although there is a *hadith* that such women must obey the rule [to cover themselves]. According to Sura Nur, a Muslim woman must observe *hijab* in the presence of non-Muslim women, which confirms this point, although there might be other points there, because infidel women may describe Muslim women's features to their men. From this, clearly the benefit of observing *hijab* goes to women themselves, not to men (pp. 84–6).

In Chapter Five, 'The Role of the Islamic Regime in Keeping Society Pure', Azari first re-emphasizes the necessity for the Islamic government to enforce *hijab*, as one of its primary duties. He then argues that Islamic punishments are the most effective way to ensure that women comply with *hijab*.

Chapter Six, 'The Role of Marriage in Keeping Society Pure', defends *mut'a*, temporary marriage, a contract with a definite duration (from a few minutes to 99 years), which only Shi'i jurists recognize as valid. It legitimizes a sexual union as well as the children born into it, yet it is socially frowned on, regarded by some as a form of prostitution, and women who enter such unions are stigmatized.[7] Azari argues that it works as a kind of safety valve for society, and should be encouraged when legal means of satisfying sexual urges – that is, permanent marriage – are not feasible. He writes:

> By legislating the ruling (*hukm*) of *mut'a*, besides the intention of preserving public modesty in Islamic society, God has given the Islamic ruler a free hand to respond to social conditions. He can expand the ruling in order to preserve society from sexual corruption when necessary; or, when society has no problem in [satisfying] sexual urges, he can limit it.

He then explains how *mut'a* differs from *zina* (sexual intercourse without marriage), taking issue with both Sunni jurists who do not recognize *mut'a* and Iranian popular culture which stigmatizes it. It soon becomes evident that Azari himself does not consider temporary marriage a proper one, and certainly not something that fathers can be proud of.

> Compared to *mut'a*, the castle of marriage (*izdivaj*) is solider, more impenetrable and more secure. Therefore Islam considers the marriage of nubile daughters to be among the good fortunes of a father (p. 104).

By 'marriage', Azari means the permanent form, the only one popularly regarded as proper – *mut'a* – is never called marriage, but simply 'formula' (*sigha*, short for *sigha-yi 'aqd*). He then preaches the virtues of marriage, to future spouses and their parents. He touches on issues such as the stipulation of dowry in marriage contracts, choice of partners, and equity in marriage. Again he gives neither logical nor juristic argument, but tries to strike a balance on moral grounds. He concludes as follows:

> Husband and wife, like two dear friends and colleagues, must lead a shared life, and neither should try to dominate the other, since both patriarchy and matriarchy are condemned and reprehensible.
>
> It is important to note that in some situations it is better to refrain from marriage. In the absence of [financial] means and other obstacles, it is better for a human being to put him/herself within the shield of chastity and abstinence. If a woman sacrifices her sexual urges for Islam, the Leader and the Islamic Republic, she will be on the same level as Mary, mother of Jesus and Asiya, wife of Pharaoh. Many revolutionary sisters have sacrificed their youth and vitality at the feet of soldiers of the Islamic Revolution [the war-wounded] and have aroused the wonder of Westernized girls. Islam and its Leader is proud of those women who have waited for many years for the return of the war prisoners and wasted their youth.
>
> It is true that God Almighty orders society and parents to prepare for the marriage of their children, and that the Prophet says:
>
> > 'marriage is my practice and whoever avoids it is not among my followers.'
>
> But, at the same time, [the Prophet] says that if you are unable to marry, wait and do not fall into the trap of the evil of lust (pp. 107–8).

With this passage, the main text of *Image* ends.[8] It has something new to say: it encapsulates the essence of the traditionalists' new narrative and the kind of dilemmas they face in reconciling their gender views with the imperatives of the Islamic Republic. But how do women relate to such a book? What is its place in the gender debates in Qum seminaries?

Zanan's response

The answers to both questions are to be found in a review that appeared in *Zanan* in spring 1994, prefaced by a short paragraph in which *Zanan* apologizes for the delay in publication, stressing the need to respond to the book's gender thesis:

> [Since] the views expressed in this book represent a current influential in shaping the movement and condition of Iranian Muslim women, we consider publication [of the review] to be necessary, however late. In this

review, we shall become acquainted with the esteemed writer [Azari]'s most important views on women, and we shall read a critique of these views based on [Qur'anic] verses and authentic *ahadith*.[9]

The reviewer, signing himself Kazem Musavi, disposes of Azari's arguments one by one, pointing out both his errors regarding sacred sources and how his text negates the Islamic Republic's rhetoric on women. Its opening paragraph reads:

> What dismays and amazes the reader of this book is the choice of *Woman's Image in the Islamic Order* for a title, and the unusually high print run for a first impression. And all that in Women's Week. In that week, the Order strives to celebrate and to illustrate the importance of the status of women, then it allows the publication of such a book!! Likewise, what attracts attention more than anything else is the way the Islamic government is degraded by suggesting that it should interfere with the voluptuous way that some women walk! by branding as infidels Muslim women whose *hijab* the writer finds incorrect; and even by creating doubts as to the correctness of the *hijab* of Holy Zahra, Holy Zainab [the Prophet's grand-daughter] and the Prophet's wives. As a result, the correct interpretation of *hijab* [according to Azari] becomes the seclusion of women. Finally, the most prominent aspect of the book is that it places such emphasis on women's sexual features – in the author's words, 'sites of stimulation' – that it could [itself] sexually excite male readers. And this, beyond insulting the status of women, belittles and denigrates men, who according to the author see interaction with women only in sexual terms.
>
> Apart from this, Mr Azari-Qumi believes that the questions now raised about women's issues are those suggested by colonialists from capitalist countries. ... What he has forgotten is that protests and objections were raised by Muslims themselves, and even by the Prophet's relatives in the Time of [his] Presence. So, the colonialists' bad record and deeds do not mean we can blame them for any question or debate. Umm Salma, the Prophet's wife, asks why only men take part in wars and women are deprived; why women should inherit half what men do; and again, why there is no mention in the Qur'an of women who came to Medina.
>
> Asma', wife of Ja'far Ibn Abi Talib [Imam 'Ali's brother], who after his martyrdom became wife of Abu Bakr [the first Caliph] and 'Ali, asked: 'Are women mentioned in the Qur'an?' She was told: 'No.' She went to see the Prophet and said 'why are women not mentioned in the Qur'an?' and after this women were mentioned in several verses. Islamic history has many other instances of women's protest which space does not allow me to mention.

The rest of the review questions Azari's mastery of religious sciences, his common sense and his political understanding, takes issue with his narrow and literal reading of the sacred traditions, and points out inconsistencies in his political vision as well as his nonsensical assertions. This is done under three sarcastic headings, corresponding to the three central arguments in Azari's text, starting with the following.

Perfect *Hijab* Means Hiding Within the Four Walls of the House!

To challenge Azari's notion of *hijab*, the reviewer quotes two passages in which he contradicts himself. In the first, Azari goes to such lengths in stressing the importance of *hijab* that he ends up defining it as an absolute ban on contact between the sexes. He finds legitimacy for this strict notion in Imam 'Ali's *hadith* addressed to his son: 'if you can, [make sure] that she does not recognize anybody but you.' In the second passage Azari attributes such a notion of *hijab* to Western Capitalist propaganda which tries to blacken the name of Islam and lead women astray, and then denies that *hijab* restricts women's social activity.

Having pointed out the contradiction, the reviewer produces four arguments to show how and why Azari errs in his notion of *hijab*.

1. Azari cannot use that *hadith*, as its authenticity can be disputed in two ways. First, it is not clear who is being addressed: some scholars hold that Imam 'Ali was addressing his son Muhammad, others that it was his son Imam Hasan, still others 'recognize this *hadith* to be among those of Ibn Muqafa' who apparently made it up to serve Bani 'Abbas rulers.' Further, the chain of reports for this *hadith* is also problematic, as the reviewer discusses at length (p. 37).

2. Azari's translation of a key term in the *hadith*, 'la ya-rafna', 'she does not recognize, or know,' is faulty:

> 'not recognize' here entails the absence of emotional and intellectual recognition, a kind of 'recognizing' that comes from frequency of dealings and exchange and entails a kind of intimacy. To interpret it as the kind of recognition based on seeing with the eyes is erroneous. Here it means that a woman should keep this recognition only for her husband, and no other person; not that she becomes blind and deaf, cut off from society, a prisoner in the four walls of the house.

3. The context of the *hadith* should be examined:

> Even if we accept this *hadith* as authentic, it is addressed to Iman Hasan as leader and Imam of Muslims or to Muhammad [Imam 'Ali's son by another wife] as an influential Muslim personality. The 'boundary' (*harim*) of the Imam of Muslims or a distinguished religious personality is different from that of ordinary people. The spouse of the Imam as leader of the Muslims was subjected to particular conditions. It is natural that nobody should recognize her in order to be preserved from danger [of assassination].

4. Azari's definition of *hijab* is absurd:

> He claims that even Holy Zahra was unable to attain the highest state of
> *hijab*; in a situation when Azari finds fault with the *hijab* of the Prophet's
> women, then pity the women of this age for whom [a jurist like] Azari sits
> in judgement and is empowered to discern Rules. [His] justification 'for
> more important duties' is an excuse worse than sin. In his logic, no other
> duty is more important than *hijab*, by which he means women staying at
> home ...
>
> According to this perspective, municipalities must draw a curtain in
> all passage-ways, streets and vehicles, because, even if women go around
> inside bags, men can still see their silhouettes, and if the government is
> unable to prevent this, then, in order to ensure observance of the *hijab* the
> author has in mind, women must not leave home.

Drawing attention to Azari's earlier encouragement to Muslim women in Iran to
follow the example of Fatima and take part in political and cultural struggles, the
reviewer writes:

> But [Azari] does not explain to the reader how to account for such
> contradictory statements. Is it that women's participation is necessary only
> in time of struggle, after which they must retire to the home? Or is
> women's participation after the struggle necessary? If so, why should *hijab*
> be such that a man cannot see a woman? And why does he consider chador
> inadequate and interpret *hijab* as the four walls of the house?

The reviewer then produces two passages from Azari's text, accusing him of
exaggeration and extremism and issuing groundless *fatvas*. I have already given
both passages: in the first, Azari brands as sinful a number of acts, such as
wearing tight trousers or perfume, a certain way of talking and walking; in the
second, he lists measures the government must take in order to protect public
chastity. Calling them '*fatva*-letters', the reviewer first points out that, besides the
fact that Azari himself confesses it is impossible to implement such a notion of
hijab, his *fatva* is not only weak on juristic grounds but contradicts his own
doctrinal stance.

> The majority of issues in this *fatva*-letter lack shari'a proof, and its
> inference from Sura Nur, 31 is so difficult that it is almost impossible. The
> proscription and the objective of the Law-Giver cannot be found by means
> of juristic preference (*istishan*) and probability (*istiba'ad*). The holy verse
> explicitly mentions *khalkhal* [women's foot ornament at time of the
> Prophet] and the emphasis is on the practice of that period. From this
> verse, a general rule cannot be deduced to the effect that whatever is
> stimulating must be sinful; and that something is sinful if it is stimulating.
> The jurist's task is to give only a general ruling, not to define the subject. It
> is up to the believer, according to his/her situation, to ascertain whether

tight trousers are stimulating for them or not. Leaving this aside, issuing such a *fatva* is not in line with his definition of the *vali-yi faqih*. From what we understand of his doctrinal basis, no jurist is in a position to give orders to the Islamic state and the government, and all jurists are under the command of the *vali-yi faqih*.

The other problem with these musts and must-nots is that they always want women not to talk, not to walk, not to have the right to choose what to wear, but they never tell sick men to close their sick eyes and purify their sick hearts and thoughts (p. 39).

Granting Men the post of Director-General of the Family

Having drawn attention to this basic contradiction in Azari's argument – that he and the political clerics are no longer in a position to declare independent judgement or to give a ruling that goes against the wish of the Islamic Republic – the reviewer turns his attention to Azari's notion of gender roles in the family. The heading refers to a passage in Chapter Three of *Image*, translated above, where Azari argues that the internal affairs of the family are assigned to women, and external affairs, which need reasoning and logic, to men. In defining men's role in the family, he uses a management term for 'director-general', *mudir-i kull*, used in Persian only in the context of governmental and private organizations, where it is an appointment carrying authority and prestige. The reviewer comments:

> This unfounded statement comes from a historic, honour-bound mode of thinking ... which confines correct legal relations of a woman after marriage to her husband and does not even give her permission to set foot outside the house to see her parents.

In a footnote, the reviewer explains that he refers to this mode of thinking as honour-bound because it concerns cultural notions of sexual honour, but it is not in fact sexual honour but a kind of abuse of men's sensitivities.

> To give religious sanction to their demands, the adherents of this mode of thinking traditionally resort to Sura Nisa, 34, interpreting it according to their own views. It must be said that His Excellency Azari does not join them on this matter, as he, unlike many others, has interpreted this verse in a realistic manner [men are a degree higher than women because they provide for them]; he resorts to a *hadith* which contains a directive for a specific problem at a specific juncture. The *hadith* concerned is about the division of labour between Hazrat 'Ali and Zahra. According to this *hadith*, tasks inside the home were allocated to Zahra and those outside to 'Ali. Now, the chores inside the home were much more strenuous than those outside: fetching water from the well, grinding grain, making bread and so

forth ... were among Zahra's duties, and collecting wood and shopping were 'Ali's. This division was altered when their situation changed and they were able to have a servant. Then again, in the period after the Prophet's death, when 'Ali was house-bound because of his opposition to the Caliph, it was Zahra who went out and dealt with political issues and campaigned for him. Therefore, if there is no weakness in the chain of reporters, this *hadith* pertains only to a specific time. To extend it to all people and all times, in all conditions and situations, is unacceptable. Besides, the actual practice of these honoured personalities ['Ali and Zahra] is incompatible with the author's perspective, because Zahra at different points in her life took charge of both internal and external affairs of her household. Even if we suppose Azari's account to be correct, other *ahadith* contradict his perspective. These *ahadith* recognize women as in charge and managers of the house and assign them responsibility for the children.

The reviewer quotes a *hadith* of the Prophet in which men and women are held equally responsible for the family and children, and ends the section on a sarcastic note:

> Therefore, on the basis of undisputed evidence and proof, we now depose men from the high post of director-general of the family!
>
> The thesis of men's superiority in reason and wisdom is groundless, even futile; it won't wash any more!

Woman: a Worthless Animal

This heading refers to a passage where Azari makes a bizarre connection between women without *hijab* and an animal's genitals, a passage so confusing that I had to paraphrase it to render it into meaningful English. The reviewer first quotes the part where Azari invokes a *hadith* of Imam Sadiq in order to suggest that in a man's eyes a woman without *hijab* is a worthless animal, then goes on:

> Mr Azari's account in this section, besides being slanderous, is ambiguous and disjointed. If, in likening [a *hijab*less women] to an animal, he has nudity in mind, it should be said that it is not clear that that is intended. Even if we suppose that it is, one cannot make a connection between an animal's nudity and a women's lack of *hijab*. A *hijab*less woman is Muslim, so she is not the subject of the above *hadith*; and even if he does not recognize her as a Muslim, his simile still makes no sense. The *hadith* refers to the act of 'looking', not the manner in which one looks!
>
> Secondly, the *hadith* compares an animal's genitals to an infidel's and does not give any ruling on that. To find the ruling we need other evidence, which is to be found in *ahadith* that forbid looking at animals' genitals, especially when they copulate. ... But Mr Azari inserts this *hadith*

in his own text in such a way that a reader unfamiliar with *fiqh* and *ahadith* will think there is something in Imam Sadiq's *hadith* that supports Azari's position. The reader will not understand that there is no link between the two, apart from the word 'animal'. Above all, the grammatical gender in the saying is masculine, which means, if we accept Azari's reading, that it only forbids members of the same sex to look at each others' genitals, that is, a Muslim man can look at an infidel woman's genitals. This defies any logic as no jurist would give such a ruling. So, can anything be inferred from Mr Azari's account, other than the fact that a woman is indeed a 'worthless animal'?

Having impugned Azari's juristic expertise as well as his common sense, the reviewer ends with two general points and a plea.

I hope this brief review has made it clear that threatening and shaming women in order to make them accept *hijab* and other religious rules doesn't work – as has been the experience of recent years – and in effect produces the opposite effect. Personal values should not be involved when relating sacred texts and deriving rules from them, and personal opinions cannot be presented as Islamic perspectives. Why can't these great men have the courage to admit that these views stem from their own understanding and their own life experiences? So that people, especially women, are not repelled by religion and can learn that there are other opinions. An Islamic jurist does not deny people God's mercy; he calls people to God, not to himself (pp. 36–40).

Conclusion

As with the ritual to which women are subjected upon entering a government office, the debate articulated in texts such as these is also carving a new space for women within an Islamic framework. It is making it possible to question old assumptions and to discuss women as not merely sexual but also social beings. This debate is more or less absent in classical Islamic legal texts, where women figure mainly in sections related to marriage and divorce.

One of the unintended consequences of the creation of the Islamic Republic and the application of *fiqh* to social reality has been that women and their legal rights are now located at the heart of jurisprudential discourse. This is so because, by the time the Islamic Republic was born, not only were women active in all fields of social and economic life, but after the Revolution the religious authorities increasingly came to rely on popular support – including that of women – for maintaining their political ascendancy. As a result, neither would women agree to give up their rights to public life nor could the clerics afford to send women back home. Thus a door from within was opened that could no longer be closed. Women have established their presence in public and in society. The two texts examined here are but two examples of the diverse ways in which this presence was debated within *fiqh* discourse.

Ayatullah Azari's book reveals the assumptions behind the Islamic Republic's obsession with *hijab* and the kinds of dilemmas that clerics face in coming to terms with the current realities of Iranian society such as women's public presence. It represents the new traditionalist narrative on gender, which informed and dominated the gender policies of the first decade of the Islamic Republic; unlike the old narrative, it is not silent on women's social roles, but accepts their participation in society and politics, while trying to retain traditional assumptions about gender. By the early 1990s, this new narrative was increasingly facing challenges from those who objected to the imposition of *fiqh* in every aspect of social life. Sa'idzadeh's review in *Zanan* was one such challenge.

By the late 1990s, these challenges eventually brought about a major shift in the official discourse and politics of the Islamic Republic. Not only did the early radical discourse of the Revolution gradually give way to a more pluralistic one, but the context and the dynamic of the debate on women's rights also changed. The turning point in this transition was the victory of Muhammad Khatami in the 1997 presidential election, which saw the emergence of the reformist movement and a free press. Both the authors of these texts contributed to – and were affected by – this transition. In 1994, Ayatullah Azari-Qumi broke all his ties with the conservative clerics at *Risalat* – the newspaper he had founded in 1986 – and returned to the seminary way of life. In December 1997, following an open letter in which he openly criticized and questioned the qualifications of the current supreme leader (Ayatullah 'Ali Khamene'i), he was put under house arrest. He died not long after, in February 1999.

Sa'idzadeh, the author of *Zanan*'s review, became another victim of the struggle between conservatives and reformists, which took a new turn following the 1997 presidential election. In June 1998, after the publication of an article in the liberal daily *Jami'a* (subsequently closed) in which he compared religious traditionalists in Iran to the Taleban in Afghanistan, he was detained. Though he was never officially charged, his crime was to have extended to the outside world debates and arguments that belonged in the seminaries. He was released five months later, but 'unfrocked' – that is, he lost his clerical position, and became 'forbidden-pen' – that is to say that his writings cannot be published.

But the debate over women's place in society and their civil rights continues to develop. In November 1999, for the first time since the Revolution, the wisdom of the policy of enforcing *hijab* was questioned publicly. This was done by Abdullah Nuri, Khatami's former Interior Minister who was impeached by the parliament in 1998 and tried by the Special Clerical Court – two bodies dominated by conservative clerics. As one of the boldest reformers, what Nuri said during his trial is significant. While defending *hijab* as a religious rule, he advocated tolerance and the recognition of reality. '*Hijab* is among our religious obligations,' he said, 'but the fact is that this religious rule is not followed by some in society (including some Muslims), and government's effort to force these people to observe the rule of *hijab* has not been successful.'

Instead of denying reality, or trying to force it into a straightjacket of legal rules and to punish those who do not conform, Nuri, reflecting the Reformist agenda, offered a different proposal: to distinguish social reality from religious ideals and rules, to give people the choice whether or not to follow the mandates of their faith, which can never be enforced successfully, as the failure of the Islamic Republic's *hijab* policy has shown. Such a radical departure from the old slogans led to a predictable reaction from the Special Clerical Court: he was sentenced to five years in jail.

But the public reacted differently, as evidenced in the landslide victory of the reformists in the February 2000 parliamentary elections. Nuri had raised the stakes by making explicit what the Reformists did not dare to say during their campaign. It remains to be seen how the new parliament – the first not to be dominated by the conservative clerics – will deal with the old wisdoms of *fiqh* and women's issues. The discussion in this chapter has sought to open a window on one of the internal debates that paved the way for this transformation. In this sense both texts belong to a moment of transition.

Notes

1 See the scene at the entrance of the Imam Khomeini Judicial Complex in Tehran, in the documentary film *Divorce Iranian Style*, directed by Kim Longinotto and Ziba Mir-Hosseini (Channel 4 TV, 1998).
2 The paper is based on research conducted in Iran in 1995 and 1997, funded by grants from the Nuffield Foundation and the British Institute of Persian Studies. I am grateful to both organizations for their generous help.
3 For *Zanan* and Sa'idzadeh's contribution, see Z. Mir-Hosseini (1999) *Islam and Gender: The Religious Debate in Contemporary Iran*, Princeton.
4 See A. Kian, 'L'invasion culturelle occidentale: mythe ou réalité?' *Cahiers d'Etudes sur la Méditerranée Orientale et le Monde Turco-Iranien* 20 (juillet–décembre 1995), pp. 73–90.
5 See A. K. Ferdows, 'Women and the Islamic Revolution', *International Journal of Middle East Studies* 15, 2, (1983), pp. 288–90.
6 For a discussion see, Mir-Hosseini, *Islam and Gender*, pp. 24–5.
7 See S. Haeri (1989) *Law of Desire: Temporary Marriage in Iran*, London.
8 In another fascinating chapter, Azari responds to 21 questions posed by 'a female student of midwifery' soon after the original articles appeared in winter 1992.
9 *Zanan* 17, Farvardin/Urdibihist 1373 (Spring 1994), p. 36.

eleven

Perceptions of Gender Roles Among Female Iranian Immigrants in the United States

Ali Akbar Mahdi

Introduction

The Immigration and Nationality Act in 1965 changed the landscape of American ethnic communities. Waves of new immigrants came to the United States with new values, norms, languages and religions quite different from the ones in the past.[1] As has been the case, the older immigrants have always worried about the economic, political and social impacts of the newcomers. The demographic, occupational and educational characteristics of the new immigrants have generated new patterns of immigrant settlement, occupational mobility and adaptation. These new patterns, along with the increasing cultural pluralism and multicultural developments, have generated new concerns about the wider and deeper impacts of immigration on the American population, namely male–female, parent–child and family–society relationships.[2] The persistence of ethnic families and their impact on the cultural norms in the host society continue to remain a major concern of the immigration studies.[3]

Studies on gender roles within the immigrant family and perceptions of gender roles among male and female immigrants are relatively new.[4] Traditionally, sociologists have paid much attention to the structure of the immigrant family, its pattern of adaptation, and its mechanisms for survival in a new culture. Receiving little attention is how male and female immigrants perceive the gender roles they bring from the homeland as compared with those acquired in the host society. The emphasis on gender roles and the power relations underlying them connects the micro and macro analysis, and helps us to understand how ethnic values are mediated in the new host societies, and what types of marital relations might emerge.[5]

The Iranian immigrant family in the United States is one of the latest varieties of the 'ethnic family.' Given this family's high level of educational and professional achievement, the study of its male–female relationships, pattern of labour division and power allocation and perceptions of gender roles warrant particular attention. Unfortunately, literature on Iranian female immigrants is scanty. What is available often consists of journalistic reports, ideological essays or politically oriented statements. Recently, scholars have begun to study aspects of the Iranian immigrant family in the USA.[6]

This study will add to this nascent literature by elucidating how Iranian immigrant women understand their gender roles within the family and society. Because these women left their homeland and had to rebuild their lives in a new society, one must examine how their views about their own roles and relationships inside and outside the family have evolved: have Iranian immigrant women's perceptions of gender roles changed due to their geographical relocation and transformative experiences? Have they reconsidered the issues surrounding women's status in response to political developments in their homeland during the past two decades? Have these immigrant women imported their traditional roles into their newly adopted environment? To what extent do their views on male–female interactions, sexuality, marriage, divorce, gendered child-rearing and religious commands about women's status differ from those they held in Iran? What do Iranian immigrant women think about the traditions, values and norms of their adopted society?

I will address these questions with reference to a survey conducted in the USA during 1995–96. The survey included 149 randomly selected subjects. I asked women how they perceive various gender roles in Iran and the United States, how they share tasks and power within their families, as well as demographic questions pertaining to their social status in the society. The data presented here includes partial results of the sample and illuminates the views of Iranian women in the United States and the shifts in their perspectives resulting from migration. This study demonstrates how Iranian women residing outside their homeland have moved away from the traditional perspectives attributed to them by some Iranian and Orientalist scholars.

Equally important, this study offers a forum for Iranian immigrant women to recount their experiences and to explain their perceptions of the everyday realities they live. Listening to these voices is crucial, for these women can and do express their own concerns – rather than ceding that right to political groups who claim to speak for them. We need to learn first hand what attitudes, beliefs, concerns and values these women have regarding their roles in the private and public sphere.

The study

In 1995, I mailed to 821 households in 41 states a questionnaire comprised of 113 questions. This questionnaire posed a range of questions on decision making in the family, women's attitudes towards female gender roles in general, and their perceptions of gender roles in the United States and Iran in particular. The results of this survey paint a statistical picture of Iranian immigrant women who regard their roles inside and outside home as different from those ascribed to them by the religious and social norms of their homeland.

The sample

The respondents included Iranian females randomly drawn from addresses of one cultural and two scholarly associations in the United States: the Iranian Cultural Society of Columbus, Ohio (680 addresses, 307 in Ohio, 373 in other states), the Middle East Studies Association (MESA) and the Center for Iranian Research and Analysis (CIRA). Although the latter two databases were biased because their records consisted of highly educated social scientists, the addresses from the Iranian Cultural Society of Columbus contained a more diverse population. Drawing from this database was weighted in order to include more non-academician subjects in the sample. The selection of more subjects from the latter would have skewed the sample towards a higher number of people from Ohio. However, an examination of completed questionnaires shows a more diffused and distributed pattern among the subjects from various states.

Of the total 821 questionnaires mailed to selected addresses, 26 were returned due to incorrect addresses, and 52 were returned because there was no female at those addresses. Of the 743 remaining questionnaires, 158 (21.3 per cent) were completed and returned. Originally, I intended to include non-Iranian women married to Iranian husbands as well as second-generation Iranian women who were born to Iranian families abroad. Although surveying such groups would provide an interesting basis for measuring the effects of migration, bi-cultural tendencies, and acculturation, the number of these respondents – only nine in the sample – did not suffice for meaningful measurement. Consequently, I excluded non-Iranian and second-generation Iranian women from the study, leaving 149 completed questionnaires for analysis.

Profile of the respondents

The respondents are Iranian female immigrants who have lived in the USA an average of 16.05 years (median = 15.98). Close to half (42.9 per cent) of the sample are between the ages 31–40, and another 30.6 per cent are between the ages 41–50 (Table 11.1). A majority of them are married (73.2 per cent), have children (78.4 per cent), work outside the home (77.9 per cent), and regard their stay in the USA as permanent (83.9 per cent). While 72.7 per cent are Muslim, 14.4 per cent insist that they do not adhere to any religion (Table 11.2).

Table 11.3 shows the occupational profile of the sample and national data on Iranian females declaring Iranian ancestry in the 1990 US Census sampling.

Table 11.1 Respondents' Age (*N*=147)

Age	Percentage
Under 20	8.9
21–30	10.2
31–40	42.9
41–50	30.6
51–60	12.9
Above 60	2.7

Table 11.2 Respondents' Religious Affiliation (*N*=139)

Religion	Percentage
Muslim	72.7
Baha'i	4.3
Christian	5.8
Jewish	2.9
Zoroastrian	0.0
No religion	14.4

Table 11.3 Occupational profile of respondents and Iranian women in the USA

Occupational category	Sample (1996) (%)	Female Iranians in USA (1990)* (%)
Managers	8.8	14.8
Professional specialty	47.4	27.8
Sales	6.9	16.8
Clerical	1.9	19.1
Service	20.2	14.7
Crafts	6.1	3.2
Other blue-collar workers	—	3.6
Housewife	7.0	—
Student	1.7	—
Total	100.0	100.0
Number of employed	137	34,259

* *Source*: US. Census, 1990, Public Micro Samples (PUMS).

While the numbers of professors, physicians, attorneys (professional specialty), nurses, research assistants, teachers and technologists (service) in the sample are proportionally very high, businesswomen and corporate managers are under-represented. Although this reflects a bias in the sample, the national data on employment of female Iranians in the United States is neither accurate nor comparable with other ethnic groups in the United States.[7]

In terms of education, over 50.0 per cent of respondents have graduate degrees, 32.9 per cent bachelor degrees, and only 3.4 per cent have just a high school diploma (Table 11.4). Respondents' husbands were even more educated, 72.6 per cent possessing graduate degrees. While respondents had a median family income of $60–75000, their own individual income averaged over $30,000 annually. Respondents earning less than $10000 comprised 13.0 per cent of the sample. Those having no income also constituted 13.0 per cent of the sample (Table 11.5).

Table 11.4 Educational profiles of respondents and Iranian females in the United States (*N*=146)

Educational level	Sample (1996) (%)	USA (1990)* (%)
None	0.0	–
Some schooling	2.0	15.3
High school	3.4	21.8
Some college w/o degree	11.6	23.7
College graduates	82.9**	39.2

* *Source*: US. Census, 1990, Public Micro Samples (PUMS).
** This is sum of three categories: Bachelors Degree 32.88%, Masters Degree 26.71% and Doctorate, 23.29%

Table 11.5 Respondents' own and household annual income

Income in dollars	Respondents' own income (%)	Household (%)
None	13.0	–
Under 5000	7.2	–
5001–10000	5.8	–
10001–15000	5.1	
Under 15000	4.1	
15001–30000	19.6	5.0
30001–45,000	22.5	12.4
45001–60000	17.4	20.7
60001–75000	4.3	15.7
75001–100000	2.9	20.7
Above 100000	2.2	21.5
N	138	121

Limitations of the study

My efforts to generalize from the results of this research are subject to two limitations. First, although the composition of the chosen sample is not too uncharacteristic of the general Iranian population in the USA, given the databases used, the sample *is highly skewed towards a more educated and professional population.* Random sampling using more mixed and diverse population lists might have produced a more representative sample. As the data in Tables 11.3 and 11.4 indicate, the respondents are over-represented in categories of graduate degrees and professional specialization. Yet we must note that Iranian women in the USA are not very representative of Iranian women in general. Iranian immigrant women are a select population possessing the educational and financial means to migrate to the USA, and they have achieved relatively high socio-economic status among immigrants overall.

Furthermore, this study *does not take into account the different migratory patterns among Iranian immigrants.* The immigration experiences of Iranians have differed depending on social class, educational background, ethnic identity and gender. Different migration trajectories generate various types of gender relations and roles. The cultural norms, traditions and values of a society are neither monolithic nor static. Even among people of the same country, such factors as ethnicity, ideology, religion and social class influence one's view of gender relationships. Although this study does not reflect these factors, I must acknowledge that a larger number of subjects in each of these categories might have shown observable differences in the views of women from varying ethnic, religious, and socio-economic backgrounds. As Hanassab has already shown, that religious background makes a difference in patterns of mate-selection and behavioural expectations in intimate relationships among Iranians.[8]

Findings: shifting away from traditional values in the search for new roles and rights

Examining answers to the questions about women's roles in family and society, I find that most Iranian immigrant women share a Western liberal view of women's role in society. They identify love as the primary basis for marriage, consider the wearing of a veil as a restriction on women's freedom, and perceive women as equal with men in all aspects of private and social life. They overwhelmingly oppose governmental involvement in defining the rules for women's clothing and restrictions on women's activities. While their views on women's sexual behaviour are grounded in an Islamic perspective, they tend to reject religious values as the sole guide for such behaviour.

Immigrant women have strong opinions on various issues – women's abilities, marriage, divorce, religious values, sexual freedom and interaction with the men, socialization of children, women's movement in the West, and career opportunities for women. Their attitudes about veiling, dating, the government's role in deciding women's dress codes, and the stance of Islam towards women, are generally negative. They disapprove of how the Iran's Islamic Republic has sought to define women's gender roles, deploring the status of women in their homeland.

With these broadly outlined findings in mind, I discuss below the perceptions of Iranian immigrant women regarding seven issues – veiling, marriage, divorce, women's rights, male-female relationships, gendered child rearing, and the influence of religion on women's lives. The following analysis reports on the median and percentages of responses to a set of statements in a Likert-type five-point scale: (1) strongly disagree, (2) disagree, (3) neutral, (4) agree, and (5) strongly agree.

Understanding women's issues

A consistent theme in the women's studies literature is the specificity of women's issues and the lack of adequate understanding of these concerns by men. This theme does not escape Iranian female immigrants. The respondents demonstrate strong support for the statement that men do not have a clear understanding of women's problems (median = 4.16). Only a quarter of the sample is neutral or in disagreement with the statement (Table 11.6).

Equality of men and women

Iranian immigrant women agree strongly that men and woman are equal and should be treated as such in both private and public life (median = 4.78). However, they are divided on men's and women's skills and personality traits. The median for the statement 'women are naturally better at doing the house chores' is 2.41. The same applies to their views on the ambitiousness of men versus women. The median for the statement 'men are more ambitious than women' is 2.61. While they have reservations about what women can or

Table 11.6 Respondents' beliefs about women and men

	Median	Mode (%)	N
Women equal to men in social and private life	4.78	5 (69.2)	146
Women better at house work	2.41	1 (30.4)	148
Military jobs not appropriate	2.73	3 (36.7)	147
Women more emotional	3.97	4 (34.5)	148
Men better leaders	1.58	1 (48.3)	147
Men more ambitious	2.61	1 (30.8)	133
Men do not understand of women's problems	4.16	4 (43.5)	147

cannot do, they uniformly disagree with the statement that 'men are better leaders than women' (median = 1.58). Thus, while these immigrant women show a higher degree of confidence in women's abilities in public life, they have not completely abandoned traditional notions of female skills and capabilities.

Feminism

Respondents were asked: 'If we define feminism as a movement in defence and support of women's rights, with which of the following would you identify yourself?' Responses to this question are found in Table 11.7. Responses included 7.6 per cent Islamic feminist, 20.4 per cent secular feminist, and 62 per cent who are not feminist but support women's rights. Women not identifying with any of the above descriptions made up 9.2 per cent of the sample.

Respondents are also divided with regard to the relevance of feminism to the lives of women in Iran. While close to 40 per cent of the sample see no relevance, another 40 per cent feel just the opposite to be the case, and the remaining 20 per cent are unsure. Worth remembering is the fact that a lack of identification with feminism does not mean that these women oppose it. As responses in this survey indicate, the majority of these women are strong supporters of what we may call feminist ideals as defined in the west. The majority of these immigrants do not identify with the label of 'feminism,' but more than half of them think that feminism has done more good than harm for western women.

However, their support for women's rights does not translate into an embrace of feminism, as indicated by these women's responses to open-ended questions at the end of survey – asking them to compare the status of women in Iran and the United States. Although these women believe in male–female equality and in the opportunities provided to women to enhance their status in society, they are not enthusiastic about the individualistic demands characterizing Western feminism.

Table 11.7 Respondents' identification with regard to the label 'feminist'

Form of feminism	Precentage
Secular feminist	20.4
Islamic feminist	7.7
Anti-feminist	0.7
Not feminist but support women's rights	62.0
Other	9.1
N	142

Islam, the Islamic Government and control over women's lives

Islam is a comprehensive religion; life in both private and public spheres is regulated for the pious Muslim. The rights of the individual are subordinated to the welfare of the society. In the case of women, this takes a special meaning because women's and men's rights are perceived differently. Apart from the major differences in biology, capabilities and responsibilities delineated in the Qur'an, Islamic jurisprudence (shari'a) and religious traditions have elaborated on these differences, outlining specific roles for women and men in their private and public lives.[9]

Consequently, this researcher wanted to discover whether and to what extent Iranian immigrant women agree with general religious imperatives regarding female roles in the family and society. In light of the post-revolutionary Iranian leadership's efforts to re-define women's rights and roles according to Islam, I sought to find out how the respondents feel about these developments in their homeland. Since the revolution of 1978–79, the Iranian leadership has passed laws restricting women's clothing, relationships with men, presence in the public sphere, choice of occupation and profession, as well as their rights to marriage, divorce, and inheritance.[10]

Answers to a series of questions on Islam's treatment of women and its role in guiding women's sexual behaviour, suggest that Iranian immigrant women object to governmental regulation of women's clothing in public (Table 11.8). The immigrant women are almost unanimous on this issue, more than on any other (median = 1.18). Only about 8 per cent of respondents favour governmental involvement in deciding what women should wear in public. Another major area of agreement is the question of fairness in Islam's treatment of women. Distinguishing between fairness and respect, about half (51.2 per cent) think that Islam does not treat women respectfully, and over two-thirds (69.6 per cent) that Islam treats women unequally (median = 1.28).

Table 11.8 Respondents' views on Islamic laws and government (1 = strong disagree, 2 = disagree, 3 = neutral, 4 = agree, 5 = strongly agree)

	Median	Mode (%)	N
Islam fair to women	1.28	1 (64.4)	143
Islam respects women	2.20	1 (35.4)	144
Women should have a say in interpreting religious texts	4.38	5 (46.4)	138
Government to decide women's dress in public	1.18	1 (73.2)	143
Women better under the Islamic Republic than under the Shah	1.26	1 (65.7)	140
Religion should guide women's sexual behaviour	1.60	1 (47.9)	144
Should not marry a non-Muslim	1.86	1 (41.3)	143

Some 70 per cent of immigrant women disagree that religion should guide a woman's sexual behaviour. They opine that women should have a voice in the interpretation of what religious texts say about them. On the issue of whether a Muslim woman should be able to marry a man of different religion, a taboo among devout Muslims, the majority of immigrant women are in favour; 65 per cent agreed and 7.7 per cent disagreed. Regarding the status of women in the Islamic Republic of Iran, immigrant women are almost unanimously negative: 85 per cent of the sample concurred that Iranian women are worse off under the Islamic Republic than under the Shah's rule. Only 7.1 per cent rejected this assessment.

Love, sex and relationships

The issues of love, sex and relationships between men and women generate much controversy within the immigrant population. The traditional Iranian family has not given primacy to love as the only basis for initiating marriage or to individual satisfaction as the main reason for continuing a marital union. Social class, tribal nexus, political alliance and status mobility were among some of the major factors influencing marital selections.[11] Moving from a traditional setting in which sexual and intimate issues are private in nature, these immigrant women find themselves in a society that approaches these issues both openly and differently. While most immigrants have shifted away from traditional Iranian views of love, marriage and sexual relationships outside marriage, many are still ambivalent about these issues. Many profess modern attitudes while still continuing traditional practices.

For instance, at the time of marriage most people identify love as the major criterion for entering into the relationship. However, in reality it is not the major factor determining marriages, especially among the more traditional sectors of various socio-cultural groups in Iran. This survey reveals that the ideal of love as the principal determinant in a relationship is slowly taking hold among female immigrants but not yet fully. While over half of the sample (54.4 per cent) see love as a basis for marriage, almost a third (29.4 per cent) adopt a neutral stand on this issue. Moreover, while three-quarters of the respondents concur that there should be no difference in the amount of sexual freedom for men and women – 8.33 per cent disagree, and close to 20 per cent are not sure about this matter – they disagree about the effects of sexual freedom on society. Close to half of the respondents (47.2 per cent) believe that sexual freedom harms both the individual and society, whereas 33.1 per cent think the opposite and 19.72 per cent are unsure. This same pattern is evident in respondents' opinions about the demonstration of intimate affection in the public arena, even between a husband and wife. While half (49.7 per cent) of the respondents approve of such behaviour, slightly over a quarter (28.7 per cent) disapproves, and 21.7 per cent take a neutral position.

Dating, marriage, divorce and husbands

As I have mentioned, more than half the respondents (54.4 per cent) regard love as the principal determinant in a marriage. Although not unanimous on this issue, they overwhelmingly agree that a woman has the right to decide whether, when and whom she wants to marry (92.42 per cent). While they are more supportive of dating prior to marriage – 61.1 per cent approving versus 16 per cent disapproving – their opinions of non-marital sexual relationships between a woman and a trusted male friend is more mixed. While 40.9 per cent approve of such relationships, 43.8 per cent disapprove and 15.3 per cent are neutral. This attitude is consistent with their mixed responses to the idea of sexual freedom indicating that Iranian immigrants have not discarded all their native norms. Many still believe that the current inter-sexual practices in the United States leave women in a vulnerable position and damage their future prospects for establishing a long-lasting marital relationship.

Apparently, the respondents distinguish between adult and teenage dating – a distinction quite understandable in the context of the traditional Iranian culture. Yet they are more liberal about their children's sexual behaviour than their own. Asked whether teenage girls should be allowed to date, 59.9 per cent agreed, 21.8 per cent remained neutral and only 18.3 per cent disagreed. However, when dating assumes any sexual connotation, the approval rate drops significantly. In other words, most Iranian immigrant mothers are willing to allow their female teenagers to date as long as it does not involve sexual contact.

As for relationships with their husbands, Iranian female immigrants are adamantly opposed to traditional arrangements that stress hierarchy and division along public and private lines. The majority (80.2 per cent) disagrees with the traditional view that a wife should generally obey her husband. This disagreement increases when the issue is the physical punishment of women by husbands – even if this results from a woman's own 'disobedience'. They categorically reject the notion that a husband can physically punish his disobedient wife by a rate of 97.2 per cent. This is true not only of 'disobedience to husband' but also of 'disobedience in the form of refusal to sexual intercourse' a behaviour for which Islam allows physical punishment by the husband.[12]

The majority of Iranian immigrant women (78.3 per cent) consider their satisfaction from marriage, especially sexual satisfaction, as crucial for family stability, and 69.4 per cent regard their own careers as no less important than their husbands' career. The majority of them (53.7 per cent) do not think that men should be the primary bread-winners in the family, as opposed to 27.9 per cent with a contrary view. Only a few women have problems with the notion of their husbands staying home to take care of their children – an idea that receives considerable disapproval by women and is generally resented by men inside Iran. Just fewer than 7 per cent of the respondents disagreed with the proposition of men staying at home and raising children while their wives work; 78.5 per cent agreed and 14.6 per cent remained neutral.

Finally, the women were dissatisfied with traditional Iranian kinship obligations and arrangements in marriage. For example, only 3.5 per cent of respondents agreed with the statement that a married woman's obligations should include obeying her in-laws. The majority of respondents attributed the success of their marriages in the host society to the relative absence of interference by their in-laws. They voiced the same disapproval towards the traditional division of property in marriage. When asked about property ownership and financial assets owned by each partner, respondents were unanimous that property in the family should be shared by husband and wife equally, and they favoured a joint bank account: 71.5 per cent agreed, 7 per cent disagreed, and 21.5 per cent were neutral.

For these respondents, divorce is the means of last resort for solving a family dispute. Both Iranian cultural and Muslim religious values discourage married couples from this practice. More importantly, women have traditionally been expected to sacrifice their own personal satisfaction and welfare for the sake of their family.[13] Historically, Iranian women have stayed in bad marriages to preserve family honour and save their children from the negative consequences of divorce. The data in this study indicate that the negativity associated with the breakup of a marriage, at least in the case of a bad one, is declining – a phenomenon taking place in Iran too.[14] The majority of respondents (81.8 per cent) reject the proposition that a woman should stay in an unhappy marriage. However, these women are still ambivalent about terminating a bad marriage when a child's welfare is involved. While half of respondents agreed that having children should not shape the decision to terminate a bad marriage, a third (30.7 per cent) disagreed, and 12.9 per cent did not indicate any preference (Tables 11.9 and 11.11)

Table 11.9 Views on Love, Sexual Freedom, Marriage, and Divorce (1 = strong disagree, 2 = disagree, 3 = neutral, 4 = agree, 5 = strongly agree)

	Median	Mode (%)	N
Love a determining factor	3.62	4 (37.0)	138
Obey husband	1.48	1 (51.0)	143
Physical punishment of disobedient wife	1.03	1 (95.1)	143
Obeying in-laws	1.17	1 (74.8)	143
Male sexual satisfaction more important for Family stability	1.44	1 (53.1)	143
Having joint bank account	4.24	5 (42.4)	144
She decides her marriage	4.78	5 (69.0)	145
Pre-marital dating	3.86	4.5 (30.6)	144
Child no obstacle to end a bad marriage	3.68	4 (35.0)	140
Better unhappy than divorced	1.36	1 (58.0)	143
Wife's career secondary to his	1.72	1 (44.4)	144

Table 11.10 Views about the veil (1 = strong disagree, 2 = disagree, 3 = neutral, 4 = agree, 5 = strongly agree)

	Median	Mode (%)	N
Veil as good protection	1.27	1 (64.8)	145
Veil limits movement	4.47	5 (47.0)	142
Women should determine what they wear in public	4.76	5 (67.1)	147

Table 11.11 Views about raising children (1 = strong disagree, 2 = disagree, 3 = neutral, 4 = agree, 5 = strongly agree)

	Median	Mode (%)	N
No teenage dating	2.23	2 (36.6)	142
Socializing daughters as wife	3.32	4 (33.1)	142
Sex-neutral child raising	4.66	5 (59.7)	144
Same freedom for girls and boys at school	4.71	5 (62.9)	143
Girls' participation in sports	4.79	5 (70.6)	143
Separation of boys and girls at school	1.88	1 (42.3)	104

Views about the veil

The practice of veiling has provoked controversy throughout this century both in and outside Iran. During the twentieth century, Iranian women have been forced by their governments to unveil and veil themselves; neither the veil's removal nor its use has been voluntary. The decision was arbitrary and imposed by the full force of law in both cases.[15] Consequently, I wished to learn Iranian immigrant women's views of this practice.

The data in Table 11.10 indicate that the veil remains one of the most disliked aspects of the Islamic approach to women's public appearance. The majority of respondents strongly disagree with the statement that the veil is good protection for women – 80 per cent. The majority (73 per cent) view the veil as an instrument that impedes women's movement. To many of these respondents, the chador symbolizes limitation and immobility, because it suppresses their physical and social abilities.

Views about raising children

The majority of respondents agree that children, regardless of their sex, should be raised the same way (87.5 per cent); enjoy the same amount of freedom while attending school (92 per cent) and be able to participate in competitive sports such as volleyball and basketball (93 per cent). The majority believe that girls' and boys' schools should not be separated (Table 11.11). While Iranian immigrant women have become fairly liberal in their attitudes toward raising their daughters, they have not completely broken away from the ideal of motherhood as the principal and ultimate role for women. When asked whether mothers should prepare their daughters to become good wives, a cornerstone of the Islamic and traditional Iranian normative system,[16] the responses were mixed. Although a third of the respondents disagreed with such a view, 45.8 per cent agreed and 23.24 per cent remained neutral. Asked whether motherhood is the highest status a woman can achieve, another major aspect of the Islamic ideology, results were similar: 43 per cent agreed 27.1 per cent disagreed, and 29.9 remained neutral.

Women's status in the west and Iran

This research posed a series of questions to elicit female immigrants' responses to the Islamic ideology disseminated by their government at home, and shared by many non-Iranian Islamists. I formulated these questions as statements with four possible responses: 'The United States,' 'Iran,' 'Both,' and 'Neither.' The respondents identified the society in which the statement was most applicable, as shown in Table 11.12.

Arguably, the Iranian immigrant women's perceptions of American women and society are more realistic than those of their compatriots back home. These women live in the United States and closely deal with the realities of gender

Table 11.12 Perceptions of women's status in Iran and the USA (percentages)

	Iran	USA	Both	Neither	N
Women have freedom of choice	0.7	79.3	10.3	9.7	145
Women are usually treated with respect	9.2	48.2	18.5	24.1	141
Women have to live with more restrictions	73.4	4.2	16.1	6.3	143
Women are obsessed with their physical appearance	9.9	30.2	43	16.9	142
Women are viewed as a source of sexual provocation	18.2	31.5	35	15.3	143
Women are safe in public places	28.8	22.3	15.8	33.1	139
Many working women are sexually harassed	4.4	29.7	49.3	16.6	138
Women think too much about sex	0.7	55.6	12.7	31	142
A man's work is viewed as more important than women's	33.8	0.7	62.6	2.9	139
Women are treated as sex objects	28.1	20.8	40.3	10.8	139
Both men and women have equal opportunity for career success	1.4	45.1	7	46.5	142

Table 11.13 Perceptions of women's status in Iran and the USA (1 = strong disagree, 2 = disagree, 3 = neutral, 4 = agree, 5 = strongly agree)

	Median	Mode (%)	N
Western women as an extension of the cosmetic industry	3.26	4 (34.8)	141
More chance of success for women in Iran than in the USA	1.48	1 (51.0)	143

relations in the west. They have lost their idealistic views of both places. They know and have experienced both societies. To respondents in this survey, in terms of security in public arenas neither place is adequately safe for women, though they acknowledge a higher degree of safety in Iran. As illustrated in Table 11.13, over a third of the respondents consider public places in Iran and the USA unsafe for women. Only a third, 28.8 per cent, believe that public places in Iran are safe for women, and a smaller group of 15.8 per cent find public places in both countries safe.

Iranian immigrant women generally view Iran as an extremely restrictive society that demeans women's abilities and limits their movement, opportunities and life chances. When asked where women endure more restrictions, a majority of 89.5 per cent regard Iran as a more restrictive society. They agree strongly that women have more freedom of choice in the USA – 89.6 per cent versus 11 per cent. (These percentages are the sums of those percentages for each country with the percentage number for the 'both' category.) These women do not perceive as much respect for women in Iran as in the USA – 27.7 per cent versus 66.7 per cent.

More than 83 per cent of respondents disagreed with the statement that 'Iranian women have more chance of becoming socially successful in Iran than in the USA.' (median = 1.48). Close to half of the respondents (46.5 per cent) sees neither the United States nor Iran as a society that gives men and women equal career opportunities. Over half (52.1 per cent) finds that the USA is the society in which such opportunities are more likely. Only 8.4 per cent of respondents think of Iran as the only society with such equal opportunities. Female immigrants agree that women's work in Iran is not valued as much as men's work at a rate of 96.4 per cent, but 63.3 per cent endorse the fact that a man's work in the USA is also valued more than women's.

Regarding the harassment of working women, the majority believes that it occurs in both societies – 49.3 per cent. Of the other half, 4.4 per cent think that it happens only in Iran, 29.7 per cent believes that it takes place only in the USA, and 16.7 per cent feel that it does not exist in either country. With respect to the objectification and commodification of a woman's body, as well as its cultural manipulation by the cosmetic industry, a view widely held among Islamists,[17] although 45 per cent of respondents agree with the statement that 'The West has really turned women into an extension of the cosmetic industry,' they view

Iranian society as a more likely place for the treatment of women as sex objects – 68.4 per cent versus 61.2 per cent. However, they felt that women are more likely to be viewed as a source of sexual provocation in the USA – 66.4 per cent versus 53.2 per cent. Women in the United States are also regarded as being more obsessed with their physical appearance – 73.2 per cent versus 52.8 per cent. These responses correspond with most comments made by respondents, comments cited toward the end of this chapter.

Finally, it is worth noting that many immigrant women have adopted a feminist view of American society and they demonstrated an increasing feminist consciousness. Close to 47 per cent of immigrants think that neither Iranian nor American women are given equal career opportunities to compete with men. Close to a third of them disagree with the stereotype among Middle Easterners that perhaps American women are more obsessed with sex. Almost half of them believe that women in both societies are sexually harassed in the workplace. Over a third of them do not find public places in either society to be safe for women. Close to a quarter of them think that women do not have enough freedom of choice in either country. Although the majority of Iranian women in the sample dislike the Islamic Republic's policies regarding women's status and appreciate their enhanced socio-economic status in the United States, a sizeable group remain critical of women's status in the host society as well.

At the end of the survey, I requested that respondents offer their opinions on the most important difference(s) they perceive between women's roles in the USA and Iran. Two-thirds of the sample addressed this question, and the majority of them elaborated on wide differences between the two societies – regarding Iranian women as largely deprived of their rights, and the USA as a place where opportunities are more readily available to women. Interestingly, however, even the most negative evaluations of women's status in Iran were followed by some reservations about American women and their roles in the family. Below, I present the voices of these respondents' divided into three categories – those who have a positive, negative or mixed view of women's status in Iran. I selected representative comments for each category. It is worth remembering, however, that these statements represent the attitudes of some respondents, but are not a statistically significant position in the sample.

Positive view of women's status in Iran

Those who view what happens to women in Iran positively may themselves be classified into two groups with opposing views about the status of women in the USA. The first group regards women's status in the USA very negatively and claims that, in the words of one respondent, 'There is a lot of myth about women's freedom in the USA. Women are more brainwashed in the US by TV and other indirect means. In Iran, at least, it is obvious and not unclear.' This group sees American society as deceptive, hiding its patriarchal and exploitative intentions behind seemingly civilized laws. Here are four representative statements:

In Iran, you have more support from your family; children are much more respectful; more emphasis is put on a person's social conduct, graciousness, honesty, etc. than on one's looks, social class, or sexuality; and there is a better sense of security (financial, gender, health, etc.). In the United States, there is too much individualism; women are less secure; families are less stable; and there is too much excess in sexual relationships.

It is said that America is a civilized country. Is it? How much civility is there between blacks and whites? How did whites treat black women during slavery? As slave mistresses. White men continue to have the same view today. Since they cannot achieve their goals openly, now these men do so more subtly through the guise of sexual freedom, women's liberation, and so on. This is not freedom. This is sexual exploitation. This is like making women walk into their own rape chamber.

Yes, women in America are free. Free to have sex. I am against this freedom of sex, make-up, and gaze. A woman, as a role model for her children, should be covered, both in appearance and in heart. She can get any job she wishes but she must not sell herself. She must cover herself. Of course, I do not mean covering her hair. I mean, she should not avail her body for male vultures to take what they wish.

There is something scary about American culture, especially for Iranian women who have female children. The last thing that an American girl is prepared for is marriage. Family has taken a back seat in this country and women are going to end up paying for this because they are the ones who are abused, raped, and divorced. Loneliness and promiscuity are the ultimate punishments God has ordained for these women.

A second group adopts a more moderate position, conceding that the USA provides better educational and career opportunities to women. However, they also contend that certain behavioural and normative patterns in the USA are detrimental to the status of women, family, and society. Iranian women lament the excessive individualism and 'self-centeredness' of the American society. American women put their own desires and wishes ahead of those of their family. For this group of respondents, sacrifice, self-denial and morality are necessary personal qualities for motherhood:

In general, Iranian women are more concerned about the future. They put the interests of their family before their own interests. ... They are more loyal to their husbands/family and would stay in a 'not-so-happy' marriage for the sake of their children and their family reputation.

In the US, women do not realize that they have the power to keep the family together. If a family is not successful in staying together, it is usually the woman who is not flexible enough to forego some things in order to keep her family together. She has other priorities.

> There are many differences. First, there is freedom, which is abundant in America and lacking in Iran. Second, there are opportunities for getting jobs and marrying someone based on love in America. Third, there is decadence, of which America has a lot and Iran some. Where in Iran can you find so many pregnant teenagers or children out of wedlock? America is a corrupt society.

For these respondents, sacrifice for the sake of their children's future, loyalty to their husband, selflessness in marriage, and chastity among Iranian women give them a more dignified status than that enjoyed by American women. While many of the respondents believe that women in Iran enjoy a higher degree of safety, respect and dignity that are absent in the USA, they do oppose the government's policies toward women in Iran. Many respondents prefer to blame traditions or patriarchal interpretations of Islam for the problems confronted by Iranian women. As one respondent declared:

> In my opinion, women's status in Iran is not based on Islam. What is being done to women is not based on Islam. Those in the government misinterpret Islam and pay no attention to what God has offered women in Qur'an. Indeed, women's status in Iran is deplorable because men choose not to allow women to live according to Islam.

Negative view of women's status in Iran

The majority of Iranian women in the USA, represented in this study, view women's status in Iran negatively. Despite their consensus on women's status in Iran, they manifest opposing attitudes on the status of women in the USA. The respondents fall clearly into religious and secular camps. In discussing the difficulties and inadequacies of women's status in Iran, the secular group gives more weight to the role of religion and religious groups than to the role of outdated traditions and inappropriate socialization by parents.

Although the majority speak positively on women's status in the USA, a minority espouse a much more radical view of what is happening in the host society. This minority, 79.3 per cent of which perceives itself as secular feminists, faults the USA for its male domination in the political and legal realms, sexist attitudes prevalent in society, discriminatory policies in the workplace, and exploitation of females by the media and Hollywood. This group's language and reasoning about women's status in Iran are varied and powerful. Below, I have cited comments by the respondents, representative of these themes:

1. Women in Iran are treated as second-class citizens. They cannot think, act and live for themselves. They have no voice. Decisions are made for them.

> American women are more independent, have more opportunities and roles in society, and are less inhibited than Iranian women. They know

what they want and can express their opinions and wishes freely at home and in society. They are not dominated by social norms, whereas Iranian women have to obey the rules set by society. Iranian women are under the influence of their fathers, brothers, and husbands. ... Important decisions are made by men, and women are rarely consulted and listened to about issues that concern both partners.

In the US, women obviously enjoy a higher degree of equality and have more control of their lives. However, this equality is mainly an illusion since we all know that women are not paid equally for doing equal work and house work and child-care is not divided between working couples. In Iran, on the other hand, women, as second-class citizens and child-producing tools (traditionally), enjoyed a temporary and shaky 'equal-opportunity' period in the 1970s. But that period is gone and the men have managed, in the name of 'Islamic respect for women' to push women back to the kitchen where they like to see them. In other words, women all over the world have a long struggle ahead of them.

2. Islamic laws are outdated, disrespectful and unfair to women. While some regard these flaws as the result of male clerical (mis-)interpretations of Islam and divest their religion from these shortcomings, others believe that these features are inherent to Islam itself. The former group believes that the ruling clergy has made a mockery of Islamic values and has turned the traditionally unfortunate situation of women into misery.

The difference is as wide as the space between the earth and sky. In Iran, a Muslim woman is forced to obey the oppressive, unequal, selfish rules of a womanizing, discriminatory, and illiterate Arab called Muhammad. She is treated like a commodity and is used as an instrument to satisfy the sexual desires of men. She has less rights, respect, and power than men and is viewed in the same light as retards, children, the penniless, and criminals. Her desires and wishes do not matter. I spit on this religion and these laws. I damn this barbaric tribe who came to Iran and turned this beautiful land of Mitra into a land of darkness and misery.

In today's Iran in which the Islamic laws are interpreted dogmatically and imposed by the wild, club-wielding *pasdaran* [revolutionary guardsmen], the role of women is seen as being a 'sexual member of the family' and a 'foot-soldier for political rallies' and theatrical political shows. Women in the US have an active and conscious role in society but in Iran they are an instrument for the government to make a Zainab or Fatima out of them for its own political propaganda. Women who are fooled into this exercise are not representative of Iranian women but stand for the few poor or misguided people who are forced to accept these conditions in order to receive a monthly salary.

Iranian women have no financial security because of religious laws. This insecurity prevents women from being able to gain equality with men. Even though I am a Muslim woman, I think Iranian laws should be changed according to the time. Women should share family property. Even at the time of divorce, women should receive equal share. The time has come for women to unite and gain their rights.

3. According to traditional Iranian family values, women should serve as good wives and mothers, ignoring their own personal growth.

In Iran, women are tied up with family matters and house chores. Family members, especially in-laws dictate what a woman must do. When punished by their husbands, American women can resort to shelters. In Iran there are no shelters. You can only go to your parent's home. But parents often refuse you safety and send you back to your husband with the expectation that you give in to your husband's desires and bear the burden of his abuse.

4. Opportunities are limited, and social and moral restrictions do not allow women to take advantage of even these limited opportunities. Women do not have much choice and freedom of action.

For an Iranian woman, restriction is the only framework within which she can think, feel, and act. Restricted at home by her parents or husband, and outside by almost everyone and in every aspect of culture in every corner of the society. Violating these restrictions often costs her dearly and may jeopardize her chances of even being recognized as a decent human. Iran is a land of kings, fathers, and boys and the Iranian culture is the epitome of misogyny.

5. Given the conditions of the Iranian women under the Islamic Republic, these women do not have a promising, independent future. They have been rendered dependent on men, the government, and religion for their identities – a dependence that denies them the opportunity to chart their own course. The Islamic regime has reduced these women to *saqir* status – the level of children.

In America, men and women are equal. But in Iran after the revolution, the personality and rights of Iranian women have been reduced below the level of those of animals. For example, look at the law of *diya* (blood money). No explanation by mullahs can justify this law and the way it treats women.

Iranian women have lost all their rights. They need their parents' permission for attending school and getting married. They need their husbands' permission for working outside of home or travelling outside of the country. Their husbands are privileged in divorce proceeding and child custody laws. Their brothers are privileged in receiving family inheritance. There is one thing that these women are privileged with in this world: Become a mother and be told that God has reserved the heaven for you!

6. The *hijab* or practice of veiling has reduced these women to a dark, shadowy and invisible element in society without an identity of their own.

> In Iran women are more limited in the society. No freedom of speech and action. They have to cover themselves with *hijab* – an antiquated tradition from dark ages. They are punished with garment, even in the most tropical areas and in the hottest days of summer, simply because they are women and men cannot stop being whimsical.

7. Men's behaviour towards women is aggressive, disrespectful, and often domineering. Spouse abuse is abundant and physical punishment is common, especially among less educated and rural men. Iranian men are chauvinist, even when they pretend to be feminist.

> Iranian society expects women to sacrifice themselves for men and forego their rights. A woman cannot claim an independent existence after marriage, and serves only to satisfy men's physical and sexual needs. When hungry and in need, everyone in the family turns to her. Iranian men, no matter how educated they are, still think like their fathers, unless they are born with a grain of social justice. ... Iranian women cannot escape from the monstrous presence of their husbands and the ghost of their family. ... These men are spoiled by their mothers who expect their in-laws to care for their sons in the same manner. These men pretend that they are considerate, understanding, and egalitarian. They are wolves in lamb's clothing.

8. Iranian society treats widows and single women harshly and unfairly. Since women's roles are defined within the context of family, those women who do not have or are not able to maintain a family are marginalized and viewed with suspicion and disrespect.

> In America, you are viewed first as a person, then as a woman, then as a married person, regardless of having any children or not. In Iran, you are first a woman, then a wife, and finally a mother. If single or divorced, then you are the victim of gossip and accusation, a prey for sexual predators, and a wretch worthy of everyone's pity.

Mixed views on the status of women in Iran and the USA

A third group of respondents adopts a middle-ground position, emphasizing the positive and negative aspects of both societies for women. They believe that Iranian women are capable, smart, and independent. They think that women will take advantage of opportunities if and when they find them. This group argues that opportunities for and restrictions on women's activities may be found in both Iran and the USA. What matters is the recognition of women's capabilities.

This third group contends that Iranian women in the USA have lost sight of the fact that much of what is offered to women in the USA is illusive and often harmful to women's dignity. 'Iranian women in the US,' says one respondent, 'pay too much attention to appearances and ignore facts.' The USA has taken steps towards removing inequalities experienced by women, but it has made mistakes on the way such as 'overt feminism and getting hung up on the sex-related issues only. It still has ways to go to reach the true meaning of equality.' Some are more concerned about broader issues such as excessive individualism and independence, the erosion of family values, and the lack of respect for adult authority. These respondents are often even-handed in their criticisms of women's status in both societies. While some blame the cultural and social structures of both societies, others put more stress on women's agency and volition in altering their own situations.

> As an Iranian-American woman, I think that I have faced sexism in both cultures. While sexism may seem more blatant in the Iranian culture, I would contend that life in the US with its capitalist culture and excessive individualism presents challenges to Iranian women as well.'
>
> In the United States women live under a civic religion which legally establishes the ideal of equality. However, equality can never be achieved. Men and women are different. As a result of this 'paper equality' women are free to try to establish a semblance of this in society. In Iran, Islamic law (as opposed to Islam itself) constricts and devalues women. Women are kept under by those claiming a certain understanding of Islam. However, these people are using selective interpretations by men insecure in their control in the public arena and therefore seeking to achieve a greater degree of control in private arena. ... Both societies are flawed. The goal of both should be 'gender parity' rather than 'gender equality.'

Conclusion: Iranian women immigrants, defying stereotypes

The public perception of Iranian women in the USA, especially after the revolution, has been largely negative. At least three factors have contributed to this perception of Iranian women – the takeover of the American Embassy in Tehran in 1979; Betty Mahmoudi's book, *Not Without My Daughter*, then a film based on this book; and the persistent images of Iranian women marching on the streets of Tehran chanting anti-American slogans. Iranian women seemed like backward masses cloaked in the darkness of a chador and traditional beliefs.

The dominant religious and cultural discourse in Iranian society has consistently promoted conservatism in gender and sexual relations.[18] However, this discourse reflects neither the realities of Iranian society, past or present, nor the views of Iranian women, in or outside of the country. Regarding Iranian women, there is a discrepancy between the ideology and reality, the ideal and the actual state of affairs, both inside and outside of Iran. While Islamic rules forbid pre- and extra-marital affairs, they have always occurred in Iran, although in varying degrees and in different forms.

At a structural level, the political and economic developments of 1970s and the subsequent political mobilization of women during and after the revolution have had profound effects on gender relationships in Iran. In the late Pahlavi period, despite the popular belief and ideological claims of traditionalist sectors within society, the increasing presence of women in the labour force and educational institutions, coupled with more progressive family laws, altered gender relations irrevocably.[19]

Although the revolution and subsequent reinvigoration of private and public patriarchy by the ruling clergy resulted in the rolling back of female rights, these events also accelerated changes in gender relations, requiring greater determination on the part of women. Arguably, the revolution itself has unleashed an unprecedented level of awareness, energy and vision among women, as evidenced by their cultural and political activities in Iran.[20] Even in today's Islamized Iran, women believe in, and demand, much more freedom in their relationships with their male counterparts in and outside the home.[21]

The attitudes of Iranian women in the United States, as represented in this study, defy the stereotypes found in the western societies. Although some of these women are ambivalent about gender roles and relations in the USA, they clearly hold more liberal views than their counterparts in Iran, even more liberal than their husbands' opinions of these matters.[22] They are generally supportive of gender equality in the family as well as in society. They perceive gender distinctions as increasingly less relevant to their lives, especially as it relates to occupation, property ownership, child-care, decision making and power-sharing inside and outside of the home. They generally disapprove of traditional restrictions on women's social and physical mobility, especially the veil. They favour more egalitarian relationships between spouses and are disdainful of any interference by outside forces – whether religion, government, parents or in-laws.

Iranian immigrant women lament the status of Iranian women in the Islamic Republic. They regard their departure from Iran as a form of liberation from various restrictions imposed on them by cultural traditions, social customs and theocratic government. Most of these women consider Iranian society traditional with regard to sex, dating, marriage, divorce and gender relation-ships. Most espouse liberal attitudes of gender relationships, sexuality and female status in the society. Although they believe that Islamic societies have treated women unfairly, they are divided on whether this injustice is due to Islam itself or male (mis-)interpretations of the Islamic scriptures.

Despite their liberal attitudes, Iranian women immigrants have neither abandoned all their cultural values nor accepted all elements of the dominant value system governing gender relations in the United States. Iranian immigrant women have similar concerns about their roles within the family and the larger society as women in Western societies, but they are more cautious and selective in their embrace of feminism as a model for redressing gender inequality within the Iranian family. While supporting women's rights, most of them do not call themselves 'feminist.' Many criticize the individualism of American women, believing that more sacrifice and dedication preserves a marriage, especially when there are children involved.

Although they value the egalitarian relations between male and females, they are more ambivalent about the degree of sexual interaction, especially among their teenagers. They proclaim egalitarian attitudes towards the sexes but do not necessarily translate these into specific actions in various aspects of their lives. There is a gap, albeit a declining one, between these women's attitudes and their behaviour, as demonstrated in their gendered approaches to female education and socialization.

Migration has been a source of autonomy for these women, providing them with better opportunities for education, employment, personal freedom and even divorce from difficult marriages. These women depend less on their husbands as they gain their own income, reduce or suspend obligations to their husbands' families, and escape the patriarchal control of their own immediate families. As other researchers have demonstrated.[23] migration to new lands has meant a breakdown of traditional norms for Iranian women. All in all, while Iranian immigrant women are moving away from traditional understandings of gender roles and sexuality, they are developing their own unique synthesis of attributes and values representing the cultural realities of both their past and present. The cultural and social characteristics of their newly adopted society and the structural fragility of their identities in a liminal zone allow them to pick and choose freely from their inherited and adopted realities.[24] The challenge for researchers is to gain a better understanding of these women's identities and to measure the extent to which their attitudes are translated into practice. Further research is necessary to understand marital arrangements between these immigrants and their husbands, how they renegotiate and restructure the original relationships, and what kind of identities they develop for themselves both in and outside of both their families of orientation and reproduction.

Notes

1 Sanford Ungar, (1995) *Fresh Blood: The New American Immigrants*, New York.

2 Thomas Sowell, (1996) *Migration and Culture: A World View*, New York.

3 Harriet Pipes McAdoo, (ed.) (1993) *Family Ethnicity: Strength in Diversity*, Newbury Park, CA; Francis Fukuyama, (1994) 'Immigration and Family Values', in Nicholas Mills (ed.) *Arguing Immigration*, New York; C. Mindel, R. Habenstein, and R. Wright, (eds) (1998) *Ethnic Families in America: Patterns and Variations*, New York and Oxford.

4 Donna Gabaccia, (ed.) (1992) *Seeking Common Ground: Multidisciplinary Studies of Immigrant Women in the United States*, Westport, CT; Pierrette Hondagneu-Sotelo, (1994) *Gendered Transition: Mexican Experiences in Immigration*, Berkeley.

5 S. Guendelman, and- A. Itriago Perez, 'Double Lives: The Changing Role of Women in Seasonal Migration', *Women's Studies*, 13, (1987), pp. 249–71.

6 Parvin Abyaneh (1986) 'Post-Migration Economic Role of Females and Patriarchy in Immigrant Iranian Families', Ph.D. Dissertation, Riverside: University of California; Nayereh Tohidi (1993) 'Iranian Women and Gender Relations in Los Angeles', in Ron Kelley and Jonathan Friedlander (eds) *Irangeles; Iranians in Los Angeles*, Berkeley; Arlene Dallalfar, (1996) 'The Iranian Ethnic Economy in Los Angeles: Gender and Entrepreneurship', in Barbara Aswad and Barbara Bilge (eds.) *Family and Gender Among American Muslims*, Philadelphia; Arlene Dallalfar, 'Iranian Women as Immigrant Entrepreneurs', *Gender and Society*, 8, (1994), pp. 541–61; Shideh Hanassab, 'Acculturation and Young Iranian Women: Attitudes Toward Sex Roles and Intimate Relationships', *Journal of Multicultural Counseling and Development*, 19, (1991), pp. 11–21; Shideh Hanassab, 'Sexuality, Dating, and Double Standards: Young Iranian Immigrants in Los Angeles', *Iranian Studies*, 31, 1, (Winter 1998); Ali-Akbar Mahdi, 'Trading Places: Changes in Gender Roles within the Iranian Immigrant Family', *Critique: Journal for Critical Studies of the Middle East*, 15, (Fall 1999); Minoo Moallem (1991) 'Ethnic Entrepreneurship and Gender Relations among Iranians in Montreal, Quebec, Canada', in Asghar Fathi (ed.) *Iranian Refugees and Exiles Since Khomeini*, Costa Mesa, CA; Mohsen Mobasher (1996) 'Class, Ethnicity, Gender, and the Ethnic Economy: The Iranian Immigrants in Dallas', Ph.D. Dissertation, Southern Methodist University; Manizhe Vatankhahi (1991) 'The Relationship Between Traditional Roles and Marital Satisfaction Among Iranian Couples Residing in California', Ph.D. Dissertation, The California Institute of Integral Studies; Sepideh Zarrinnejad (1992) 'Immigrant Status, Acculturation, Stress, and Depression among Iranian Women in the United States', Ph.D. Dissertation, Los Angeles: California School of Professional Psychology.

7 Mehdi Bozorgmehr and George Sabagh, 'High Status Immigrants: A Statistical Profile of Iranians in the United States', *Iranian Studies*, 21, (1988); Mehdi Bozorgmehr 'From Iranian Studies to Studies of Iranians in the United States', *Iranian Studies* 31, 1 (Winter 1998).

8 Hanassab, 'Acculturation'; Hanassab, 'Sexuality'.

9 Motahhari, Morteza (1357/1976) *Nizam-i Huquq-i Zan dar Islam* (The System of Women's Rights in Islam), Qum.

10 Vahidi, Mohammad (1373/1994) *Ahkam-i Banivan* (Legal Judgements Regarding Women), Qum.

11 Mahdi, Ali-Akbar (1975) *Dar Jami'a-shinasi-yi Khanivada-yi Irani* (On the Sociology of the Iranian Family), Tehran.

12 Parvin Ardalan and Forough Khaksar, ''Aya ta bi Hal Shuda Hamsaritan ra Kutak Bizanid', (Have you ever hit your wife?), *Zanan*, No. 18, Khurdad and Tir 1373/1994, pp. 6–19, esp. p. 19.

13 Seyed Javad Mostafavi (1374/1995) *Bihisht-i Khanivada* (Family as Heaven) 2 Vols., Mashad; Motahhari, *Nizam-i Huquq-i Zanan*.

14 Ziba Mir-Hosseini (1993) *Marriage on Trial: A Study of Islamic Family Law: Iran and Morocco Compared*, London.

15 Morteza Javafri, Soghraa Ismailzadeh and Masuumeh Farshchi (1373/1994) *Vaqiha-yi Kashf-i Hijab; Asnad-i Muntashir Nashuda az Vaqiha-yi Kashf-i Hijab dar Asr-i Reza Khan* (Unveiling Event; Unpublished Documents from Reza Khan Period), Tehran: Office of the Documents of the Islamic Cultural Revolution and the Institute for Cultural Research and Studies; Ali-Akbar Mahdi (1983) *Women, Religion, and the State: Legal Developments in Twentieth Century Iran*, WID Series, No. 38, East Lansing, MI.

16 Hossein Haghjoo (1371/1992) *'Ayin-i Khanidari* (Housekeeping Rules: Women's Role at Home and in Society), Tehran.

17 Gholamali Haddad Adel (1359/1980) *Farhang-i Birihnigi va Birihnigi-yi Farhang* (The Culture of Nudity and Nudity of Culture), Tehran; Ruhollah Khomeini (1365/1986) *Sahifa-yi Nur,* (The book of light: Collection of Khomeini's messages, letters, and announcements), Tehran, Vol. 3, p. 101 and Vol. 2, p. 44; Amoli Javadi, Abdollah (1369/1990) *Zand dar 'Ayina-i Jalal va Jamal* (Women in the mirror of beauty and honor), n.p.
18 Hammed Shahidian, 'Iranian Exiles and Sexual Politics: Issues of Gender Relations and Identity', *Journal of Refugee Studies*, 9, 1, (1996), pp. 43–72.
19 Kaveh Mirani (1983) 'Social and Economic Changes in the Role of Women, 1956–1978', in Guity Nashat (ed.) *Women and Revolution in Iran*, Boulder, Colorado.
20 Parvin Paidar (1995) *Women and the Political Process in Twentieth-Century Iran*, Cambridge; Ali-Akbar Mahdi (2000) 'Caught Between Local and Global: Iranian Women's Struggle for a Civil Society', in Ali Mohammadi (ed.) *Iran Encountering Globalization*, London.
21 Ali-Akbar Mahdi, 'Transcending the Revolution?' *Middle East Insight*, 11, 5, (July–August 1995); Eric Hooglund, 'Islamic Feminism', *Middle East Insight*, 11, 5, (July–August 1995); Eric Rouleau, 'The Islamic Republic of Iran: Paradoxes and Contradictions in a Changing Society', *Middle East Insight*, 11, 5, (July–August 1995).
22 Shireen Ghaffarian, 'The Acculturation of Iranians in the United States', *Journal of Social Psychology*, 127, (1987), pp. 565–71.
23 Zahra Kamalkhani (1988) *Iranian Immigrants and Refugees in Norway*, Bergen; Janet Bauer (1991) 'A Long Way Home: Islam in the Adaptation of Iranian Women Refugees in Turkey and West Germany', in Asghar Fathi (ed.) *Iranian Refugees*, pp. 77–102; Tohidi, 'Iranian Women and Gender Relations'.
24 Hamid Naficy (1993) *The Making of Exile Cultures: Iranian Television in Los Angeles*, Minneapolis; Ali-Akbar Mahdi, 'Ethnic Identity among Second-Generation Iranians in the United States', *Iranian Studies*, 31, 1, (Winter 1998).

twelve

Communities in Place and Communities in Space

Globalization and Feminism in Iran

Asghar Fathi

Introduction

It is generally believed, by Iranians as well as non-Iranians, that the present theocratic regime in Iran has total control over the women in that country. Some even say that the ruling religious establishment has taken the status of women completely backwards. It is the contention of this chapter that there are certain social forces in support of increased power and status for Iranian women which are beyond the control of the present rulers of Iran. Although in some situations the Iranian religious leaders have reluctantly adjusted their rule to these forces, in others the battle continues. The objective of this chapter is two-fold. First, to show that, on balance, the status of Iranian women has improved since the turn of the century, in spite of discrimination by the Islamic regime since 1979. Secondly, to discuss the factors responsible for this situation.

Historical background

In the last decade of the nineteenth century Mirza Malkum Khan, a French-educated Iranian, wrote in his newspaper, *Qanun* (Law), published irregularly in London, that half of the population of every nation consists of women, and no improvement in society is possible without the co-operation of women. Hence, he advocated respect and appreciation for Iranian women.[1]

Sayyid Jamal Va'iz, during the Constitutional movement of 1905–11, recommended education for women from his pulpit. He also preached against temporary marriage and polygyny.[2] There is also the story of the newspaper

Suhbat (Conversation), published in Tabriz. It was the bastion of constitutionalism during that movement, but was closed down and its editor banished from the city because it had implicitly criticized the inferior position of women in Iran.[3] These examples demonstrate that very few people in Iran talked about the status of women at the turn of the century and the topic was taboo at that time.

After the confusion and the disintegration of the Iranian government during World War I, Reza Shah Pahlavi emerged in the mid-1920s as a dictator. In 1935 he decreed the removal of the veil by women. This and other changes during Reza Shah's time created a western appearance in the country, but did not substantially change the mentality of Iranians and the status of women. As a result, with the departure of Reza Shah after the invasion of Iran by the Allied forces in 1941, most Iranian women reverted to the veil.[4]

Following the overthrow of Prime Minister Muhammad Musaddiq in 1953, Muhammad Reza Shah Pahlavi began his dictatorial rule and cosmetic reforms. Women were permitted to vote and became deputies in the rubber-stamp parliament. They were allowed to become judges and members of the cabinet. However, Muhammad Reza Shah, like his father, did not or could not change the traditional attitudes and norms in society, including those related to the status of women.[5] As a result, in spite of an outward appearance of westernization, the world-view of the majority of Iranians, especially in provincial towns and the rural and tribal areas, had remained more or less unchanged since the pre-constitutional period.

Thus with the ascendancy of the religious leaders to power in 1979, only a small group of women in Tehran, the capital, recognized the threat to the relative freedom they had enjoyed during the Pahlavi era.[6] The majority of Iranian women, especially those who lived outside the large urban areas, were either indifferent to or supportive of the Islamic policy of discrimination against women.

Therefore, it is not just the brute force of the religious leaders that has restricted Iranian women in their social roles and treated them as second-class citizens today. The power of the present theocracy in Iran is based on its legitimacy in the eyes of the majority of Iranians. Realistically speaking, one can even say that the present regime enjoys more legitimacy than the Pahlavi regime because, unlike the latter, its legitimacy is based on deep-rooted religious beliefs of the majority of Iranians. With respect to the status of women, it is the perception of traditional and religious-minded Iranian men and women that the discriminatory policy of the Islamic regime is not only just but that it is also divinely ordained. In other words, change in the status of women, like any other social change, depends on changes in the mentality and world-view of the members of society.

Now, if this conclusion is correct, how can one explain the present regime's concern with the status of women, especially after the death of Khomeini? For instance, we hear frequent references made by the Supreme Leader, the President and the Speaker of the Parliament to the superiority of the status of Iranian women over that of women in the rest of the world. We read about a special bureau devoted to the affairs of women as part of the office of the President, the Office of International Relations for Women in the Ministry of Foreign Affairs, and similar bureaus in other government organizations.[7] In the 1997 presidential election, Muhammad Khatami, who won the race, declared that 'guaranteeing women's rights on paper is not enough!'[8] We also see that some women journalists and some women deputies in parliament are openly demanding more protection and power for Iranian women.[9]

Such a high degree of preoccupation with the status of women on the part of government officials and journalists did not exist even during the rule of Muhammad Reza Shah, who considered himself the champion of women's rights, much less during his father's regime and before. What are the explanations for the fact that in recent years the status of women in Iran has become, more than ever before, a contentious public issue?

In my view, the answer to this question is the high level of consciousness on the part of a significant proportion of Iranian women today about their role in society in comparison to the turn of the century, the time of the constitutional movement, and the period of Reza Shah. I believe that this higher level of consciousness is the result of two factors – more educational opportunities for Iranian women and their ever-increasing involvement with the globalization of feminism.

Educational opportunities for Iranian women

In my opinion, the most significant of Reza Shah's reforms with respect to the status of women was not his decree for the forcible removal of the veil. Rather it was his establishment of a nation-wide modern educational system in which female students had the same opportunities as males.[10] But he could not have done this without first laying some preliminary foundations. Thus he began by creating a standing army to bring the marauding tribes under his control and restore security and tranquillity in the country after the chaos and the disintegration of the government during World War I. Then he modernized and centralized the government with the introduction of a European-style bureaucracy. Finally, and no less importantly, he reduced the influence of the religious leaders who were opposed to any social change, especially when the model was western.[11]

After the confusion of World War II and especially after Muhammad Reza Shah's return to power with the help of the American government in 1953, westernization (read Americanization) of Iran went to extremes. But one positive aspect was the increase in the number of Iranian students (male and female) sent abroad. For example, just before the upheaval of 1979, Iranians were the largest group of foreign students in the United States.[12]

As a result, the sheer number of literate and educated women in Iran today, whose sources of knowledge and awareness are not limited to their parents and husbands or the preacher in the mosque, is many times larger than at the turn of century, or in Reza Shah's time. Today there are many women who have college degrees and professional training and who are aware of their own accomplishments and abilities in comparison to the average Iranian man, who enjoys more privileges and freedom than they do.

Again, although the present regime in Iran is a theocratic one, the country has a modern bureaucracy, a western-style educational system, and factories and hospitals that need professional, educated and highly-skilled workers which are scarce, a situation aggravated by the emigration of many male officials and professionals since the downfall of the Pahlavi regime. Hence there is an acute need for the existing educated women – a need felt even by the religious leaders who run the affairs of the country.[13] Under these conditions those officials and leaders cannot afford to be insensitive to the feelings of this influential minority. Besides, some of these religious leaders' wives, daughters and daughters-in-law are part of this minority. Hence the lip service to the significant status of women in Islamic society, occasional concessions, and here and there a token recognition of women as equal to but separate from men.

Global feminism and Iranian women

The second, and in my view more important factor responsible for the rise in the consciousness level of Iranian women is the globalization of feminism or the emergence of feminists as a community in space. To explain this process we have to briefly digress.

Globalization generally means that the lives of the people on planet Earth, even those people living in traditional settings, are increasingly affected by events far removed physically. Globalization is the outcome of modernity – a set of institutions and modes of behaviour which appeared first in post-feudal Europe but in the twentieth century has spread world-wide. Modern institutions and social relations are based on the widespread use of inanimate sources of material power or machinery, a situation that produces and requires new modes of communication and transportation.[14]

Thus modernity is inseparable from its own media: the printed text and subsequently, the electronic signal, which play a major role in the separation and re-organization of time and space.[15] In other words, in the pre-modern era, for most of the ordinary activities of day-to-day life, time and space remained essentially linked through place. The 'when' of activity was often directly connected to the 'where' of activity, via the mediation of place or locale. For example, almost everybody spent his or her working days on the same farm or shop and was involved more or less with the same persons; and on holy days they all gathered in the same place of worship situated in their own neighbourhood.

With modernity, social relations and organization take the form of the co-ordination of actions of many people physically absent from one another. The 'when' and 'where' are often connected without the mediation of place. For instance, thanks to the mediation of the printed text and increasingly the electronic signal, people can conduct business and entertain and be entertained without the benefit of proximity in place or even time. This increase in the space–time distanciation opens up many possibilities of social change by breaking free from the restraints of local customs and practices.[16]

The emergence of community in space

Modernity has brought about major changes in the relationship between people throughout the world. One such change is the weakening, if not the disappearance, of the local community in the traditional sense, where the inhabitants of a locality had face-to-face contact with one another and were interdependent physically, emotionally and intellectually. This situation produced similar attitudes, manners, tastes and knowledge, which in turn gave rise to a rigid culture which was oriented toward the past. Today, because of the space–time distanciation, this community, which was rooted in place, is now being supplanted by another type of community which is in space, mobile, and its members are connected over vast distances by interest.[17] On the other hand, what structures the place or locale is not simply that which is visible in the scene. Nowadays locales are penetrated and shaped by social influences quite distant from them.

For instance, today homosexuals are no longer isolated groups. The homosexuals in San Francisco are aware of other homosexuals in New York, Manchester and Tokyo. With the help of all sorts of publications and the electronic media, homosexuals in various parts of the world learn about one another, create shared feelings and common orientations, consolidate their identity, and even form pressure groups.[18] In other words, they are part of an emerging community in space whose geographically scattered members share a distinct culture and are capable of promoting their own interests. Thus communities of taste, habit and belief become detached from place and from the confines of the nation.

Therefore, because of communities in space, culture today is no longer constrained geographically. Communities in space globalize orientations, sentiments and identities. They develop collective ideologies and plans of action across borders. There are many global communities with distinct cultures, such as environmentalists and human rights activists. Feminists are one of the more visible and vociferous of these communities.

Globalization and reactive traditionalism

Globalization and the resulting social consequences of the separation of time and space should not be seen as a unidirectional development, in which there are no reversals or which is all-encompassing. Like all trends and developments, it has its dialectical and contradictory features, provoking opposing characteristics. For instance, the revival of local nationalism and ethnic identities, is associated with, and is in part a reaction to, globalizing influences.[19]

To explain, the free flow of information that is the characteristic of globalization, has resulted in a post-traditional social order.[20] In a post-traditional order, traditions have to explain themselves; reason and justification have to be offered for them. However, the distinctive quality of tradition is that it presumes the idea of a revealed truth, and this is the origin of its authority. Again, traditions have their guardians, priests, wise men and patriarchal fathers who have privileged access to the revealed truth. Hence the appearance of reactive traditionalism along with globalization is not accidental. Thus globalization often leads to an insistence on defending and re-enforcing the local cultures, linguistic minorities and the revival of the traditional beliefs and values.[21] For instance, during the last two decades in the Middle East religious fundamentalism has become a formidable political force as exemplified by the situations of Iran and Afghanistan.

Iranian women as a part of the global feminist community

There are ample signs that many literate and educated women in Iran today are becoming part of the global feminist community. According to the anecdotal evidence presented in the appendix to this chapter, they seek information about the status of women around the world, they celebrate the successes of feminist leaders in other countries, and exchange ideas among themselves in Iran and with feminists world-wide, in addition to participating in international conferences and inviting foreign women to Iran. Also there are women in the west who are sensitive to the problems of women in Third World countries, and are willing to support them in their struggle against the forces of reactive traditionalism.

On the other hand, the Islamic regime in Iran tries very hard to stop the intrusion of the 'decadent culture' of the west and preserve the 'Islamic way of life', including the traditional status of women. For instance, in addition to imposing a strict dress code for women and separating men and women in public places, the authorities maintain firm control over the internal mass media and have banned satellite TV dishes. But in this era of the burgeoning influence of global relations, it is impossible to deny Iranian women access to Persian and foreign language broadcasts and publications from abroad, or to stop long-distance telephone calls and the internet.

Conclusion

Comparing the status of Iranian women in the first and last decades of the twentieth century, there has been a substantial increase in the number of literate and educated women in the past 90 years and many of them have become part of the global feminist community, which provides them with information, role models and sympathetic support. As a result, it appears that women in Iran are on their way to becoming a significant social force in their struggle for freedom from inequality and servitude, and their quest for a fulfilling and satisfying life by various means, including global connections of many kinds.

Appendix

The following random pieces of evidence are presented in order to demonstrate that many literate Iranian women are part of the global feminist community.

A. In one issue of *Zanan* (Women), a popular Persian magazine published in Iran,[22] out of the 17 published pieces, seven were translations from western sources. In addition, there were two reports about prominent non-Iranian women in this issue – one about the successful re-election of the Pakistani Prime Minister Benazir Bhutto, and the other about Toni Morrison, the American novelist and feminist who had just won the Nobel Prize for literature (with the names of other women winners of the Nobel Prize since 1909 along with the list of Morrison's novels). In the same issue there was an article criticizing a previously published speech by Mehrangiz Kar, a well-known Iranian feminist lawyer, followed by a critique of this rebuttal. Again, in the same issue there was a review of a film made in Iran called 'Who really is Sara?'. The identity of Sara is the centre of discussion in this review. The reviewer is hostile toward the 'rotten' traditional norms that have enmeshed Sara.[23]

B. In an issue of the *New York Times Magazine*, an American female reporter who was visiting Iran writes about being invited to a gathering of an Iranian women's group.[24] She describes Fatemeh, the daughter of the previous President of the Islamic Republic, A.A. Hashemi-Rafsanjani, dressed in stylish clothes, lacquered hair, careful make-up, a perfectly tailored lime-green and white chanel-style suit, pale hose and pumps,[25] gasping as outraged and uncomprehending as any western feminist in her reaction to a report about the harsh treatment of women in Afghanistan by the fundamentalist Taleban that has captured a large part of the country in the on-going civil war there. The American reporter writes of Fatemeh as a member of a small group of women connected with the regime who have entered Iranian politics to negotiate extremely carefully for more rights, more important jobs, equal pay, work benefits and promotion, the right to divorce and custody of their children, within the confines of Islam.

C. In September of 1997 it was reported that a scheduled visit to Iran by four American and one Canadian women representing various non-governmental organizations had been postponed because their hostess Fatemeh Hashemi-Rafsanjani, the president of an Iranian women's organization, had been taken ill and flown to Canada for emergency treatment.[26] The same report adds that some Iranian newspapers had been opposed to this visit, and that the real reason behind this change of plans was that the Supreme Guide (the Iranian head of state) had apparently forbidden the visit, in spite of the fact that the American women's group had sent visitors to Iran previously.

D. As mentioned before, religious leaders in Iran are essentially against any changes in the status of women, and the changes that have occurred have been largely due to forces beyond their control. However, to stem the tide, all sorts of rearguard tactics are constantly employed. For instance, in a bill recently passed by the parliament, along with banning the publication of pictures of women without proper Islamic cover, the publication of materials in defence of the rights of women which could be suspected of challenging established Islamic practices or creating a rift between the sexes also would be considered un-Islamic and forbidden.[27] However, it is interesting to note that the Iranian magazine *Zanan* had already criticized the bill before its ratification, because it treats women in Iran as they are treated in Afghanistan.[28]

E. During the Conference on Gender and Society in the Muslim World Since 1800, at the Royal Holloway University of London in July 1997, Azam Taliqani, the daughter of Ayatullah Sayyid Mahmud Taliqani (a prominent Khomeini supporter who was assassinated after the revolution of 1979) was one of the participants. She also distributed copies of the September 1992 issue of *Payam-i Hajar* (The Message of Hagar [The second wife of the Biblical prophet Abraham]). In this English language organ of the Islamic Women's Institute of Iran of which Taliqani is the founder, editor and manager, we find part of the speech delivered by her at the Third International Peace University Conference held in Helsinki, Finland in October 1985; a reprint of a UN message on the 'Issues of vital importance to women and the recommended measures' in order to end gender discrimination, and an article, by the editor, disputing the general belief that in Islam men are superior to women.

F. In the summer 1997 issue of *Homemaker's* a shopping guide published eight times a year in Canada and delivered at no charge to 1300000 homes, the editor in chief has an article, along with photos, in which she reports on the ten days she had spent with Afghan women who had taken refuge from the Taleban regime in Northern Pakistan. The author deplores the fact that in Afghanistan the schools for girls have been closed, that women can no longer work outside their homes, that they can only leave their homes in the company of a close male relative and only if covered from head to toe, and that they are not allowed to be treated by a male doctor. She also criticizes the insensitivity and lack of action by other countries and especially the UN, to help the Afghan women. In one place the author writes, 'When I tell Samar [a female Afghan physician she interviewed] that Canadian women will be outraged when they learn the facts of the lives of these women ...', the Afghan physician replies, 'No one has tried to help. We need other women to speak out.' Finally, the editor tells readers that if they want to voice their opinion about women in Afghanistan they can write, fax or e-mail the magazine. She promises to forward their letters to the United Nations.

The rest of the story is found in the 2 December 1999 issue of the newspapter *The Globe and Mail* which has an article on Sally Armstrong, the former editor-in-chief of *Homemaker's* it is reprted there that her 1997 piece on the treatment of women in Afghanistan generated 9000 letters to the magazine which were subsequently delivered to the U.N. by the Canadian Foreign Affairs Minister.[29]

Notes

1 *Qanun*, No. 7, p. 3. This newspaper has been reprinted by Homa Nateq. Mirza Malkum Khan (1833–1907) was an Iranian reformist. For more about this controversial intellectual see Fereshte Nuraii (1352) *Mirza Malkum Khan Nazim al-Daula*, Tehran, among others.

2 *Aljamal*, No. 1, p. 4 and No. 11, p. 1. Sayyid Jamal al-Din Va'iz (1862–1908) was a popular pro-constitutional preacher. Some of his homilies appeared in 36 issues of a newspaper called *Aljamal*. For more on Sayyid Jamal see Asghar Fathi, 'Seyyed Jamal Vaez and the Aljamal Newspaper in Iran,' *Middle Eastern Studies*, 33, 2 (1997), pp. 216–225, among others.

3 Ahmad Kasravi (1336) *Khaharan va Dukhtaran-e Ma* (Our Sisters and Daughters), Tehran, pp. 3–4.

4 On Reza Shah Pahlavi see Amin Banani (1969) *The Modernization of Iran: 1921–1941*, Stanford, California, and Gholam-Reza Vatandoust (1985) 'The Status of Iranian Women During the Pahlavi Regime', in A. Fathi (ed.) *Women and Family in Iran*, Leiden, pp. 107–30.

5 *Ibid.*.

6 Several thousand women demonstrated in Tehran against the dress restrictions and for women's rights during 7–12 March 1979, according to *Middle East Journal*, 33, 3 (1979), p. 355.

7 Hayeda Moghaisi, 'Cultural and Social Deadends in the Islamic Republic', *Iran Times*, 18 November 1994, p. 7.

8 *The Globe and Mail* (Canada) 20 May 1977, p. A15.

9 *Iran Times*, 8 October 1993, p. 1; *Iran Times*, 8 December 1995, p. 1 and *Iran Times*, 14 February 1997, p. 6. Also, see section D of the Appendix to this chapter.

10 Banani, *The Modernization of Iran* and Vatandoust, 'The Status'.

11 *Ibid.*

12 According to *Time* magazine, 29 January 1979 (p. 63), there were 235000 foreigners (many of them graduate students) on colleges and university campuses in the USA in 1978; there were even more in 1979. By far the largest foreign contingent was 36000 or so students from Iran.

13 Moghaisi, *Iran Times*, 2 December 1994, p. 9.

14 The theoretical discussion in this section is based mainly on works by Anthony Giddens, more specifically his *Consequences of Modernity*, 1990; *Modernity and Self*

Identity, 1991; *Beyond Left and Right: The Future of Radical Politics*, 1994; and Anthony Giddens and Christopher Pierson, *Conversations with Anthony Giddens: Making Sense of Modernity*, 1998, all Stanford, California.

15 Giddens, *Modernity and Self-Identity*, pp. 23–7.

16 Giddens, *Consequences of Modernity*, pp. 17–21; and Giddens and Pierson, *Conversations with Anthony Giddens*, p. 13.

17 James W. Carey, 'The Communication Revolution and the Professional Communicator,' in Paul Halmos (ed.) (1969) *The Sociological Monograph: The Sociology of Mass Communication*, Keel, pp. 23–38; James W. Carey (1975) 'Canadian Communication Theory', in G. J. Robinson and D. F. Theal (eds) *Studies in Canadian Communications*, Montreal, pp. 27–59; and Joshua Meyrowitz (1985) *No Sense of Place*, New York.

18 Carey, 'The Communication Revolution'.

19 Giddens, *Consequences of Modernity*, p. 19 and Giddens, *Beyond Left and Right*, pp. 5–6.

20 For a more accurate and systematic discussion of this process see the concept of 'reflexivity' as elaborated by Giddens, *Consequences of Modernity*, pp. 36-9; Giddens, *Beyond Left and Right*, pp. 46–9, 81, 83–5.

21 *Zanan*, 2, 14, Mihr and Aban, 1372 (October–November–December, 1993). In another issue, Farvardin and Ordibihisht, 1377 (March–April–May, 1998), there are pieces such as 'Patriarchy and Cruelty to Women', translated from western publications and an article on difficulties that Iranian women face in getting a divorce. There are, of course, other women's publications in Iran such as *Zan-i Ruz* (Woman of Today), which follows the official party line.

22 *New York Times Magazine*, 'Chanel Under the Chador', 4 May 1997, pp. 46–51.

23 The world of fashion is another type of community in space to which many well-to-do Iranian women usually belong.

24 *Iran Times*, 5 September 1997, p. 1.

25 *Iran Times*, 21 August 1998, p. 5.

26 *Iran Times*, 12 June 1998, p. 7.

27 Also, see the report about an international feminist coalition that was seeking to get Iran banned from the 1996 Olympics for discriminating against female athletes. *Iran Times*, 20 January 1995, p. 1.

Contributors

Sarah Ansari is Lecturer in World History in the Department of History at Royal Holloway, University of London. Her main area of research and writing has been on South Asian Muslims in general and the Pakistani province of Sind in particular. She is currently working on partition-related migration between India and Pakistan, and has published on issues relating to gender and womanhood in Pakistan since 1947. In addition, she is editor of the *Journal of the Royal Asiatic Society*

Asghar Fathi is Professor emeritus of sociology at the University of Calgary in Canada. He has studied at the American University of Beirut (public administration), Tehran University (law) and the University of Washington (sociology). His major interests and publications are in the fields of media and public communication (including the Islamic pulpit), social change in developing countries and the intellectuals in the Middle East.

Gulnar (Guli) Eleanor Francis-Dehqani was born in Isfahan, Iran, where she lived for the first thirteen years of her life. Following the Islamic Revolution, she moved to England. She graduated from the University of Nottingham with a BA Hons in Music, and in 1989 began working for the BBC, first as a studio manager at World Service Radio and later as a producer in the Religious Department of domestic radio. In 1994, Guli completed an MA in Religious Studies at the University of Bristol, and was awarded her PhD in 1999. She was ordained in 1998 and began working as curate within the Church of England Southwest London.

Azadeh Kian-Thiébaut is Associate Professor of Political Science at the University of Paris 8, and a researcher at Monde Iranien, Centre National de la Recherche Scientifique. Her publications include (1998) *Secularization of Iran: a Doomed Failure? The New Middle Class and the Making of Modern Iran*; (1999) *Avoir vingt ans à Téhéran* (with Isabelle Eshraghi); (1998) *L'élection de Khatam: le printemps iranien?* special issue of Les Cahiers de l'Orient, n°. 49; (2000) *L'Iran: uncertain avenir?* special issue of Les Cahiers de l'Orient, n°.60.

Shireen Mahdavi was born in Tehran, Iran, and was educated at the LSE, University of London, and the University of Utah. She holds a PhD from the University of London. Prior to the 1979 Iranian Revolution, she taught at the Institute of Social Research, Tehran, was involved in research in the field of social affairs, and served as an advisor to the government. Currently she is an independent scholar, affiliated to the Department of History, University of Utah. She has written extensively on various aspects of Iranian history, with special emphasis on the nineteenth century and the position of women. Her latest publication is (2001) *For God, Mammon and Country: a nineteenth century Persian Merchant*, Boulder, Colorado.

Ali Akbar Mahdi is Chair and Professor of Sociology at Ohio Wesleyan University, Columbus. He is the author of (1998) *Iranian Culture, Civil Society, and Concern for Democracy*, (1992) *Sociology in Iran* (co-authored with Abdolali Lahsaeizadeh), and (1975) *On Sociology of the Iranian Family*. He has also written a large number of articles and reviews on women in Iran, Iranians in the United States, Islam, and Iranian politics in various journals, including *Contemporary Sociology, Critique, Journal of Iranian Research and Analysis, Iranian Studies, Middle East Insight, Michigan Sociological Review, Resources-for Feminist Research, International Journal of Middle Eastern Studies, Middle East Journal, Historian, Sociological Focus, International Social Science Review*, and *Feminist Forum*.

Vanessa Martin is Reader in Modern Middle Eastern History at Royal Holloway, London, and is on the Councils of the British Institute of Persian Studies and the Royal Asiatic Society. She obtained her M.A. and Ph.D. from SOAS, London. Her publications include (1989) *Islam and Modernism: the Iranian Revolution of 1906* and (2000) *Creating an Islamic State: Khomeini and the Making of a New Iran*. She is currently researching for a book on the lives of ordinary men and women in nineteenth century Iran.

Ziba Mir-Hosseini is an independent consultant, researcher and writer on Middle Eastern issues, specialising in gender, family relations, Islam, law and development. She is currently Research Associate at the Department of Social Anthropology, University of Cambridge and also at the Centre for Near and Middle Eastern Studies, SOAS, University of London. She is the author of (1993) *Marriage on Trial: A Study of Islamic Family Law in Iran and Morocco* and (2000) *Islam and Gender: The Religious Debate in Contemporary Iran*; and co-director of two feature-length documentary films: *'Divorce Iranian Style'* (1998); and *'Runaway'* (2001)

Farian Sabahi is Visiting Fellow at the Graduate Institute of International Studies, Geneva, and currently carrying out research on oil policies in the Islamic Republic of Iran. In 1999 she completed her PhD at SOAS, University of London. Her publications include (2000) *La pecora e il tappeto: economia tribale in Azerbaigian. Il caso die nomadi Shahsevan*, Milan, and (2001) *The Literary Corps in Pahlavi Iran (1963-1979): political, social and literary implications*, Lugano. She has also contributed articles to journals, as well as 'Link between education and state control on nomadic tribes in Iran', in F. Jabar and H. Dawood (eds) (2001) *Tribes and Powers*, London. As a freelance journalist specialising on Islam and the Middle East, she regularly writes for the Italian daily newspaper, *Il Sole 24 Ore* and broadcasts on Radio Svizzera Italiana.

Hossein Shahidi has been a journalist for more than 20 years, working in Iran and Britain. Currently he is Manager of Journalism and Production Training at the BBC World Service. In addition to training BBC journalists, he has taught radio journalism at the Palestinian Bir Zeit University and organised training courses for print journalists in Iran. He compiled and edited the first textbook to be used by the BBC World Service [the Handbook of Radio Journalism], and writes on professional journalism for specialised periodicals in Iran.

Azam Torab is currently a non-stipendiary Research Fellow in Social Anthropology at Clare Hall, University of Cambridge, and a Research Associate at SOAS, University of London. She studied Ethnology at the University of Basle and completed her PhD in Social Anthropology in 1998 at SOAS, based on fieldwork in Tehran on gender and ritual. She is presently completing a monograph and conducting further research on gender and ritual in Iran.

Anna Vanzan received her laurea in Oriental Languages and Literature at the University of Venice (Italy) and her PhD in Near Eastern Studies at New York University. She has taught courses on Persian history and language at the University of Bologna and is currently adjunct professor at the University IULM of Milano-Feltre. She has written widely on different aspects of Islamic culture, and has translated both classic and modern Persian literature for Italian readers. She focuses in particular on women's writing in contemporary Iran.

Michael Zirinsky was born in Brooklyn, New York, to the children of east European immigrants, during the battle of Stalingrad. After education in the public schools of New York and the Tehran Community School of the Iran Mission of the Presbyterian Church (USA), he took degrees in politics and history at Oberlin College, the American University, and the University of North Carolina. His research centres on western relations with late Qajar and early Pahlavi Iran. He teaches modern history at Boise State University, Boise, Idaho.

Index